Getting There

'To travel hopefully is a better thing than to arrive.'

ROBERT LOUIS STEVENSON, 1881

Getting There

Journeys of an accidental adventurer

Sue Williams

NEW HOLLAND

First published in Australia in 2001 by
New Holland Publishers (Australia) Pty Ltd
Sydney • Auckland • London • Cape Town

14 Aquatic Drive Frenchs Forest NSW 2086 Australia
218 Lake Road Northcote Auckland New Zealand
24 Nutford Place London W1H 5DQ United Kingdom
80 McKenzie Street Cape Town 8001 South Africa

National Library of Australia
Cataloguing-in-Publication Data:

Williams, Sue, 1959 Apr. 2– .
Getting there: journeys of an accidental adventurer.

ISBN 1 86436 623 0.

1. Williams, Sue, 1959 Apr. 2– .Journeys. 2. Travelers.
3. Voyages and travels. I. Title.

910.4

Publishing Manager: Anouska Good
Project Editor: Sophie Church
Designer: Peta Nugent
Typesetter: Midland Typesetters
Printer: Griffin Press

This book is typeset in 10/16.5 pt Arrus.

For Jimmy,
to whom it is always wonderful to come home.

With heartfelt thanks to Jimmy, Selwa, Jane-Anne,
Tim, Louise, Adrienne and Linley.

contents

ENTRY ECUADOR
POLICIA — MIGRACION
MAR 11 1987
008   30
ENTRADA — QUIT

prologue

It all started with the piercing shrill of a factory whistle to signal lunchtime—at 2.30 in the morning. I turned to the woman slumped next to me in the row, and took advantage of the sudden quiet of a few hundred machines being switched off at once to ask her name, and how she'd ended up in a hell-hole like this, with nothing to look forward to but eating meat pudding and chips in the middle of the night.

I knew why I was there. I was on holiday from university in between terms. I needed money, and the night-shift at this toy car factory was the only casual work around for desperates. But the woman beside me smiled. She worked here for three months every year, she said, to earn enough money to enable her to spend the rest of her time travelling the world. *Travelling the world*? I stole a sly sideways look at her as we trudged off to the canteen. She looked sane enough, all right. None of the obvious signs of factory fever: dishevelled, harried appearance; burbling non-stop at the first chance to speak after solitary hours spent at the deafening machine-face; or dribbling with excitement at the prospect of stale meat pudding.

But, as she finally began talking, my chips grew cold on the plate. She regaled me with tales of far-flung, exotic destinations and far-flung, exotic people across Pakistan's Khyber Pass, along China's Yangtze River, down in the deep US south and up through the tangle of the Parisian streets of Montmartre in the spring. I was enthralled. And, slowly, the idea of travelling to savour such far-flung, exotic experiences *myself*, began to take hold.

Before long, I was spending every spare moment pushing my university books aside to pore over maps. I was sitting up all day reading travel books, both old and new, then going back into work each night, red-eyed and exhausted. My mind was spiced with images of dusty lives in remote villages around the Congo, tall men in vivid blue gowns shimmering on horses through the Sahara, lusty pageant days in Guatemala and peasants crammed onto boats cleaving their way up China's Yellow River.

Previously, I hadn't had any idea of what I was going to do after university, but now I knew. I'd work for a bit, then travel for a while. Work and travel; travel and work. So, each night, as I snapped tiny pairs of plastic axles on a pad ready for a machine to hammer in the wheels, I sat and dreamt. The more I dreamt, the more enthusiastic I became. And the more enthusiastic I became, the more accidents I had with the machine, often finishing my shift bruised and bleeding, which only served to harden my resolve. For it really didn't matter. My life suddenly had a new direction, a new purpose, a new meaning.

● ● ●

After finishing my degree, and working at an office accounting job by day and in various bars around London at night, I set off on my first trip in 1981, at the age of 22, supposedly from the UK to South Africa. It ended disastrously, and very prematurely, but nothing was going to put me off. Sure, I'd loathed the bad times, but the good ones were priceless. I'd discovered travel, and had become hopelessly addicted.

I started living a kind of half-life when I was back home in Britain, with all my time spent working for cash, saving slavishly, rationing my consumption of electricity and existing on a diet of toast and Marmite, all so I could go away again, and as soon as possible. My only break was to train as a journalist, and then work as one until the travel bug bit again. I returned to Africa, then went to Hong Kong, to China, through Europe, to Latin America, to New Zealand and, finally having settled in Australia, I made trips to Borneo, to Fiji, to India and to Pakistan.

'But *why*?' friends and family would regularly interrogate me. 'Why Africa? Why Latin America? Why China? Why not a package to a Club Med somewhere nice?' And, usually, 'Why alone?'

The truth was that I had found I just adored arriving in new places—the more different from the ones I knew, the better—looking around and getting to understand how things worked. I loved meeting people who lived completely unfamiliar lives, listening to their quite diverse points of view on the world and getting to know them, however briefly. And I loved the freedom of wandering around, able to go and explore some new region, sight or landmark on a whim, and tackling the challenges that invariably threw themselves up...and often all over me.

Sure, I love relaxing holidays in big luxury hotels as much as the next person. But they're not enough. What's the thrill of actually managing to get somewhere if someone else has arranged it all in advance for you? Where's the excitement of crossing new boundaries if they simply appear on an itinerary delivered to your hotel room, and you're back again for tea? How can you possibly rub shoulders with the locals, live with them as equals and, sometimes, rely on them to help you out of trouble, if you're travelling in air-conditioned comfort, peering at them through tinted windows and taking photos from a distance?

As for travelling alone, for a start, I knew no-one else who wanted to put their lives on hold while they roamed the world. Even if I had, travelling with someone on very little money, poor food and sometimes in terrible conditions I found could, and certainly did, wreck many a healthy friendship. But, more than that, I revelled in the freedom of being on my own.

There was nothing like standing on the edge of a mountain and knowing you'd got there all by yourself. There was nothing that could compare to setting a point on the map and then managing to get there, despite a woeful sense of direction and a chronic shortage of petrol, or a train having been derailed, or the only boat being marooned on a sandbank in the middle of a great, fast-flowing, crocodile-infested river. And there was nothing that could beat the simple, life-affirming experience of being alone in a foreign land, with little more than a change of T-shirt, a pen knife and a sleeping bag, and surviving. Sure, you might be arrested and told you're about to be shot by a pair of embittered soldiers, you might be thrown into a prison cell and told you'll probably die there, or you may well even be attacked by a lecherous local who believes that being white, a woman and alone is an invitation to, well, anything he's ever imagined. But, happily, you get through—and are a much stronger person for it.

Of course, being a lone woman has its fair share of difficulties but, somehow, with a fair dollop of luck and a pretty cool head, I've always managed to get through. I survived a multiple bicycle pile-up in Beijing by lying quietly at the bottom until everyone else was lifted off me; I avoided the clutches of a Peruvian hotel porter who let himself into my room—and my bed—in the dead of night by waking just in time and screaming loudly; I survived and escaped from a car in Kenya whose driver refused to stop by yanking the steering wheel so hard that he only narrowly avoided crashing into a tree.

More recently, I even decided to risk a travel trip with my partner. As a dedicated five-star Western comforts man, it was tough persuading him to give it a go. But the result of our trip to India was a revelation, for both him and me.

Yet later, back on the road on my own, I did feel like I was, at last, coming home. Back on my own steam. Travelling alone to new and different places. In short, getting there.

chapter one
DESTINY IN A DUSTCART
destination: Africa

Up ahead, I could see a long, narrow wharf jutting out into the ocean. It looked deserted, lonely and dangerous. I felt my body tense—I had to do something.

'Look guys,' I said, as firmly and as coolly as I could manage, 'I think we should go back to town now.' With a shock, I heard the words come out as a nervous squeak. The three men said nothing. The car just continued heading towards the dark wharf. 'Now, come on guys,' I chirruped again.

The man in the front twisted around to glare at me. 'We want to show you our sights,' he said, 'and then we will...'

His voice was interrupted by the wail of police sirens, a flash of blue and a blinding white light that snapped on, flooding the entire area. We screeched to a halt. Suddenly, we could see we were surrounded by five police cars, with uniformed police and half-a-dozen others in dark suits pouring out onto the road. They crouched, one knee on the ground, holding machine guns trained directly on us. One shouted something through a megaphone, and the driver opened his door and slowly climbed out, raising his hands in the air. He was immediately grabbed, twisted around and slammed back against the car. They called for his mate in the front. He got out and was shoved back to land, spread-eagled, against his side. Then they wrenched open one of the back doors, and pulled the third man, sitting next to me, out onto the road, kicked him and hoisted him over the car.

Immediately, they were frisked and an arsenal of guns pulled from various pockets. I gasped with horror. Why on earth had they been carrying guns at all, let alone two or three each? I sat frozen in the back, until one of the officers barked at me through the open door. I didn't move. He shouted louder to me to get out. I tried, but my legs just didn't seem to be working. My brain was reeling. My God! I was only two weeks into my trip-of-a-lifetime around Africa and I was obviously already in deep shit. And I hadn't even got to Africa yet! I felt faint. This whole experience was fast turning into a nightmare from which I felt I'd never wake...

•••

When I'd seen a magazine ad for an overland trip from Europe to Johannesburg, it had instantly caught my imagination: Africa—by truck! With a small group of similarly fascinating and daring adventurers! It was a chance to explore the inaccessible, authentically fabulous places ordinary tourists can never reach, to meet friendly locals in their own backyard, to share precious knowledge of traditional cultures, to learn and discover about the world and—along the way—myself!

Having finished college six months before, I'd been anxiously searching for an acceptable way of putting off making a decision on what to do next. This looked perfect. I'd always fancied doing a bit of travelling, and this seemed a neat compromise between overly organised and ferociously sanitised package travel, and striking out into the heart of the unknown alone, defenceless and, let's be honest here, *scared*. Instead, with an overland trucking trip, I'd be with a few like souls, pretty safe, yet still able to experience the edge, however muted, of independent adventuring.

I'd eagerly signed up and handed over my life savings before it had even occurred to me to ask the skinny, curiously unfriendly New Zealand organiser I met a few days later even the basic questions: what kind of vehicle would we be travelling in? (a converted dustcart); who are the other people? (an extremely motley assortment of, quite possibly, the world's greatest misfits); and, most importantly of all, why so cheap?

Ah, that one was answered very quickly. Five nights on from the start of the trip, lying squashed on the floor of that rickety old truck between two fellow travellers—with whom I'd been huddling closely in a desperate attempt to keep warm—the miserable truth was beginning to fill me with horror. We weren't even a week into our epic four-month journey, and already I was beginning to bitterly regret not having done the tiniest bit of homework before quitting my job, packing a rucksack with a few carefully coordinating T-shirts and skirts, and surrendering my destiny to a dustcart astonishingly ill-equipped for the journey we were undertaking.

•••

Life rarely works out quite how you imagine and travel even less so. It had started to go horribly wrong, horribly early. The first sign of impending disaster came on the fifth night of the trip. We were parked in a little town close to Mont Blanc on the French–Italian border in the middle of the bitter winter of 1981. The ground had been too hard the night before to drive in tent pegs so we could sleep under the tattered set of canvasses that masqueraded as our 'comfortable accommodation'. The only firewood we could find was far too wet to do anything but sputter as the flames of our pathetic matches died. Our driver constantly got lost, and we'd all been rendered speechless when the trip's organiser, Tim, had waved us off airily with the farewell, 'I'll see you in Africa! Europe's far too cold at this time of year for me!' We could see nothing of the spectacular scenery through the icy fog. And, to cap it all, there was some problem with the paperwork that meant we wouldn't be allowed through the border for days—and that's even if the vehicle's diesel lines *hadn't* frozen solid in the cold.

I spent that night, like the previous ones, hunched in a summer-weight sleeping bag (we were off to Africa, why would I need anything warmer?), dressed in all three of my pretty outfits at once, crushed between my similarly unwashed, hungry and increasingly irritable travelling companions. The floor was wet and slippery with ice. I couldn't feel my hands. My back ached. I could no longer remember why I'd ever even wanted to leave home.

I woke suddenly in the middle of the night, struggling for breath. There was a head on my chest, pinioning me to the ground; an arm, flung across my throat, about to cut off my air supply; and a foot against my mouth, encased in a crusty sock that smelled as if its owner had died inside. Life, I thought, as I pushed the foot away with one frozen hand and tried to roll the head on my chest off me with the other, simply couldn't get any worse than this. If only I'd known.

'Oi!' complained English fireman Dan as I slung his arm back towards his body, and tried to sit up. He sniffed, slurpily, and immediately rolled his bulk to take up the space my torso had just vacated on the floor.

'What the fuck?!' immediately came the yell from Australian plumber Trevor, whose smelly-socked foot was now lying jammed between the floor and Dan's right shoulder. 'Hey! Get OFF me!' he kicked.

I struggled to my feet and tiptoed between the bodies to the back of the truck. Quietly, I pulled back the fluttering sheet of thin plastic supposed to be keeping us snug from the icy winds blasting through from outside. I clambered over the tailgate of the truck and lightly went to step on the first rung of the ladder to the ground. There was nothing there. The ladder had been pulled up. Instead, I fell heavily onto the ice below, and an excruciating pain shot up my leg. I lay crumpled on the ground, moaning, and wondering how much it would cost to hole up in a hotel room near the border until I could decently return home, pretending to friends and family that, in all my time in Africa, I hadn't passed a single post box.

'What are you doing?' came a voice from the blackness. 'You can't sleep there. Bloody stupid. You'll catch your death.'

I looked up. It was Mark, a tall, strapping New Zealander, standing enveloped in the big, floor-length sheepskin coat that the rest of us had been coveting since he'd first climbed onto one of the two bench seats running the length of the truck. It was the first time I'd actually heard him speak. Every day, he'd merely nab the best seat by the back of the truck, scowl at the rest of us and stare moodily out at where the scenery might be. I grimaced. 'I fell,' I said, weakly.

He looked at the back of the truck. 'Well, you should be more careful when the ladder's not there,' he snapped, and dissolved back into the night.

I pulled myself to my feet, and limped back and forth to try to keep myself warm. I'd never been so miserable in my life.

Half-an-hour later, another foot came into view from over the back of the tailgate. 'Watch out!' I whispered. 'There's no ladder.' The foot was pulled back in, and a face appeared.

'Hey! What are you doing out here?' hissed Jenny, the cheery Londoner who'd been the only one to return my greeting the first morning on board. The rest had simply looked away, haughtily, as if acknowledging that having other people in the truck somehow diminished their own standing as highly accomplished, world-weary travellers. I told Jenny about falling, and then helped her down.

'I *have* to have a pee,' she said. 'Can you see anything?' I shook my head. 'Oh, well,' she said, 'nothing for it...' She dived under the truck and peed underneath. I admired her style and wondered where Mark was. He surely wouldn't have approved.

'It's bloody freezing in there,' said Jenny, emerging a few minutes later, doing up her jeans. 'Trevor wouldn't lend me his jumper or his spare socks. He says he needs them all.'

Somehow, that didn't surprise me at all. Sometimes in life you meet people you instantly warm to, and sometimes you meet people who chill you to the core. I liked Jenny; I loathed her boyfriend Trevor. As far as I could see, he wouldn't deign to pee on a burning man unless he had a signed guarantee he'd receive a handsome cash reward and a Humane Society medal. The evening before, the three of us had bought a bottle of wine for ninety Australian cents. Trevor, blonde and athletic, had insisted on contributing only fifteen cents. He said he'd probably only have one glass. I fumed silently as he helped himself to a second.

In fact, as the days wore on, it became harder and harder to imagine a more mismatched bunch of people, or a group less emotionally, physically and intellectually prepared to make the journey we were now undertaking.

There was Dan, the big, brutish fireman, dragging his mousy wife Debbie along under angrily sullen protest, in search of a new life in South Africa. The old one had proved so dull, he reasoned, anything would be an improvement. There was cockney Jenny, the skinny blonde who'd never ventured outside London yet was impressively exuberant about every possibility; and her boyfriend Trevor who bragged about the host of exotic travels he'd undertaken in the past, yet was inexplicably silent on why, then, he was sitting meekly on this truck with us amateurs, rather than striding alone across Africa with a bottle of water and a spear for catching his own lunch. Instead, he merely complained about everything and everyone, without ever doing a thing about either.

There was weedy, gnome-like South African Stewart, desperate for a woman—any woman—just as long as she was white; and sweet Lisa, an Australian flowerchild, and a veteran of travels all over Bali, Thailand and India, who laughed gaily at Stewart's racism as it never seemed once to occur to her that everything he said was in deadly earnest. They became quite friendly, until she discovered he wasn't joking, and he discovered she thought he was.

Then there was Erica, a quiet English rose—until provoked, when her thorns could rip the toughest flesh; and Nina, an Aussie with a deep love of Asia and, unfortunately, an instant loathing of anything African. There were Mark and Ryan, two remarkably silent Kiwis, affable enough, but who probably uttered only a handful of words during the entire journey. There was one American, Jonathan, eager to encounter any new experiences, as long as he could eat, snort or inject them. Claire and Wallace were two eccentric English women; Mickey, the put-upon driver's Australian assistant; and Tim, the führer in charge of the trip, the driver-mechanic-tactician-organiser who, it became clear as soon as he deigned to join us in Africa, would allow you to travel in comparative comfort in the front seat, and get first pickings from the food cupboard—but only if you slept with him first.

Jenny, Erica and I hit it off from the start, but with Trevor I struck up an immediate antipathy. And, to be fair, it was mutual. I quite liked Stewart, however, and he me, until it became obvious that I would never sleep with him, under any circumstances. Then he joined in Trevor's crabby mutterings, the pair looking for all the world like the elderly Muppets on the theatre balcony, bitching and moaning for all their worth.

But they had plenty to complain about. The weeks it took us to cross France and Italy were agony. We spent our nights either in the truck or shivering four to a two-person tent, doing our best to keep warm on frozen fields because all the camp grounds were closed for winter. We spent our days heaving the truck out of mud, because Tim had ordered his Europe-leg driver, Mickey, not to use the four-wheel drive as it ate up too much petrol and therefore his profit margin.

•••

In Sicily, the weather brightened and so did we. The capital, Palermo, was a cheerful little city, full of wide streets, stylish shops, grassy squares and elegant Sicilians strolling and eating ice cream. The port town of Trapani to the west, from which we planned to catch the ferry over to that great African continent, was dotted with carts heaped with tangerines, the first fruit we'd seen around for weeks. Our spirits soared when we saw a stray ray of sunshine breaking through the clouds. Africa suddenly felt so close. Tunis, the capital of Tunisia, might be only a hop, skip and jump over the water, but it was going to be so different from Europe. We couldn't wait. Unfortunately, we had to when we discovered we'd just missed the ferry.

Luckily, there was another scheduled for the next day, so we had only one more night in Sicily. The local campsite, of course, was closed, so it was a choice between a night sleeping on a patch of concrete just outside town, or the truck again, or splashing out on a bed in a nearby hotel in Palermo. Jenny and I merely looked at each other when Tim pointed out the hotel. I could even feel those starched white sheets, and, closing my eyes, could just see the bubbles on a steaming hot bath. I knew she felt the same. Sadly, Trevor would have to come too, but the cost of a room divided by three would make it eminently affordable. We agreed that, if they'd allow the three of us in one room, we'd toss a coin for the bed. If I won, I'd have it alone. If either of them won, they'd share it. No problem. I just wanted that bath and a warm night under a roof, between walls. It didn't seem too much to ask.

Inside the hotel, on tall stools propped against the reception bar, three men, each in their mid-twenties, were drinking coffee out of tall glasses. There didn't seem to be anyone else in charge. We explained what we wanted.

'Why three people in one room?' one of them immediately asked, looking flushed. 'You are very good friends, I think.' The three giggled.

Hastily, we explained that we were broke, but were craving just one night in a warm room, between cool, white sheets. They poured coffee for us and we sat and drank it gratefully, feeling almost human for the first time since we'd left London.

'So what do you do tonight?' asked the one who'd seemed totally unconvinced by our explanation. 'You go straight to bed?' That prospect loomed invitingly for the one—or two—of us who'd win the toss, but we all had the presence of mind to look non-committal.

'Not sure,' I said. 'Maybe we chat, read a book...' Out of the corner of my eye, I noticed Mickey and Claire walk in through the front door to our left, stop dead in their tracks when they saw us, grab a key off the wall rack in the distance and then slide guiltily up the stairs, obviously hoping they hadn't been spotted. The truck's first romance, evidently. 'Or maybe we sleep, yes,' I continued, lapsing into that strange phrasing English-speakers often use to foreigners, in the bizarre belief that somehow that was much easier to understand. 'We haven't had much sleep for a while.' The men smirked again.

'No, I know!' boomed the quiet one of the trio, whose name turned out to be Pierero. 'You must come to my house for dinner.' Jenny and I looked at each other, almost drooling at the thought of a real meal, but suddenly school-girly reticent about over-friendly men of an unfamiliar cultural background. We knew Trevor wouldn't be much help if the going got ugly.

Pierero must have noticed our hesitation. 'My mother,' he kissed his fingertips, 'is a wonderful cook.' At the mention of a mother, we relaxed, as we were probably supposed to, and Trevor said we'd be delighted to accept the invitation.

We signed the guest book and all piled into the massive Mercedes, which apparently belonged to the one called Angelo, parked outside. We purred off. 'But first we go to my house,' said Angelo, 'for an aperitif, you understand.'

His house, oddly, seemed a very long way away indeed. We drove out through the outskirts of town, past lifeless, rubble-strewn squares and along a snaky tar road fringed with woodlands. I started feeling nervous. 'Where are we going?' I ventured, as the evening sky darkened.

'Oh, we're not far now,' said Toto, sharing the backseat with us. 'We wanted to show you this view of the sea.' It was true: up ahead we could see a wharf disappearing into the dark sky above what must be the sea. I felt scared. Why had we agreed to this? These guys could be...anyone.

I said we should go back, but they took absolutely no notice at all. And then, just as Toto started saying he was only showing us the sights, it happened. We'd screamed to a stop, the three Sicilians had been forced out of the car and slammed over it, and we three were sitting, terrified, in the back, as the police continued to point their machine guns straight at us and yell at us to get moving. Jenny was the first to stir. 'Money!' she hissed, suddenly. 'They must be after our money!' Hastily, we pulled our money from our bags and stuffed it down our knickers.

'Out!' shouted the man again. We climbed awkwardly out of the car, where everything looked as though it was going on in slow motion. How could this be happening? I'd always believed in expecting the unexpected, but not *this*!

The plain-clothes policemen took turns to frisk us. My knees shook as they patted me down. I tried to hold myself still. They might think I was trembling because I had something to hide. The very thought made me shake even more. I looked over at Trevor, standing tight-lipped as he too was searched. Wasn't it he who'd agreed to the meal so rashly? Jenny and I, left alone, would certainly have been more cautious. In fact, I wouldn't have minded staying in the hotel room for the evening. There might even have been a bath down the corridor, with hot water and bubbles and soap... Yes, suddenly, it all seemed

Trevor's fault. Much later, I overheard him discussing the incident to Stewart. 'I told her it wasn't a good idea to go off with those men,' he said. 'But she wouldn't listen...'

When the officers had finished searching us, the one who seemed to be in charge looked us up and down. He probably grasped the situation. He didn't speak to us again. We stood to one side, while the police and our new friends got on with their business. The police pulled the car apart, lifting the cushions from the seats, yanking off the hub caps, searching the boot, taking everything out of bags, and lifting the bonnet to shine a torch inside. After half-an-hour, it seemed they had turned up nothing. Snarling, they handed back the guns, much to our amazement, and gestured at us all to get out of their sights.

With knees knocking, we climbed back into the car. Even the men were subdued. 'Are we going back now?' asked Jenny, brightly.

'No,' replied Angelo, quietly. 'I live nearby. I am sure you would now like a drink.'

We drove in silence for a few minutes, then stopped outside a nondescript apartment block. We followed the others out and walked up two flights of dark stairs. Angelo threw open a door, and gestured at us to walk inside. I gasped. It was the most magnificent home I had ever seen. The huge lounge, with tiger skins draped across the floors, had as its centrepiece a brightly illuminated black marble bar. Long, low, white leather sofas sat along the other side. In the first of the three bathrooms, was a massive sunken bath, again in black marble. Peeking into the bedroom I passed along the way, I caught sight of a king-sized bed, covered in fur. It was like a spread out of *Hello* magazine for an apartment you'd imagine Dudley Moore might use as his bachelor pad, between wives.

It was a shock. How could a young man, who couldn't be any older than, say, twenty-seven, afford a place like that? He waved away the question impatiently. Trevor gave me a filthy look. To him, the answer was obvious: in a place like Sicily, one of the most loosely run gateways between Africa and Europe, it had to be drugs.

We each stiffly drank a whisky (or was that drank a stiff whisky?) refused a second and then made our way out. Angelo's mood seemed to improve. He drove us straight to a restaurant, where he was greeted warmly by the proprietor, and ordered enough food to have fed the whole truck for a week. Maybe two, on our rations. Sadly, however, my stomach still hadn't recovered from the earlier shock, and I could only pick at the platters of antipasto, pastas, steak and vegetables. When the guys then offered to put us up for the night, as a way of apologising for the fright 'our stupid police' had given us, all three of us were adamant. Thanks very much, but we were eager to get back to the hotel.

When they finally dropped us off, however, the hotel was dark—and locked up. After trying the door and looking in vain for a bell, we gave up and made our way glumly back to the truck, ready for another night huddled on the floor. Hopefully, our fortunes would change when we eventually reached Africa. After all, it sat waiting for us, just over the dark Sicilian Channel. Tunis—it sounded warm, exotic, exciting and a world away from Europe. Our first taste of Africa. It was going to be so memorable.

The voyage the next day certainly was. The water was so rough, I spent six hours of the eight-hour trip throwing up the previous night's whisky and spaghetti. By the time we sighted land, I was past caring which continent it was—just as long as it didn't sway about when you walked on it.

But as we prepared to dock, I felt the excitement begin to rise again. We were soon going to be in Africa, the place I'd been dreaming about for so long. It was going to be hot, exotic and immensely exciting. The adventure was about to begin. And, surely, everything was going to be perfect from here on in.

chapter two
NAKED AND ALONE
ON THE WASTELAND

destination: Zaire

It was quite possibly the worst camp we'd ever had. Just 20 metres away, the body of a bloated horse lay on its side, its eyes covered with flies, its nose and mouth swarming with maggots and its legs stiffly out in front of it, like a plastic toy. Rats shuffled past us all night, stopping to sniff at any bags containing food before being shooed away by whoever was taking their turn on guard duty. It was hugely depressing.

We'd taken only twelve days to travel south through Tunisia, Algeria and Niger before entering Nigeria, the most heavily populated country of black Africa. Now we were in hot, dusty Kano, the capital of northern Nigeria, all sleeping on a patch of wasteland just outside town, close to a railway line. We'd gone to bed early, since there seemed precious little else to do at night in Kano. And, even worse, it was my birthday. I felt I just could stand it no longer. 'Does anyone fancy a drink?' I shouted out, after an hour of struggling fruitlessly to get to sleep. I glanced at my watch. It was only 9.30pm. I wondered if everyone else, apart from Mark on guard, was already asleep.

I thought I'd try a different tack. 'I'm buying,' I added, in a slightly smaller voice. Immediately, there was an enthusiastic chorus of voices, and a scrabbling of legs out of sleeping bags and mosquito nets.

A small group of us made for the nearest big hotel, a gleaming white building, conspicuous both for its size and its obvious wealth, with its own row of swish shops, a swimming pool and a little crowd of prostitutes hanging around outside. As we approached, they wolf-whistled at Mark, Ryan, Stewart and Trevor. 'Hey, big boy!' one in a short, tight leopard-print dress cried, fastening herself onto Mark. 'You like some fun?'

Mark coloured, but smiled at her. 'How much?' he asked. She stood on her toes, beckoned at him to bend down and whispered a figure in his ear. He straightened up. 'You must be joking!' he bellowed. 'That's five American dollars!'

The woman looked crestfallen. I walked on. I couldn't bear this. Where else in the world would sex come that cheap? How dare he try to barter down a woman for such a paltry sum of cash!

Inside, the bar seemed full of white expatriate oil company workers, all taking a break from their compound nearby. I bought a beer and then waited for the others. They soon caught up, minus Mark and Ryan who had apparently struck an acceptable bargain over a two-for-one deal. I bought a round, and stood awkwardly through a chorus of 'Happy Birthday'. The expats joined in, then came over and seemed eager to chat to us. They'd spent the last six months talking only to each other; different faces and conversation were a welcome diversion. Very soon, they were also buying rounds. It wasn't long before I noticed people's faces were starting to swim before my eyes, presumably on a tidal wave of alcohol.

'Are you all right?' Jenny asked me, noticing I'd suddenly fallen quiet.

'Yep, I'm fine,' I mumbled. It was a hot, steamy night, and I felt like I badly needed a breath of fresh air. Just outside the bar was the hotel pool. It glittered invitingly under the lights. On a whim, I wandered outside. And on another whim, I decided I'd dive in. It was only once I'd hit the surface that I remembered I was fully clothed.

Still, it did make me feel a great deal better. Sufficiently emboldened, I decided I'd head for 'home'. Jenny and Erica joined me. Back at our camp, I tore off my clothes, tossed them into the back of the truck, climbed into my sleeping bag on the ground nearby and immediately fell soundly asleep.

Waking up in the morning, I didn't feel bad at all. I stretched my arms in the air. I yawned. I looked around to see who else was still sleeping. I couldn't see anyone. Suddenly alarmed, I reached for my glasses inside the sleeping bag. I pulled them on and looked again. No-one; nothing. The wasteland was completely bare. The truck must have driven off earlier and I hadn't heard a thing. Now there was just me left behind—naked inside my sleeping bag.

No doubt, the others had parked up in town to buy provisions and assumed I'd come and catch them up. And I would have, if I'd had any clothes. But they, I remembered, were in the truck. I lay very still and tried to consider my options. That didn't take long since they were so extremely limited. In fact, they came down to just two: keep lying there and hope someone would come back to find me; or try to hop, in my sleeping bag, the 5 kilometres to town. So I stayed. And stayed. And stayed. Just as the sun reached its highest point and I was trying to keep smiling at the curious group of Nigerians who had ambled over from God knows where to stare at me, no doubt wondering what on earth I was doing, I heard Stewart shout my name in the distance. I yelled back, at the top of my lungs. Soon, he came jogging into my field of vision. I'd never been so pleased to see anyone in my life.

'I saw a little pile of wet clothes on the floor,' he gasped, out of breath. 'I asked around, but no-one claimed them. Then I thought they might be yours.' He handed them over and I tried to put them on while still in my sleeping bag, avoiding the eyes of the little group of locals watching me with interest.

'Thanks, Stewart,' I said, struggling with my trousers. They were wet and clammy and I was having trouble getting them past my knees. 'You don't know how grateful I am.'

It was a rare moment of warmth between any of the truck's motley crew. For if I'd thought the trip would suddenly acquire its own rhythm as we started our long drive from Tunis, through sub-Saharan Africa, through Nigeria and on to Cameroon and the Central African Republic (CAR) en route to Zaire, the half-way point of our journey to South Africa, I was sadly mistaken. In fact, things were taking a stark turn for the worse. While the scenery slowly changed from the dusty pale yellow of the desert to the grey, stubbly fields of Nigeria, and then the dirty green of Cameroon and the CAR, conditions inside the truck were deteriorating daily. My only hope was that once we got to Zaire and were able to take a bit of a break from each other—splitting up to take a boat down the Congo along with other 'real' people—life might improve. There'd be so much to see and do in Zaire, with the Lonely Planet guidebook describing the country as a place of genuine adventure, an archetypal explorer's dream with rainforests, mountains, volcanoes, rivers and teeming wildlife, that surely we'd start really enjoying the trip. For we sure weren't at this point.

For a start, Tim had finally joined us in the Tunisian capital, looking bright and refreshed. We'd been pleased to see him. It wasn't a sensation that lasted for long. I'd expected him to take charge with effortless ease, oiling our arrival in Africa with some well-chosen wisdoms about the continent, perhaps the odd lecture on the mores of the different countries we were passing through and, naturally, a thorough understanding of the peoples. Instead, it quickly became evident that he quite simply regarded each new country as a fresh hurdle to clear, and each and every African as his enemy. It didn't matter whether they were startling sapphire-robed Tuaregs who'd appear suddenly from nowhere, racing through the featureless Sahara Desert on their horses, or the squat-legged, square-jawed Hausa of northern Nigeria who'd simply turn and stare, amazed at the sight of so many white people sitting in various states of disarray in a converted dustcart. They were all no more than awkward distractions. Tim's focus was on getting his precious truck to South Africa as quickly and as cheaply as possible, so he could make some 'real' cash running two or three-week safaris for well-heeled tourists.

'They're all the same,' he sneered early on, as we were all gazing in wonderment at a group of the Tuareg tribesmen on horseback galloping by. 'They're always giving you hassles. Bastards. Rob you as soon as look at you.' It was an attitude that poisoned every transaction. Shopping at markets, Tim insisted the stall-holders were intent on cheating him, just because he was white and they assumed he could afford a couple of cents more than the old man down the way who'd just sold half his children for a bag of rice. At night, he warned, the locals all turned thieves, hatching plots in the dark to come and steal our tent pegs; or the wheels off the truck; or a few of our rotting bananas. And expressly to stop them, he regularly did the unforgivable: he'd give the biggest bloke in the village a big stick and a handful of coins if he whacked anyone who came within a cooee of our camp.

Suspicion, distrust, ignorance and contempt, he encouraged at every turn. He used soap to wash in rivers, regardless of whether they also functioned as the local drinking water supply. He tried to rip people off at every opportunity: 'They'll do it to you first, otherwise,' he said.

One day in the CAR, we'd camped close to an old broken down shack, which Tim tore apart for firewood. Two hours later, we were horrified to see an elderly man collapse in tears, arriving back to see his home destroyed. Not knowing what else to do, I went and sat in my tent and cried. I couldn't look at the old man a moment longer. I felt so ashamed, so angry, so disillusioned with my pretty little fantasies of waltzing around Africa, meeting people, befriending them and creating a beautiful, mutual understanding. Instead, I was part of a monster blundering around the continent, achieving the seemingly impossible in leaving people's lives even poorer. Of course, it would have helped the old man far more if I'd organised a whip-round for him, or even gone over, shaken his hand and apologised, but at the time it felt like nothing could possibly help.

Another day, driving through Cameroon, the truck went over a bridge and caught a wheel on the edge, snapping part of the wood and becoming caught in the structure. Tim gathered together a mob of locals to push and pull us out. As we drove off after a three-hour struggle to free us, he threw money at them, leaving them to scrabble in the dirt for the coins. Only later did he inform us that he'd tossed old Zaire coins to them, utterly worthless even in Zaire.

I tried to confront Tim over the way he treated people, but he would have none of it. 'What do you know?' he growled. 'You bleedin' heart liberals...all the same.'

When I talked to the others about banding together against him, they were fearful. 'But what'll we do if he drives off without us?' asked Nina. 'I don't have much money. I'll be stranded.' She had a point. The price of the trip to Jo'burg had been an all-inclusive one, with our travel, a few sights and all our food thrown in. Few of us had much spending money left over.

'Things might improve when we get to Zaire,' suggested Lisa. 'He might just be behaving like this because he's a bit stressed. Once we get to the half-way point and we have all those miles under our belt, he might relax a little bit. I don't think he's a bad person, he's just a bit under pressure. Let's wait till Zaire and see how he is then.'

Stewart snorted. 'Hey! I quite like him,' he said. 'He says it as he sees it. What's wrong with that?' I gave up.

It wasn't as if Tim was much nicer to us. The water tank soon sprang a leak and, too mean to fix it, he merely filled it each day from rivers, streams and lakes. Very soon, the state of each other's bowels became a favourite topic of conversation as we battled various potencies of dysentery. Washing was a rare luxury—only if we happened to stop in a campsite with showers, or came across any large puddles in the road or a river that we hoped was safe enough to bathe in. Those of us who still cared became adept at washing our entire bodies, and cleaning teeth, in no more than a wine bottleful of water.

Frequently we'd end the day putting up tents in the pitch black of darkness as every road we travelled down seemed to be rougher, and progress so much slower, than Tim had allowed for. The tents were so often soaked from heavy rainy season downpours, that they rarely had time to dry out. Wet sleeping bags were unfurled every night. People regularly injured themselves falling out of the back of the truck in the dark when the ladder hadn't been propped up. The fires we lit at night with green wood would usually only take with generous swigs of kerosene, and would often spark and catch someone standing too close. I felt inordinately grateful to Nina one evening in the north of Cameroon for hurling some of her precious teeth-brushing allowance of water at me when my trousers, unbeknownst to me, caught alight.

On the couple of occasions we saw other, professional overland expeditions travelling in luxuriously appointed trucks, we could only stand and stare at their up-to-the-minute camping equipment, imagine their gourmet meals and wave at their happy, smiling, contented faces, as they excitedly discussed the next stop on their fabulous itineraries.

In our truck, the food cupboard and kitty soon ran out of the basics, and our all-expenses-trip was quickly reduced to a one-meal-a-day journey. Those who could afford it bought bread, cans of sardines and bananas along the way, and ate them lovingly for breakfast and lunch in front of those of us who couldn't. Those of us eking out extremely limited budgets existed between evening meals on a diet of dried potato granules from the 'Cadbury's Smash' drum in the emergency provisions section. With hot water, they made edible instant mashed potato. Without any water at all, eating them was rather like crunching on gravel, a torture akin only to the party game where you eat as many Cream Crackers without a drink as possible. The only difference was there was never a party drink available after the Smash.

The cupboard soon sported a huge padlock to which only a couple of trusted lieutenants—Mickey and his new girlfriend Claire—had keys. Naturally, the rest of us began to loathe them both. We were all steadily losing weight; Claire looked unnaturally healthy. And even when you lashed out and bought food, like sardines, a ripe avocado, a stub of bread, it wasn't always safe. You were always on your guard against anyone dipping a casual hand into your pack beneath your seat. Because it did happen. Often.

While all of us muttered darkly that Tim wasn't treating us fairly, there was little chance of a united front. Erica was now sleeping with Tim, so didn't want to do anything to jeopardise her place in the cab with him, or her extra rations; Stewart was still torn between hunger and a sneaking admiration; Mark and Ryan wouldn't comment. Divisions and enmities were also tearing us apart, provoked by personality clashes, our different expectations of the trip, and the gnawing hunger and persistent sickness we all routinely suffered.

Dan and Debbie bickered constantly. 'I never wanted to come in the first place!' you could hear her shrieking from their tent. 'I was quite happy to stay at home. But you, oh you, you *promised* me this was going to be wonderful. Huh! Why do I ever listen to you?'

He, on the other hand, seemed oblivious to her complaints. He'd adapted utterly to the deprivations of the trip. Soon, there was a scramble every day to sit the furthest possible from him in the truck. He completely gave up washing and stank to high heaven. He no longer washed his hair, saying its natural oils would soon replenish the sheen itself. He ate with his hands. He caught and killed chickens when it was his turn to make the evening meal. 'This is fantastic!' he said, one night, hacking into two dead chickens. 'This is *really* living.' Memorably, he once even defecated in the double sleeping bag he shared with Debbie, as she slept beside him. That night, her screaming woke us all up.

It wasn't easy sustaining even civil relationships in such conditions. There was fighting over food, water and money. Trevor and Mark once came to blows over a piece of firewood, when each claimed they'd spotted it first and so should be let off washing-up duties. It was *Lord of the Flies* without the island, a story of how quickly civilisation pares down into a miserable fight for survival when the going gets tough.

In retrospect, it was a ridiculous way to try to travel. We were a tiny microcosm of Western culture sliding through the continent. We barely touched, or were touched by, the lives of those we observed, always from a distance. Instead, we became obsessed with our own discomfort and festering animosities. Africa flashed by outside the truck, unnoticed.

Our contact with the people who lived outside our little world inside the truck was pretty minimal. It was difficult for locals to make the first move; our sheer numbers were terrifying. Often, the kids were happiest to approach, eager for some time, some attention and, hopefully, a plastic biro at the end of it all. In former French colonies, like the CAR and Niger, sometimes a crowd of children would gather around the back of the truck and their chant would grow deafening. '*Donnez-moi un bic!*' they'd shout in unison. '*Donnez-moi un bic! Donnez-moi un bic!*'

Sometimes, it was just as easy with the adults. In tiny villages in Cameroon and the CAR, they didn't tend to see many outsiders so were just as curious as their kids. In cities, naturally, relations tended to be much more complex and problematic. Still, the novelty of seeing a bunch of *mzungus* (white people) travelling around in such a bizarre way often broke down barriers in itself. In Tunisia and Algeria, strangers would throw lemons and cigarettes into the back of the truck as gifts to their odd visitors. At one point, we even considered rigging up a net to catch their offerings. One afternoon, stopping for a break as we walked behind the truck, creaking up a steep incline in southern Niger, a woman came out of her hut, disappeared back inside and then re-emerged, with a saucepan of little doughy cakes to give to the strangers. In one tiny cluster of huts just over the border in Nigeria, a family standing with only bark strips around their waists waved and smiled at us so much, I went over and asked if I could take a photo. They happily agreed, but then disappeared back inside their hut. They re-emerged a few minutes later to pose proudly in torn T-shirts with American slogans and tattered trousers.

For the influence of the West was increasingly obvious everywhere. In Kano, we passed a little house built entirely of Coca-Cola cans. Nearby, huge, thick power poles had recently been erected to feed electricity to the oil workers' compound a few kilometres away. One had been placed immediately outside the front door of a little house, which meant its residents could no longer open it. They had to climb in and out of a window along the side. 'Well, the plans said we had to put it there,' laughed the English oil workers I met later that day in the bar on my birthday. 'The exercise'll do them good.' Those same men had also just finished putting speed humps along the main roads of the town in an attempt to slow down traffic. Instead, the road toll shot up. Locals, having little idea they'd been put in, and no idea what they were, died in terrible numbers after their elderly cars hit the bumps at speed and disintegrated completely.

Everywhere, there were still great hoardings for face cream that could lighten black skin and make its owner so much more attractive, despite the knowledge that the hydro-quinine in those bleaching mixes quite literally ate away the skin. Happy photos of mothers nursing bouncing babies extolled the virtues of powdered milk over breast milk, even though doctors knew the water often used to make up the formula did the kids so much damage. Cigarettes, said posters plastered all over big towns, were good for your health. It depressed me that big corporations were still so keen to press products that they must have known were decimating the health of so many, onto Africans.

Some of our contact with the locals, on the other hand, wasn't quite so welcome. We were parked in Bangui, the capital of the CAR, close to the Zaire border when the 1981 elections took place. The CAR had always been run as the personal fiefdom of the massively corrupt and brutal, self-declared emperor, Jean-Bédel Bokassa. His authority, however, had been waning for years and had fallen apart completely two years before when the army, said to be acting on his personal instructions, massacred schoolchildren peacefully protesting his decree that they wear expensive uniforms made in his own factory. In September 1979, he was overthrown by a French-backed coup led, ironically, by the President he'd previously deposed, David Dacko, and fled into exile, while Dacko's date for fresh elections for office coincided with our arrival. He, of course, won, and riots immediately broke out all over the country, with locals claiming the election had been rigged by the French. The new government immediately slapped a curfew on the capital, and Zaire closed its border with the CAR. We were caught, waiting, hoping, it wouldn't be too long before they opened it again.

Our campsite was a stretch of mud in the middle of nowhere, used by any travellers coming into the city. Very soon, there was quite a crowd of us sitting there every day by our vehicles, waiting for the border to open. We were perfect prey for thieves, and there they were among the most skilled in the world. Trevor, lying on the ground one afternoon listening to his transistor radio, happened to notice a long break between tunes. It had been stolen as it lay just a couple of inches away from his ear. A couple driving a Kombi around Africa, and sleeping inside, were astonished to climb out of their vehicle one morning to see it propped up with bricks, after thieves had stolen the tyres during the night as they slept. Four Danes locked their Land Rover while they went into town. When they came back, it had been stripped of everything and anything of value, inside and out.

One day, wandering around the dusty, deserted city, Jenny and I were hailed by a white couple driving a Swedish aid worker jeep. It was a real novelty, they explained, to see other whites in that part of the world; would we come over to their house for tea later? Gladly, we accepted. We arrived at 4pm to find them leisurely setting about making dinner for us. And I mean leisurely. By 6pm, there was still no sign of food, and we began to get nervous. The curfew began at 7.30pm every evening, and we had to be sure to be home—on our patch of wasteland outside the city once more—by then.

'No problem!' Jans airily waved off our concerns. 'We'll drive you back. Don't worry about that.' So we relaxed, and ate and drank and chatted, enjoying the chance to mix with other Westerners well away from our truck and the conflict ever-broiling inside. Come 10pm, however, we said we'd have to go, and looked expectantly at Jans. 'Damn!' he said. 'I forgot! I've drunk far too much to drive you back tonight.' We waited meekly, hoping for an invitation to stay the night. It never came. 'You'll be fine!' Jans simply exhorted. 'Just wave and smile if the military approach!'

We said our farewells, suddenly feeling far more sober, and stepped out of the front door into the road. No more than two minutes later, an army jeep roared past and screeched to a halt at the sight of us. We smiled and waved, as instructed. It seemed to have the opposite effect to the one intended.

'Stop!' shouted one of the group of five soldiers. 'Curfew! Curfew!' He waved an old machine gun at us. He didn't have to tell us twice—we froze.

Another army van pulled up alongside them. A soldier in camouflage gear climbed out, levelled a museum-piece rifle at us and said, in a low, cold voice, 'Get in!' He pointed his gun to the back of the van and strode over to the wire door. Another man leapt out, put a huge key into the over-sized padlock, turned and opened the door. 'Get in!' the soldier repeated. 'NOW!!'

We quickly went to the door and peered in. Inside were perhaps fifteen people squashed into a space probably intended for no more than five. One look back at the soldier's glowering face, however, and we quickly pushed our way in, as those already inside vainly tried to squash themselves against the walls to avoid us. 'English,' we whispered to them. 'English. Not French.' Well, it wouldn't do us any good for them to think we were the enemy. But we were, anyway. Whites. In a police van. They could only mean trouble.

The van drove around for another half-an-hour, obviously looking for anyone else violating curfew. Inside, it was hot and unbearably stuffy, but no-one spoke. Everyone avoided everyone else's eyes. Occasionally you'd catch someone curiously looking you up and down, who'd immediately look away, embarrassed. But sitting hunched together and on top of each other, there was barely any room for modesty. Still, Jenny and I were too terrified to utter a single word. The soldiers stopped only once more, to pick up two more women, in tight little dresses and high-heeled sling-backs, pushing them on top of us, before we set off once more.

Finally, the van pulled up for the last time. The wire door swung open and the soldier jerked his head to tell us to get out. We were at the city army barracks. Jenny and I exchanged worried looks. 'English,' we said, feebly. 'English.' No-one took any notice. Our group was herded into the front of the barracks, where we were divided into men one side, and women the other. Apart from the barking of the soldiers, not a word was spoken. Everyone abjectly ambled to one side or the other, eager not to attract attention to themselves by being slow, or difficult, or at all argumentative. We were all then herded down a long, dark corridor, which stank of urine. Two of the four holding cells were already full, packed with men wailing and grumbling, which paused for a fraction of a second to turn into interested chatter the moment the inmates noticed two white women in the female group. Our men were pushed into one of the empty cells. The women were ushered into the other. Jenny and I were stopped as we started to walk in. We were told to wait outside, while the soldiers strode back up the corridor we'd just walked down.

We stood outside the women's cell, looking in. Obviously, most of them were sex workers, dressed breezily in little dresses, high heels and over-bright lipstick, except for one woman who'd just been rushing back home from visiting her sick mother. Her husband would be so worried, she moaned. And who would feed the children in the morning?

The others tried to comfort her. We'll be out of here by 11am the next morning, they reassured her. It didn't seem to have much of an effect. 'But my husband!' she wailed. 'He needs his breakfast!' The others shrugged and turned away. They didn't have too much sympathy. She was lucky—at least she *had* a husband.

There was an argument going on between the soldiers who'd brought us in, and those obviously in charge of the place. Their voices became raised as they gestured towards us. I suppose we were a problem. They seemed not to be prepared to put us in a cell with the others, but that left them with the problem of what to do with us. Finally, they seemed to reach a resolution. The burliest of the soldiers came over to us. We stiffened.

'Come here!' he ordered. We were walked back to their front office, a bare room with a table, a single chair and three big wooden cupboards against one wall. 'You, stay here!' he said, before turning on his heel, marching out and slamming the door shut. It immediately bounced open again. We took turns sitting on the chair. We tried to lie down on the table, but it was just a little too short for comfort. After about an hour, when it became obvious this was our spot for the night, we both laid down on the floor, exhausted, ready to sleep.

A few minutes later, one of the soldiers walked back in. He glanced over at us, and then opened the door to one of the cupboards. There was a great clatter as a couple of dozen rifles fell out into a heap on the floor before his feet, and a number of grenades rolled across the floor. He looked at us apologetically, then gathered up the grenades and pushed them back in the cupboard, and took an armful of rifles and walked straight back out. Curiosity piqued, we got to our feet and nonchalantly strolled over to the other two cupboards. Again, they were stuffed with rifles. If we had half a mind to launch an escape attempt, the odds were in our favour, I mulled over to myself. Then, finally, I fell asleep on the hard floor.

It must have only been a couple more hours when there was a sudden shouting, the scuffling of a dozen pairs of army boots running up the corridor and the thud of armaments being thrown into a truck. Jenny and I sat up in alarm. We went over to the door and peered out. Catching sight of us, one of the soldiers in charge ran over.

'We go now,' he said. 'There is trouble. We leave you in charge.' And, with that, they roared off in their selection of trucks and jeeps. In charge! Well, we had enough armaments to start World War Three and enough prisoners to continue it, at least for a bit, but we merely retreated back into our room and hoped they wouldn't be away for too long. Of course, we could have released the other poor souls who'd been arrested alongside us, but what if they really were villains, what if they attacked us, and what if the soldiers came back while we were seeing all their inmates off? It was safest to do nothing, we agreed. We went back to sleep on the floor, hoping nothing would happen while we were holding the fort.

By daylight, we were woken by the revving up of the vehicles that had just returned and the shouting of a few more prisoners. A couple of the soldiers opened the door to our office. 'You can go now!' one called out. We didn't have to be told twice. We scurried out into the dawn, relieved that we'd been treated so well, and our period in charge of an army camp in one of the most bloodied parts of Africa had been totally without incident. It was a lucky escape.

Two days later, we were granted permission to leave the CAR and, eagerly, we boarded the ferry for Zaire. Zongo was waiting for us on the other side of the Oubangui River, marking the start of a huge new country, full of rainforest, fascinating new people, strange animals, exotic birds and a whole new experience. It was our half-way mark, the point at which we all desperately hoped the trip might improve. As the ferry chugged to a halt on the sandbank that signalled Zaire, hope rose inside me. I caught Jenny's eye and smiled. She beamed back. Life was now going to improve. It *had* to.

chapter three
HOW FAR NOW TO NAIROBI?

destination: Nairobi, Kenya

Crossing over that river from Bangui to Zongo, Zaire, was a symbolic moment for us all. Zaire represented a big deal. We had passed the half-way point of the trip, and we were now on the home-run. Zaire, formerly the Congo and later to revert back to the Congo, felt like the very heart of Africa, the kind of place where anything could happen—and sometimes did. It was a country of lush, impenetrable rainforest, split in half by the mighty Congo River snaking 4380 kilometres through the hinterland to the Atlantic Ocean in Angola and the towering Ruwenzori Mountains, the so-called Mountains of the Moon, soaring 4.8 kilometres into the sky.

After the excitement of Zaire, we'd be moving into Rwanda, then Tanzania and on to the tourist-friendly watering hole of Kenya. There, we'd be able to have a taste once more of the Western life we'd left so far behind: eat chips and ice cream, see a movie, sleep in a hotel room between clean sheets, watch *Dallas* on TV. All of us were looking forward to Nairobi. We'd be able to go our own ways for a couple of weeks and have a break from each other, before returning to that God-awful truck for the last leg down to South Africa.

Yet our arrival in Zaire heralded no monumental shift in our fortunes. Even when the sights around us were absolutely breathtaking, few of us were in any position to appreciate them as fully as we should. Early in the trip, we had been stunned into silence by the sudden appearance in the undulating featurelessness of the Sahara Desert of the stately Hoggar Mountains near Tamanrasset, Algeria, until it was discovered that the truck's water supply had been seeping out steadily all the way from Touggourt in the north. We had been entranced by the striking round straw and daub huts nestling in the folds of volcanoes near Yaounde, the Cameroon capital, with its promise of the Africa we always hoped still existed, until the truck was surrounded by a group of hostile men wielding machetes, waving us on. And now, it was the same story all over again. Passing by the Mountains of the Moon, we all gazed awestruck at the magnificence of the dark green giants, their peaks wreathed in mist—until we were struck down, as one, by a violent stomach-ache from something Lisa had cooked the previous night.

Money was also a constant cloud over us. Firstly, we never seemed to have enough, since Tim had under-budgeted so badly for the trip. All of us ended up having to fork out more if we wanted to do any of those activities advertised so alluringly, like visiting the Rwandan gorillas or staying in some of the East African game parks. Some of us auctioned off our meals to raise the extra money. Even so, doing game parks on the cheap became an intensely hazardous exercise. Having to slip out of your threadbare tent into the pitch black night in the Serengeti to relieve yourself, with the communal torches long since run out of batteries, became a heart-stopping experience. Especially when the morning sun would reveal the paw prints from a pride of lions just feet away from your squatting position. It made wonders of nature, that might previously have seemed tremendously exciting, suddenly a distinct threat. One day in the Rwandan capital Kigale, a great hawk swooped down on a samoza I'd just bought and snatched it away out of my hands. I should have been enchanted. Instead, it was as much as I could do to stop myself bursting into tears.

Secondly, there was the hassle over getting hold of local currency in each country we passed through. In each place, the strength or weakness of the currency reflected the current economic and political circumstances. Tunisia, for example, being run as a moderate pro-Western Arab state under the stable leadership of president-for-life Habib Bourguiba, had an extremely strong currency. Just before we'd arrived in early 1981, Bourguiba had announced that opposition political parties could finally be formed, and the currency firmed even further at half a *dinar* to a US dollar.

In neighbouring Algeria, on the other hand, the *dinar* was extremely weak, reflecting the political instability of a country which had chosen to remain non-aligned and support various liberation struggles going on in the continent, from the ANC in South Africa to the Polisario Front in Western Sahara. In the banks, one US dollar was worth four *dinar*. On the streets, among the black market money-changers, the same dollar was worth twelve *dinar*.

Naturally, countries were extremely keen to stamp out their currency black markets as they undermined the official exchange rates. Tourists were required, as a result, to show official exchange receipts as they left the country, proving they'd changed money at banks. For me, this posed a real dilemma. It might be bad enough visiting Africa in such an artificial way, I thought; it would be twice as bad to harm struggling economies at the same time by changing hard currency on the black market. It soon became obvious, however, that I'd never be able to survive if I stayed with the official rates. Besides, often the banks were only open at odd times on various days that were impossible to predict. And sometimes the bureaucratic red tape simply proved all too much.

One day in Goma, the tidy little town on the shores of Lake Kivu in western Zaire, close to the border with Rwanda, I really despaired of good intentions. We'd been sleeping *al fresco* on a field of slated volcano lava into which it was impossible to drive tent pegs, close to the palace of the country's president, the immensely wealthy and horrifically corrupt Mobutu Sese Seko. His palace, indeed, was the biggest building for miles, gleaming magnificently in the morning sun while his people eked out a living nearby in little mud huts, or rickety wooden sheds. The palace was guarded by the kind of dogs whose bark suggested vicious, over-sized wolves, interrupting our sleep all night, growling and howling when anyone walked past the ornate gates.

Trevor, Jenny and I had walked the 3 kilometres into town, to try to change some money at a bank. For such a small town, Goma really did have an awful lot of banks—at least four just by the main street, and all housed in grand, airy colonial mansions, that looked bizarrely out of place in such a modest setting. Inside, however, the real Zaire endured. In the first, a group of ragged staff dressed in an assortment of ill-matched Western clothing, rushed over to take a look at us when we walked in. When we asked to change money, they looked alarmed.

'You want to change *dollars*?' asked an older woman, dressed in a red and white striped T-shirt over a yellow and purple print dress. She looked incredulous. '*American* dollars? Why don't you change outside, on the street? You get a much better rate.'

'No, no,' said Trevor, firmly. 'I want to change them *here*.' He hadn't a single bank stamp on his form and he dearly needed one before he went through customs later that week.

The five people behind the counter looked at each other, confused. Evidently, few tourists had ever made such a demand on their services. Besides, it turned out, they only had one pen between them. They scuffled around for forms, jostled for the pen, laboriously looked up exchange rates, and finally processed the US$10 note Trevor handed them. In return, they carefully counted out the US$5 commission, then handed him 15 *zaires*, in stark contrast to the 100 *zaires* he would have received a few steps away, outside.

Unfortunately, I had only traveller's cheques and after taking one and passing it around admiringly, they then handed it back to me with a shrug. They'd never seen such a thing before. Surely it wasn't real money?

On to the next bank. No, they couldn't change traveller's cheques either. The next could—but not the brand I had. The fourth looked unsure, so I pressed my need to change it. After much shaking of heads and protest, the man in charge finally consented to phone his head office in the capital, Kinshasha, to ask permission to change the cheque. He told me to come back in the afternoon to await the outcome. I wandered round town for a few hours, and then returned.

He was beaming. 'Yes, you are very lucky,' he announced. 'They have said we can change this.' He handed it back to me.

I passed it back to him. 'Well, let's do it,' I said.

I sat down on the floor while the calculations were done and the forms were all filled in, in triplicate. They then had to be inspected by everyone in the bank to make sure no-one had made a mistake. Finally, I was called back to the counter and handed all the paperwork. I looked at it and blinked. After changing a US$20 traveller's cheque, minus the tax and commission, I actually *owed* them four *zaire*. I could do nothing but laugh out loud. The bank manager looked downcast. 'Yes, it is a little unfortunate,' he said, slowly, 'but that is the best we can do.'

I was trapped. I also needed the stamp on my form and, if that's what it cost, then so be it. I told the manager to hang on a moment and walked outside to look for a money-changer. There was one loitering on the steps, no doubt in the full knowledge of what the bank would be offering me. I changed

US$20 cash with him, then went back into the bank, paid my fee and decided the paperwork would be a nice souvenir. Sometimes, the odds were just stacked against you.

The next day, life seemed just as bizarre. I'd befriended a couple of locals I'd met on a walk and they invited me back to their village. I picked up Jenny on the way. Once there, they gave us thick, soupy tea and then started touching our hair. I suppose a couple of blondes would be bound to excite some curiosity. Two older women then came over and started to braid our hair in tight little plaits all over our heads. They then dressed us in brightly coloured sarongs and stood back and admired their handiwork. We must have looked a sight.

But then came visitors no-one could have expected. There was the roar above our heads of a helicopter and our new friends ran into their huts in terror. We stayed rooted to the spot as a green camouflaged army helicopter hovered into view and slowly started to descend. It landed nearby and Jenny and I simply stood and watched. The door opened and two white soldiers climbed out then stood stock still in disbelief as they caught sight of us. 'Hi!' yelled Jenny, above the noise of the blades. 'Welcome!'

They were the French Army on a training exercise, probably getting ready to go into the CAR to help quell the riots that had seemed to be picking up momentum. Still, we had a civilised cup of tea together while they regarded our hair and outfits dubiously. 'I never would have expected to see two white women in a place like this...looking like that!' said one.

'Well,' I replied, 'neither did we.'

Meantime, back at the truck, the fighting continued undiluted by our exotic geographical progress. Ructions, particularly between Lisa and Jonathan, were growing far more ferocious by the day. Darkly cynical about life and all who lived it, Jonathan couldn't bear Lisa's ingenuous innocence, he said, a moment longer. Nina, older than the rest of us, joined his attacks and, later, his tent. The pair muttered morosely between themselves about Lisa's floaty dresses, the flowers she'd put in her hair, her friendliness to Africans and the way she acted as though a good hug was a panacea for all ills.

'You're just two dried-up horrible people,' she'd scream back when the digging all got too much. 'You're bitter and twisted.' And she was probably right. Physical conditions didn't help any, though. Mosquitoes invaded the tents every night, making sleep impossible, and everyone was tired and cranky during the day. At various places in Zaire in the evenings, swarms of tsetse flies would descend, biting us all through even the thickest of socks and pants. The state of one's bowels became the only topic of conversation. When we travelled, the person with the worst diarrhoea would be left to thump the loudest on the door between Tim's driving cabin and the rest of the truck, to plead for him to stop. According to his mood, he'd either agree to stop, or smile evilly and not. Erica, still up in front with him, often joined in the pleas for him to give us mercy stops. He was just misunderstood, she insisted.

Lisa retreated more and more within herself to avoid the ugly realities of daily life in the truck. She'd frequently buy big bags of marijuana and make cookies with it at night, in order to drift off into blissful nirvana during the day. Regularly, however, she'd only just avoid trouble. The day before we were due to go through the border between Zaire and Rwanda, she panicked when she realised how much she still had stored in her pack. So, that night, she cooked up a whole batch of dope cookies and the next day she ate the lot. By the time she had to show her passport, she couldn't even stand. Jenny and I swore to the guards she was desperately sick and we were eager to get her to hospital in Kigale.

Another day, still in Zaire, she hopped off the truck when we were driving slowly over a particularly rough road, to look for butterflies. It wasn't until the next day that someone realised she was missing. Tim, at first, refused to go back for her. But in the nearest act to rebellion so far, the rest of us—bar Nina and Jonathan—insisted he turn around and find her. Eventually, we came across her ambling up the muddy highway with a whole village-full of children behind her, Mary Poppins-like, singing songs.

For, to be fair, there were moments when some of us managed to connect with the people we'd actually come to see. It was easy to make friends with the kids standing staring at us in every village. Most of them were scared of white people, so just a movement towards them and they'd back off in terror. Then, if you laughed, they realised you were playing, and you could spend hours chasing them, screaming and laughing, until you all collapsed together in a heap. One day, in a village near Douala, Cameroon, I nearly came a cropper when a little boy I was chasing fell over and bumped his head. His dad, sitting doing some knitting nearby, leapt up and came racing towards me when he saw me bending over his son, sitting shaking in floods of tears. Luckily, on his way, the other kids told him what had happened, and he ended up shaking my hand and inviting me into his hut for a glass of tea. Another day, a man in northern Tanzania, with an economy-sized Blue Band margarine can pushed through a gash in his ear for decoration, presented me, with great ceremony, with a plastic biro.

'These people,' Nina would drone on, 'know nothing. Look, they don't even grow things on their land.' And she'd sweep an arm across a sharply steeped piece of dusty land as we passed Rwanda's Virunga mountain range. 'If this was Bali, they'd be selling us tomatoes and banana pancakes. What's the matter with these people? If they just *tried* to make money, they'd be so much happier...'

Stewart would then chime in. 'People may criticise South Africa,' he'd say, 'but at least the blacks have enough to eat. They're not so stupid as the people here. They know where their bread is buttered.'

For God's sake! They were equally dismissive when we arrived in Rwanda to discover we weren't going to be allowed to visit the famous gorilla sanctuary on the slopes of the Visoke volcano because guerilla activity in the area, with rising tensions between the Hutu and the Tutsi, had escalated dangerously. 'Don't these people realise they need money from us tourists?' snarled Nina. 'You'd think they'd have a bit more sense.'

It was the same ignorant laughter at the consequences of a decision by Tim to accuse a local, who'd come to our camp selling oranges, of stealing a few pieces of cloth from the truck. Sure, he'd done it, but when the townspeople heard they summonsed the police, who beat him, then made him stand all day under the burning sun, holding a heavy rock in each hand. We begged the police to let him go; the cloths were worth nothing and how could we, who had so much, blame him, who had so little, for such a trivial theft? Besides, we were horribly embarrassed and ashamed. Nina and Stewart, on the other hand, were triumphant. It just showed how cruel and inhumane Africans could be to Africans. 'You see, these people don't even behave well to their own,' said Stewart. 'They can't be trusted.'

Can't be trusted? Oh yes, that would be with the aftermath of a colonial history that destroyed traditional ways of life, created new tensions between black and black, distorted the meaning of justice and corrupted any sense of fair play. But in Nina's and Stewart's eyes, they were probably to blame for colonialism too. After all, Europeans would never have put themselves out to vanquish the continent in the first place if they'd have known the natives would be so plainly ungrateful.

Time and time again, it shocked me to the core that people of such ignorance and such arrogance would even opt to travel around Africa. Nina spat back that she was here 'despite the Africans', coming to see—huh!—the mountain gorillas of Rwanda, the Mountains of the Moon in Zaire, the lions of Tsavo. Stewart had joined the ride as a way of getting back home to Jo'burg cheaply, with a few more notches on his adventure belt. Tim was there just to make sure his truck arrived intact, and with as little expenditure as possible. Jonathan was there to have fun.

His share of that fun, however, came to an abrupt end in Zaire. One morning, he started complaining of a blinding headache. By the next day, it was no better. On the third day, he couldn't even raise his head. We stopped off at a doctor's little compound. The verdict: typhoid. Passing through Kinshasha, we dropped him off at a hospital, and nobody ever saw him again.

Mark and Ryan weren't much happier. They had caught some sexually-transmitted disease or other after their shared night with the prostitute in Kano. They'd been so heartily back-slappingly 'boysy' about that night, I couldn't help but smile looking at their tight, grim faces a few weeks later. 'How do you feel today?' I took real pleasure in asking them both, felicitously. 'Any better?' They both, individually, would do their best to grin, stoically.

The phrase most often heard however, was, 'How far now to Nairobi?' None of us were in top form. We'd all suffered various bouts of amoebic dysentery, others had regular attacks of malaria, being washed out for days at a time before the fever ebbed. Three people contracted Hepatitis A.

It'll be all right when we reach Nairobi, became our daily mantra. There, we'll be able to see good doctors, and eating some decent food will build up our collective strength no end. As we rock-and-rolled over lumpy roads in northern Tanzania to use a little-known border crossing into Kenya Tim had heard rarely charged entry fees, the thought of Nairobi kept everyone smiling as we were thrown around the truck. What did a few bumps and bruises matter, we asked. We'll soon be able to go into a chemist shop and buy plasters. Who cares that we're now so low on food, we're down to one meal a day? We'll soon be eating curry out of hollowed-out pineapples and sorbets frozen inside coconut husks.

Tim noticed our spirits soar and chose his moment well. The night before our border crossing into Kenya, he made a rare appearance outside his driver's cab and said he had an announcement to make: he'd run out of money and would no longer be taking us down to South Africa. The trip would stop in Nairobi instead. But before we had even summoned up a complaint, he got in with his counter-attack. 'You know, you've only got yourselves to blame,' he growled. 'If you hadn't been such pigs at the beginning and eaten so much, there would have been plenty of food for us all. And if you'd have helped me more in organising things, then our funds would have lasted all the way to Jo'burg.'

We all looked at each other, dumbstruck. There seemed little point in arguing—his mind was obviously made up. And did any of us *honestly* want him to recant, and continue this terrible trip down to South Africa?

So, after all that, Nairobi was to be the end of the line. Still, it was going to be a pretty bloody wonderful end of the line. As we drove through the border into Kenya, then started the two-day drive to the capital, I began to plan everything I wanted to do and see there, and then what I'd do next. On the first day, however, I started feeling rough. On the second, Jenny peered at me hard and exclaimed that my eyes had turned yellow. Nairobi was holding so much promise but, for me, promise that wouldn't be fulfilled. I had caught Hepatitis A and, rather than explore the fabulous delights of the place, I spent a week in bed, too weak to go out to buy food and living only on the kindness of the hotel owner who brought me fresh water to drink every day. If he hadn't taken pity on me, I realised later with a jolt, I could have ended my days in that room—especially if I'd pre-paid for any length of time.

When a doctor finally came, he told me I'd probably need at least another six weeks of complete rest to start my recovery. It was just too long. I had no choice but to fly out, back home, for some TLC. I'd come all that way and seen nothing of my destination. But Africa wasn't done with me yet...

chapter four
SO, HOW ARE *YOUR* BLACKS?

destination: Great Zimbabwe Ruins, Zimbabwe

That truck trip through Africa had been my first experience of group travel. It would also, I vowed, be my very last. Nothing, but nothing, could be worse than travelling with a bunch of ill-matched people in such ghastly conditions. Except, perhaps, the option I eventually plumped for.

Malcolm and I had been friends at uni, perhaps not the best of friends, but certainly not the worst, either. We felt we knew each other pretty well. He longed to travel; I was determined to return to Africa to finish off the disastrous journey that had ended so abruptly in Nairobi. He didn't have the confidence to go it alone; I'd been bombarded with dire warnings from friends about the dangers of a woman travelling solo. 'A Rape Every Three Minutes' was the headline on a *Newsweek* magazine article a friend thoughtfully sent me about South Africa, over which she had scrawled, 'Malcolm better than going it alone??!!' Another offering came over the fax from a former work colleague: 'Death in Paradise', a newspaper story about a lone female tourist who'd been attacked and murdered in Bali.

I phoned Malcolm. 'Let's do it,' I said.

On paper, it looked wonderful: Cape Town to Cairo, taking in everything and anything in between. There'd be mountains, deserts, swamps, game parks, elephants, lakes, rivers, hippos, monuments and pyramids. We'd be hitchhiking, catching buses and trains, hopping onto boats and planes, riding on horses, donkeys and camels, walking, climbing, jumping, skipping... and all with trusty Malcolm by my side—someone to talk to, to marvel over incredible sights with, to protect, and to be protected by.

It wasn't long, however, before I started regretting the decision. About three hours, to be precise. We argued on the plane. He snored. He sniffed. He sneezed. He turned the pages of his novel too noisily. Everything he did started to get on my nerves. I spent most of the flight wondering where would be a good place to part.

'Do you think there'll be a bus from the airport to town?' Malcolm asked, six hours away from Johannesburg. 'Do you think long trousers would be better than shorts? Will there be anywhere to change traveller's cheques on the way? What will the weather be like? Do you think I should just go take a running jump now and save you the trouble of smashing this window and throwing me through it?'

The problem seemed to be that suddenly I'd been cast as the guru of travel, by virtue solely of having survived one trip around Africa. But if only he knew what that trip had been like! I hadn't a clue about catching buses from airports or the delicacies of choosing appropriate clothing. The most I'd learnt about Africa from the previous trip was how to wash in a spitful of water; how eating pawpaw seeds helped diminish the effects of a dysentery attack; and how to swallow instant mashed potato granules without getting your throat scratched to buggery.

I was as nervous as Malcolm so obviously was but felt, somehow, less prepared to show it. Still, there were some certainties in the equation, I reassured myself. For a start, in Johannesburg, we'd both been invited to stay at Stewart's house. Yes, Stewart, the guy who'd also been on the last ill-fated trip around Africa. Yes, sure, I hadn't liked him much then, but maybe he just reacted badly to stress, I told myself. I'd also found him a terrible racist, but he did insist he wasn't. Back in South Africa, he'd told me, he actually lived on a commune, with black and white. Maybe I'd been a little harsh on him. Dan and Debbie were also living in the city, and I'd written to say we might be calling in.

I had other people, too, to visit. Goy, a much-loved school-teacher originally from Cape Town, still had family living there. If I was going, he said, could I drop in on them and report back? Goy had been classified in apartheid South Africa as a 'coloured', one of those living in a no-man's land between black and white. Unwelcome back in his homeland after various bouts of anti-government activity, he longed to know, first-hand, how they were all doing. I was happy to oblige. Later, I was to be shocked by what I found.

I was far more enthusiastic, however, about moving on north from South Africa, through Botswana, to Zimbabwe. It was 1982, and just two years had passed since Zimbabwean independence. I was eager to celebrate a country that had finally kicked out its racist past and was redefining itself, in a mood of tremendously joyful optimism, along black–white egalitarian lines. And in the south of the country, near Nyanda, lay the Great Zimbabwe Ruins, first occupied in the third century by early Iron Age people. As the second biggest structure in Africa, after the Egyptian pyramids, it was meant to be a fabulous sight.

After finally landing in Johannesburg, Malcolm and I caught the bus into the soulless, grey, high-rise jumble of the town, then wandered around until we found another bus to Stewart's suburb. That was a surprise in itself. It was obviously a smart, uptown kind of area, with tidy green lawns and large white free-standing homes. His house was particularly large—nothing like my idea of a 'commune', as he'd so lovingly described it. It was quite luxurious, with its own swimming pool and quota of black servants. Back on the truck, he'd banged on about the fact that he and his housemates provided accommodation, free, for their two servants. It turned out to be little more than a shed at the end of their garden. And a pretty basic shed, at that.

'But otherwise, Merlie and Madarak would have to travel to their homeland every night and then start out at four the next morning to get back here in time for work,' said Stewart, obviously annoyed this subject had come up so early.

'What time do they start work?' I asked. 'Couldn't they just start later?'

'No, everyone starts at 7am,' he explained. Black people that was. Whites were strictly nine to five. To allow blacks to start later just wasn't an option. 'Besides,' added Stewart, sounding irritated now, 'if they were living away, they'd have to get back in time to feed their children.'

'What? They have children in that shed too?'

'Yes, four,' he replied.

'Two adults and *four* children in that tiny shed?'

'Well, maybe they should have thought of that,' barked Stewart, 'before they had so many.'

We moved on swiftly. Stewart looked more wizened and even more gnome-ish than I'd remembered, but everything was going marvellously, he insisted. He'd settled nicely back into his old job as a teacher after his last fabulous African adventure. He didn't put it quite like that, of course. 'I decided after that bloody truck, that I never want to leave home again,' he declared. 'I have everything I want here. Everything else I can read about in books.' He'd met up with fellow truck refugees Dan and Debbie only once since we'd parted in Nairobi. I was surprised. They lived a mere fifteen minutes away in one of the poorer suburbs of town. 'No, they're not really my type,' said Stewart, pouring a beer. 'In fact, I think of them as white trash. Do you remember how Dan stopped washing?'

•••

The next day, Malcolm was up early. He woke me with a cup of tea in bed. 'Well, what shall we do today?' he asked.

'I don't know,' I said. 'What would *you* like to do?' He looked anxious.

'I don't know,' he shrugged. 'What do *you* want to do?'

I sighed. 'Well, we could go and see Dan,' I suggested.

'Yes!' he said. 'I was thinking that earlier. I thought that.' It wasn't even 9am and already I felt like strangling him. This wasn't looking good.

We went out and wandered around town until I saw a bus with the name of Dan's suburb on the front, and jumped onto it. Malcolm and I asked a couple of people, and soon found their house. It was in the middle of a row of similarly dingy buildings, with a couple of scabby dogs sitting scratching by the doorstep. I banged on the door. Dan opened it, and his eyes widened to see me. We hugged in delight. I noticed he smelled of Palmolive soap. That was an improvement, at least.

Sitting drinking beer in their tiny front room, Dan said he loved South Africa. 'Apartheid,' he said, thoughtfully, 'is a media invention. The government really feels that each should look after their own. This way, the blacks look after themselves in their own place, and we get on with our lives in our areas.'

Still, he and Debbie were planning to move on soon, this time to Namibia. They needed more space, he said, they wanted the room and the opportunity to really extend themselves. In Johannesburg, he'd found the perfect job selling firefighting equipment to local councils. In Namibia, he could do the same thing, but sell to rural communities.

'How about Debbie?' I asked. 'How does she feel about all this?' He looked out of the window. He hadn't yet got around to telling her, but he knew she'd be thrilled at this new challenge.

When Debbie came home, she looked exhausted. She'd found work helping out at a hospital, but it was too many hours and for too little money. She hoped it wouldn't be for much longer, though. 'We're planning to start trying for a family soon,' she confided in the kitchen, as she made tea. 'You know, Dan's finally settled down here. It's great. Back in England, he had itchy feet all the time, always wanting to do other things. But, at last, I think he's found his place.' I kissed her warmly on the cheek in congratulation. Secretly, I wondered how much longer their marriage could possibly last. (I didn't have to wait long to find out. I received a postcard from Debbie a month later, from the UK, breaking the news that the couple had split. Dan had indeed gone on to Namibia; she, at last giving up on her dream of a 'normal' life with a nine-to-five husband, had gone home to mum.)

We went back to visit the couple a week later and Dan told us his boss Dave had invited us all to his home for a *braai* (barbecue). We went along, and he was generous in his hospitality. He seemed a perfectly nice man. Under normal circumstances, I could imagine enjoying his company. Yet in a country where the 'situation'—and the anxiety to justify it—was a national obsession, there seemed to be only ever one subject up for discussion.

Standing basting lamb steaks over the fire in his sweeping garden, with a couple of black maids on hand in case he grew tired of the chore, Dave waxed lyrical about his country. 'You people just don't understand our blacks,' he said to Malcolm and me, as the maids cast their eyes to the ground. 'You don't realise they've only just come out of the bush, they're not civilised, they don't know the things we do. They just can't be trusted with anything but the most menial jobs. They can't handle responsibility. Yes, they might complain at that, but they've got to learn to run before they can walk.'

This wasn't the first time, and I knew it wouldn't be the last, I'd hear the self-justifications of people who knew they were living privileged existences. Hitching through South Africa, east down to the seaside city of Durban, and then right along the coast to Cape Town in the south, became a torment of listening to white drivers' takes on race relations, knowing that to argue meant being turfed out of their cars in the middle of nowhere. Sometimes, you had to do it. Sometimes, you shut up and put up. Malcolm often went completely quiet. 'Oh, I could have blasted his argument to pieces,' he'd often say after a particularly tense stand-off. 'But I thought I'd better not.'

Instead, he invariably left me to withstand the heat. There was the elderly Afrikaans farmer, chatting amiably about how blacks were generally grateful for whites assuming the responsibility of running the country for them. There was the middle-aged salesman who talked cheerfully of Africans being like children: capricious, silly and ultimately untrustworthy. Then there was the church minister who condemned blacks as a people who loved drink too much, were hedonistic, incapable of serious thought and far too sexually promiscuous for their own good. It sounded like plenty of white people I knew.

Finally, just as we were coming into the flashy city of Durban, there was the woman who noticed a little cat lying injured by the side of the road. She stopped, wrapped it in her jacket, put it on the driver's seat and carried it, with misty eyes, to the local vet. Her name was Elaine and here, at last, seemed to be a feeling, kindly human being. When she offered us a bed for a couple of nights in town, we were thrilled.

The next morning, we awoke to the sound of her yelling. Peering out of the window, I saw her shouting at the man doing the gardening. He flinched with every word. He wasn't cutting the grass short enough, but was pruning the bushes too vigorously. He had pulled up a plant with the weeds. He was lazy and stupid and ignorant. Their relationship seemed to be based solely on fear, and communicated in loathing.

When her husband, Peter, returned home that afternoon from his job driving petrol tankers, my unease only increased. He stank of whisky but was friendly enough as he welcomed us warmly to their home. He invited us to have a drink with him. We did. A couple of hours of solid drinking later, Peter announced we were all off to a party.

The crowd at the *braai* in the next suburb on the outskirts were a group of middle-aged men and women, the women in little summer dresses and pearls and the men in short sleeved shirts and pale slacks. Malcolm and I were introduced around, and smiled genially. The drink and the talk flowed. It followed the usual path: the country was going to the dogs; the blacks were getting too uppity. I could hear Malcolm telling a man in the corner how he'd been planning this Cape to Cairo trip for ages, and that I'd tagged along on a whim.

A podgy man, with a particularly bad jet-black toupée, kept digging me in the ribs to emphasise his every point. I'd tried to move away, but he simply followed. 'These people aren't civilised,' he went on as he chewed at the fat sausage in his hand, showing me the masticated contents of his mouth with each word, grease dribbling down his chin. 'They don't know nothin'.'

I started to speak, but my words were interrupted by the sound of glasses smashing, screaming and shouting. We all rushed towards the kitchen. Peter, by now pretty much blind drunk, was swinging his fists at a man who was trying to restrain him. A tray of broken glasses lay on the grass. Elaine, so drunk she couldn't stand up, was sitting on a chair nearby, screeching a steady flow of invectives at him. The host was asking them both to leave.

I drove us home and we all went to bed. A couple of hours later, we were woken by the sound of gunshots. Feeling sick to my stomach, I pulled on a T-shirt and raced downstairs, fully expecting to see Elaine lying face down on the ground. Peter turned, his rifle in his hands, as I walked into the dining room. 'Bloody blacks,' he spat. 'Bastards. I thought I heard one of their kids in the garden. Don't know if I got him, though.' I stood still, stock still. I didn't trust myself to speak. 'We've had kids in here before, they stole some of our apples,' Peter was saying. 'I'll get them one day.'

There was a ring on the doorbell. Peter turned unsteadily, put the rifle down and went to the door. It was the police. One of his bullets had ricocheted off the garage and imbedded itself in a neighbour's house. They'd complained. It seemed far more serious than the risk of a black kid being killed.

Later that morning, after breakfast, Malcolm sat down on the bed. 'Well, what shall we do today?' he said. I looked at him.

'I think we should go,' I replied, starting to toss things into my pack.

'Yes,' he said, 'I thought that.'

I felt the hairs on the back of my neck prickle in a way that was becoming increasingly familiar whenever Malcolm was close. 'Well, why didn't you say it then?' I felt like screaming. He would never suggest anything but always insisted that anything I came up with he'd already come up with five minutes before. 'I know' and 'I thought that' were fast becoming his catchphrases. I bit my lip and carried on packing.

• • •

Moving down along the picturesque stretch of coast towards Cape Town, we met other whites far more relaxed about the situation. 'No, we and the Africans are very happy,' one man, who looked strangely like Benny Hill, told us hitching through Port Shepstone. 'There are no problems at all. It's just that we don't like to socialise together in the evenings.' A soldier in the South African army giving us a lift to Port Elizabeth asked me curiously, 'So, how are *your* blacks?' What do you say to a question like that? And an Indian businessman on his way to Mossel Bay insisted on buying me a portion of chips when he stopped to buy his own lunch on the way. 'You must be very careful if a coloured stops to pick you up,' he whispered, conspiratorially. 'It may be dangerous.' I was stunned.

'But you're very nice,' I whispered back.

'Yes, but it's the others you can't trust,' he replied, ingenuously. I should try only to travel with whites, he urged, they were the best. 'And if a black stops to pick you up, refuse. They are bad people.'

Only once while hitching were we picked up by a black man. That wasn't really surprising. Most of the cars on the road were driven by whites, and besides, if you were black in South Africa, would you really want to do any white person a favour? This man, however, seemed not to begrudge us a lift. It was a terribly slow ride as his truck full of supermarket goods groaned uphill and creaked downhill for 100 kilometres, but gradually he started to relax in our company, chatting about the country, his friends in the ANC and the hope that one day the country would be a completely different place.

We arrived in town just as night fell, and Mala said he couldn't possibly leave us in the middle of the city when we knew nowhere to stay. Besides, he felt we were his responsibility. He insisted on taking us to the home of his employer. He would happily put us up for the night, said Mala. He was a kind, good man. But just one thing. 'Please, please,' he begged, 'do not tell him anything I have said to you today. Please. I have a family. I do not want to lose this job.'

• • •

I went to visit Goy's sister and her family, as promised, and had a delightful time being shown around Cape Town, one of the most beautiful cities in the world. Even at some of the stunning lookouts around the place, however, it was hard to forget apartheid—there were separate benches for blacks and whites to enjoy the views. Two Africans dancing to a band playing in a square as part of the annual Cape Festival, were marched away by police, wincing as their arms were pulled up behind their backs.

In the evening, Mary cooked us a wonderful meal and talked about her niece, who left South Africa to live in Zimbabwe, whom nobody had heard from for years. 'We write to her, but have never heard back,' said Mary. 'Do you think you could look her up and check that she's all right on your way through?' I said I'd be happy to.

As they dropped Malcolm and me back at our youth hostel, we asked them in for coffee. Mary looked at the floor. 'No, sorry, we don't have time,' she said. 'We must be getting back.' It was only later I noticed the sign at the gate: 'Whites Only'. Perhaps it was just as well.

'What did you eat?' asked one of the South Africans staying there after he saw us climbing out of their car. Confused, I thought back.

'Rice, salad, vegetables, chicken...' I said.

'Hah!' he exclaimed, sneering. 'They were obviously trying to impress you. All they'd normally eat would be mealie meal.'

The next morning, I got up early. 'What do you think we should do?' I asked Malcolm. I think I already knew his answer.

'I don't know,' he said. 'What do *you* think?' I said I was ready to start our long journey north. I was eager to make a move on to Zimbabwe. 'Yes, I thought that,' said Malcolm. I could feel the irritation rise within me. I tried to quell it. Moving on would be good. Botswana was meant to be a beautiful place, and Zimbabwe would prove a wonderful change of mood.

We were lucky in finding transport all the way through. We stopped in Mafeking, the sandy little town that, in 1899, was the site of the famous siege of 9000 Boer troops against 1000 British soldiers. It was an eye-opener. Alongside the old newspaper cuttings of British commander Robert Baden-Powell pompously claiming all the glory—saying that locals ran away when the trouble started—were the official documents stating how those very same locals were, in fact, the ones to dig the trenches and do much of the dangerous scouting. To add insult to injury, many of them were even driven out of Mafeking when food began to run short, to face certain death at the hands of the enemy. Baden-Powell wasn't even popular among his own side. When the relieving troops arrived, tired, hungry and worn down by hardship, they were stunned to find how healthy those under siege looked. In the end, the liberators had to be fed by those they were supposedly saving.

From there, we hitched to the capital Gaberone, a smart new town with very little character, and then lurched over a very badly rutted mud road, in a truck with no clutch, on to Maun, a little cowboy town in the middle of nowhere, whose only claim to fame was as the nearest settlement to the Okavango Delta. There, luckily, we bumped into some other travellers and all chipped in to hire a plane together to get to the swamplands. They were wild and beautiful, an incredible network of narrow green rivers meandering through clumps of bushland and fields of reeds, teeming with wildlife. We spent a couple of days paddling quietly in a canoe along the rivers, peering at crocodiles, elephants and wildebeests.

One day, a local worker at the nearby camp took a few of us on a walking safari. With his spear held aloft, he crept through the undergrowth, signalling at us to follow. After half-an-hour, when we'd started to relax as we hadn't seen much at all, we saw his body suddenly tense. A massive bull elephant came crashing out of the trees towards us. My first instinct was to run like hell in the opposite direction but our guide gestured at us to hold our ground. We stood, frozen to the spot, for what felt like an hour. I finally understood what it was like to watch your life flashing on rewind before your eyes. In truth, it was probably only a few minutes before the elephant raised his trunk, made a kind of 'Oh, I can't be bothered with this' snuffle and clomped off in the opposite direction. Strangely, we all found we'd lost our enthusiasm for our foot safari after that. It had seemed tremendously exciting at first to have a guide with a simple spear to protect us. Now we all agreed we'd only feel safe with a whole battalion of them, armed with machine guns. We feigned tiredness from the hot sun, and asked our guide to lead us back.

We weren't quite so fortunate with transport on the way back. From Maun, the only lift Malcolm and I were offered was in the back of an open pick-up truck. We bounced along for about five hours, choking on the thick brown dust from the road. One of the be-suited men in the front even got concerned enough at one stage to stop and walk round to ask how we were faring. 'Only a couple of hours to go now,' he said cheerily. 'And then we'll have a present for you.' As he climbed back in the front, careful not to get any dust on his suit, Malcolm and I looked at each other, and then at the huge watermelon that had been rolling around in the back with us. They must be intending to give us that. My mouth watered at the thought. My throat was so dry I could eat the whole thing myself.

Three hours later, we finally got to civilisation. The two men both helped us out of the truck, as we were almost too stiff to manage it ourselves. 'And now,' said the first man, 'we will give you our present.' We smiled. I tried not to look too eager. It was as much as I could do to stop myself lunging for that big, juicy, beautiful, slurpy watermelon. I'd already worked out how we could cut it open with my penknife, divide it and then dive straight in with our hands. It was going to taste so good!

With an enormous effort, I wrenched my eyes back to the two men. The second man was fiddling around in his briefcase. 'Hurry up!' I wanted to say. 'I'm so thirsty!' He, however, seemed otherwise engaged. Finally, he seemed to locate what he wanted and pulled out a little booklet and some leaflets with a sigh of satisfaction.

'Here,' he said, proudly. 'You will enjoy reading these.'

I watched them, wordlessly, as they smiled at each other, climbed back in the truck and pulled away, with the melon wobbling in the back and a cloud of dust billowing back right in our faces. I didn't even have the strength to close my eyes. I looked down at the papers he had given us: 'Marriage: the Bedrock of the World' said the booklet; 'Love and Marriage' was the title of the leaflet. Both were produced by the Seventh Day Adventist Church. I felt so bitterly disappointed, I could have wept.

The next day, we headed into Zimbabwe. Not far now to those ruins. I wanted to have a taste of the past, before I had a flavour of the future. Parliament was due to re-open in a week and I knew you could buy tickets to see President Canaan Banana, Bishop Abel Muzorewa and their new Prime Minister Robert Mugabe in action. I felt in need of a healthy dose of black politics.

Not everyone, however, seemed to share my enthusiasm. I'd naively assumed that the whites who hadn't fled down to South Africa on independence—the famous 'chicken run', named after Mugabe's election symbol—would be those intent on making the place work. They weren't. They just couldn't bear to walk away from the privilege and wealth they'd enjoyed there. They were angry, they were bitter and they were racists—an exceedingly dangerous combination. Hitching north through the country, they talked angrily of the government taking away their guns, but how many they'd secretly managed to stash away. Then they regaled us with tales of whites who'd wired their homes up with bombs before racing down to South Africa on the pretence of going there for the weekend. When the nightwatchmen turned the lights on in the evening, the place went up. 'They'd rather no-one had it than let the blacks take it,' said these sick, pathetic people, admiringly. And often they'd add, 'If only I had the nerve to do that.'

A white ambulance officer who worked close to the stunning Victoria Falls in the west of the country, on the Zambian border, boasted to us that he'd roar to the scene if a white was injured in an accident, but take his time if the victim was black. In stark contrast, as I was trying to cross a busy street in the bustling city of Bulawayo, south of Harare, a black man caught my arm and helped me over. 'Hey sister,' he said, cheerfully. 'Welcome to Zimbabwe! We don't want to lose any of our tourists!'

Just outside Bulawayo, I tried to track down Mary and Goy's niece. She'd moved since the last address Mary had for her, but neighbours gave me the new one. Finally, I found the house, in a neat, affluent suburb of town. I rang the bell and a very pale white woman opened the door. I was confused. 'Sorry,' I said, 'I'm looking for Jan Clifford, I must have the wrong house.'

She smiled. 'Yes, that's me,' she said. 'How can I help you?'

I told her I was on a mission from Mary, and she blanched. She stepped outside, looked around and then bundled me into the house. There, she made me a cup of tea in silence. 'Does anyone else know you're here?' she asked, nervously. I shook my head. 'Have you told Mary my new address?'

'No, not yet.' She sat down and sighed with relief.

'It's all so difficult,' she said. I didn't understand and told her so. She looked at me, hard.

Finally, she seemed to come to a decision. Yes, she was coloured, but she had been born paler than any of her brothers and sisters and could, at a pinch, pass as white. As a result, she'd fled South Africa, destroyed the passbook that classified her as coloured and come to Zimbabwe to start another life. Here, she lived as a white and had even married a white man, who had absolutely no idea that she was anything other than she said. Naturally, she had to be forever vigilant to keep her secret safe. She avoided the sun religiously, in case it tanned her, and would only go out once or twice a week during the day when she had to, wearing dark glasses, a hat and sun cream for protection. She had also never had children, for fear one of them would turn out darker.

I listened, horrified, as Jan talked on about the way she now lived her life. Secrets and lies, secrets and lies. Her husband, Stan, hated blacks and coloureds alike. If he ever found out, he'd leave her, without a doubt. If her neighbours in this nice white suburb ever discovered, they'd hound her out. She talked and talked. It seemed a relief. She'd cut off all contact with her family back home, in case they took it into their minds to visit. She avoided making close friends. Her greatest regret was the children. She'd told Stan she had a medical problem that stopped her getting pregnant. But if circumstances had been any different, she would have loved a little boy and a girl... As the sun went down, I said a sad goodbye to Jan and promised never to breathe a word about her to her relatives.

I walked back into town, slept fitfully, and we started hitching early the next morning on the main road east to Nyanda and the ruins. I wanted to be entranced by the great stone walls that had withstood so many centuries; I wanted to gaze in awe at the sight that was believed by some to be the mysterious site of King Solomon's mines. I wanted some sanity, some sunshine for the soul. If we were lucky, we might get there before nightfall.

chapter five
THE SNAKES! THE SNAKES!

destination: Mt Kilimanjaro, Tanzania

I was fast asleep in the tent when suddenly there was a terrified yell from beside me. I opened my eyes in alarm.

'The snakes! The snakes!' Malcolm shouted, sitting up in his sleeping bag beside me. 'The tent's full of snakes!'

I gasped in horror. Malcolm seemed frozen to the spot. Heart pounding, I reached over and snapped on my torch. I pulled my knees as far into my chest as they'd go, and shone the light on the ground by the tent opening. There was nothing. I looked at Malcolm. 'SNAKES!' he was still hollering. I realised, with a start, that he was in the middle of a nightmare.

'It's okay, Malcolm,' I said softly. 'I'll get rid of the snakes. They're all gone now. Don't worry. Just get back to sleep now.' He mumbled something, and lay back down. I was still trembling so hard, it took me an hour-and-a-half to get back to sleep.

The next morning, I asked him if he remembered anything from the previous night. He looked at me blankly. 'No, should I?' he asked.

'Oh, you just had a nightmare,' I said casually.

'No,' he said, firmly. 'I would remember if I had.'

'But you did,' I insisted.

'No,' he replied. 'You must have had a nightmare and now you're blaming me.'

By the time we'd reached the pleasant modernity of the Zimbabwean capital, Harare, travelling with Malcolm had reached the stage of a bad marriage, where you can agree on nothing and no longer remember why you're together, or why you even thought it might be a good idea in the first place. Of course, since we were just friends—'were' fast becoming the operative word here—it wasn't like we were staying together for the sake of the children, for fear of losing the marital home or even for the occasional brief pleasures of a sex life. In short, the only things keeping us in tandem were Malcolm's tent and the fear of being alone. And, lately, even that had assumed an overwhelmingly attractive allure of its own.

The months of bickering, simmering warfare between us had taken its toll. These days, we argued about everything and anything. I liked Marmite on bread as our staple, cheap meal. Malcolm preferred jam. He ate more bread than me, so shouldn't he contribute more to each loaf we bought? No, because I used more topping than he did, he claimed. I was looking forward to arriving in Tanzania, eager to climb Mt Kilimanjaro. He said I didn't have the right shoes, the right jacket, the right attitude. I said he was being childish. He said no, I was. I said no, no, no, no, no, he was.

We'd start every day with an argument. 'Well, what shall we do today?' he'd say, waking up in the morning. I'd make a suggestion. 'Yes, I thought that,' he'd reply, or 'Yes, I know'.

It would drive me mad. If the plan ended badly, in getting hopelessly lost or left in a bog without a dry patch to pitch the tent, I'd get blamed for my 'dumb' idea. If it worked out well, invariably he would claim the credit.

Deciding to hitch over to the eastern highlands, close by the Mozambique border, our first lift even ended in yet another fight, in a shady lay-by just off the main highway. 'Why the hell did you say that?' he yelled, after we were turfed out of a nice, fast car when I'd argued with the driver that black brains weren't necessarily inferior to white. 'You have to spoil everything!'

But Malcolm was equally mortified the day I shut up and said nothing as some idiot, quite rightly assuming a captive audience, described how female brains were the weakest of all. 'You really should have said something,' he chided.

I snapped. 'Well, why didn't *you*?' I demanded.

'Oh, I thought it better that I didn't systematically crush his argument,' he declared airily. He was deathly serious.

Our approach to life was just very different. Malcolm became stressed easily: by a lack of food; by an absence of any traffic at all on a road where we might be trying for a lift; by worry over where we were going to sleep that night. I was far more easy-going: we could both do with losing a few pounds; a vehicle would come along sooner or later and it wasn't as if we were in a blazing hurry; we could always bed down by the side of the road. I thrived on the unpredictability of a travelling life—the very thing he hated most. The more I laughed and made light of adversity, the more uptight he became. That made me even more determined to laugh louder and harder. He was fast turning into a nervous wreck...and I a malicious bitch.

Our relationship had reached the point where the end was clearly in sight. All through Zimbabwe we ended up hitching separately, often only a few yards from each other, because he said one place would be better, and I said another place would be. Naturally, when cars stopped for me and not for him, it wasn't necessarily that my spot was better; it was merely that drivers are far more likely to pick up a lone woman than a lone man. It gave me spiteful satisfaction every time, however, to watch him run at full speed, with his heavy rucksack swaying on his back, to join my lift. In truth, I was becoming even more irritable from a lack of sleep as a result of those ghastly night-mares. 'The spiders! There's spiders everywhere!' was another favourite. They'd only happen, on average, once a week, but the other nights I found myself lying tensely waiting for them. Every time I'd die a little in fright at the terror in Malcolm's voice before recognising another nightmare. We even began sleeping separately—I slept much better outside his tent, swathed in my sleeping bag inside a mosquito net. It meant I was kept awake by neither those night-time visitors nor his snoring.

In truth, there seemed very little point in us travelling together anymore. I was no longer sharing his tent, and the alternatives to being together surely couldn't be any worse than this constant irritation that overshadowed everywhere we went, and everything we did.

One evening, camping out among the high rolling hills of Zimbabwe's Nyanga National Park on the fringes of a cool green forest, the tension finally exploded into violence. We had opened a bottle of wine that a friendly driver had given us and were sitting outside the tent in the soft blue evening, drinking from our plastic beakers. Both of us were steadily becoming more and more snitchy over who had drunk the most. Our voices grew louder and we started dragging up festering animosities. He accused me of losing one of his tent poles, which meant the ceiling now always drooped; I said he couldn't hold his drink. He taunted me over my hopeless sense of direction; I said he'd never survive here without me. He had a quick temper and I took great pleasure in baiting him. That night, we both overstepped the mark. He became so angry, he leaned back, put his weight on his hands and took a scissor kick at my stomach. I was speechless, but more from shock than pain. Silently, I crawled away from his stupid saggy, baggy tent and into my sleeping bag nearby, horrified by the depths to which our relationship had sunk. In the morning, I rose just before dawn, packed up my stuff and walked off towards the road where I managed to hitch a lift north almost instantly. I didn't see Malcolm again until we bumped into each other two months later in Nairobi, Kenya.

•••

Now I was, at last, on my own. On the plus side, I was as free as a bird to do whatever I wanted, and to go wherever took my fancy. On the down side, I felt suddenly much more vulnerable. But why? What exactly was I scared of? Death? Rape? Being attacked and injured by someone? Well, any of those things could happen back home—or even in a shared tent—and being with someone might not prevent those worst case scenarios. Did I not think, alone, I'd be up to the big challenge I'd been looking forward to for months in Africa: climbing the continent's highest mountain, Mt Kilimanjaro? Well, why wouldn't I be able to do it alone? Or was it simply the 'being alone' I was nervous of? Maybe. But then I soon came to find that, in Africa, a white woman travelling alone never actually is.

Locals, sometimes wary of a white couple together, will approach a lone woman much more freely, I quickly discovered. You're not a threat, and hardly a danger. With a pack on your back and hitching rides, you're obviously not untouchably rich, either. From my point of view, I realised that moving around as a couple turns you into a self-contained unit, while travelling alone *makes* you chat. You're dependent on others for company to keep you sane.

Hitching westwards through the emerald green hills of central Zimbabwe towards the vast concrete monolith of the great Kariba Dam, with my shiny new tent balanced on the top of my pack, I found African women starting conversations with me far more often as I wandered around pretty little towns waiting for lifts. Before, it seemed, they'd been put off by the presence of a man. Now, they were simply enormously curious about what on earth was wrong with me that meant I was on my own, and they felt free to ask. On the springy banks of the vast blue expanse of Lake Kariba, I was surrounded by a little group of women walking back home from doing the washing.

'Why you have no man?' they quizzed me. When I said playfully that I just couldn't fathom what was wrong with me, they screamed with laughter. 'You smell bad? You are barren? You are cursed?' they each ventured in turn, giggling.

Of course, there were also bound to be some difficulties. Crossing the border from Zimbabwe to Zambia, I tried to shrug off the warnings customs officers on the Zimbabwean side gave me about the Zambian capital, Lusaka, just 100 kilometres north. It would be dangerous for a lone white woman there, they said. People were more aggressive. There were many thieves. There was much violence. Outwardly, I smiled. Inside, I quailed.

Certainly, there seemed to be an awful lot of broken glass embedded into the top of high concrete walls surrounding security compounds all around the busy roads of Lusaka. The city streets were full of guys leaning against walls, smoking cigarettes and idly watching people. Somehow, the atmosphere felt tense. Perhaps those men were just waiting for a chance to jump unwary passers-by. Or perhaps it was me being over-jumpy after so many cautions. I checked into a cheap youth hostel and went to bed early, after sorting out my planned route on the map into Malawi. The next morning, I just needed to change some money, and then I could be off.

I went out early the next morning to find someone operating on the black market. It didn't take long. One of those men propping up the wall, smoking, seemed only too happy to help. He introduced me to a second man, similarly engaged, who flashed me an envelope full of Zambian *kwacha* notes. I handed over my US dollars and he passed me the envelope. It would have been too rude to have counted the notes in front of him. Instead, I waited until I was around the corner to check. Opening the flap, I was horrified to find it packed tight with a wad of newsprint—he must have swapped the two when I wasn't looking. I went back around the corner but, of course, there was suddenly no sign of any men hanging around. I went back to the hostel and checked in for another night.

Later that same afternoon, wandering around the wide, modern streets of the city centre, I was approached by a man who said the doctor he worked for wanted to change cash. He had a bad lisp, and it took me a while to understand him. When I did, I was pleased. This would be much safer. Doctors often wanted to change money, and I was pleased that he wanted to do it in the waiting room of his surgery. Anyone could be taken for a ride once—I'd just been unlucky.

My man asked for the money on the threshold of the surgery and I handed him my cash in an envelope. He then went straight to the door marked 'Doctor', and I settled back in a chair in the waiting room. This was easy. After fifteen minutes, I started to become suspicious. After thirty, I felt downright worried. I went up to the doctor's door and opened it. He looked up, startled, from examining an elderly woman's breasts. I apologised, but asked if he'd just seen a man with a very bad lisp. 'Yes, yes,' said the doctor, sounding annoyed at the interruption. 'He had a stomach-ache. But don't worry. I've given him some pain killers and he's probably now safely back home, tucked up in bed.'

I went cold. 'But...but I've been waiting for him out here,' I said, indicating the waiting room.

'He went out the other way,' said the doctor impatiently, nodding his head towards the back door of his office. I apologised and withdrew, feeling thoroughly beaten.

I was determined not to extend my time in this town. If I was very careful with what local money I had, and only ate the food I was carrying with me, I'd be able to get through. The next morning, I walked for an hour-and-a-half out of the city before I hit a main road that looked busy enough to hitch beside. Luckily, outside the capital, people were far friendlier.

One night, while pitching my tent on the outskirts of a small town of squat brown brick shacks, I was invited home by one of the villagers and his family to dinner. I hadn't eaten anything all day and had been looking forward with almost indecent glee to opening a tin of sardines, slicing a squashy tomato I'd bought along the way and cracking open an old packet of biscuits I'd been hoarding for an emergency. I was downcast, but knew it would have been terribly rude to have refused such a fine offer of hospitality. I thanked them, and handed over my sardines in a similar gesture of friendship, secretly hoping they might serve them up. Unfortunately, they put them away for later. I, instead, was served possibly the most disgusting meal I've ever experienced: a greasy, grey stew that tasted rather like boiled old hides. Its authenticity as meat was, however, confirmed when an eyeball suddenly floated to the surface. As I stared back at it in horror, the whole family exclaimed on my good luck. Almost gagging, I closed my eyes and swallowed hard. I spent the next couple of nights in a cold sweat at the memory of that choice titbit.

I crossed into Malawi at the rundown old town of Chipata, changed some money, celebrated my newfound affluence with a packet of cream biscuits and caught a bumpy bus south to the new capital, Lilongwe. It was disappointing. Modern and spread-out, it was utterly featureless and felt curiously empty. I moved on straight away, catching another bus a couple of hours later to the old capital, Blantyre, further south. What a contrast. It was a charming, character-filled place of elegant old buildings, buzzing markets and women wearing blouses and skirts made from material bearing the stern countenance of the country's president, Hastings Banda. After the celebratory feeling of Zimbabwe and the confidence of Zambia, it was like stepping back in time to another world. Banda had ruled with a rod of iron since he became Prime Minister, on independence from white rule in 1964.

Going for a walk one day in a pair of cotton jeans, I was hissed at for an hour by locals before discovering that it was against the law for women to wear trousers. Beards for men were banned, too. And the place still felt almost feudal in the relationship between black and white people. Travelling in rural areas outside the main cities, I was taken aback to see black women curtsey as I approached, and black men bowing, all with eyes downcast and a timid, 'Good morning, ma'am', whatever the time of day. It was actually illegal for a mixed race couple to have sex, despite the persistent rumours that swept the country about Banda having a white mistress.

For the first time since I'd left Malcolm, I felt quite lonely. Locals, although unceasingly polite, would rarely stop and chat. They seemed far too nervous. Only twice did I manage to break down the barriers. The first time was when I climbed Mt Mulanje east of Blantyre—a pretty, and quite gentle, walk up through trees wreathed in old man's beard and alongside waterfalls and streams. I was fine—until I somehow lost the path back down. I wandered for what seemed like hours in the gathering dusk until a man appeared from nowhere.

'Which is the way down?' I asked him. He looked bewildered, then pointed straight down. 'No, I meant, how do I get down?' I laughed. He laughed too. The light was failing fast, and he was so black, I could only see the whites of his eyes and the flash of his teeth as he grinned.

'You are lost?' he asked me. 'You are alone?' For a moment, I felt as if it might be wise to deny both. After all, wasn't I vulnerable enough, without admitting my nearest ally might still be sitting in a tent in north-west Zimbabwe, wondering, for all I knew, what to do that day? But then how silly would it be to pretend I knew exactly where I was and that I was simply the forward scout for a whole rambling club following on just behind?

'Yes,' I said, cheerfully. 'I am both lost and alone. Do you know the way?'

'Yes, of course,' he replied. 'I was born here. You follow me.'

'Oh, thanks!' I said. And then he disappeared. I looked around me. I'd never been able to see very well in the dark. Now I could see nothing. There wasn't even a moon. All I could hear was the rustling of pine needles in the wind.

I stood on the spot, stupidly, for a full five minutes before he came back. 'What are you doing?' he said, with interest, from right beside me, making me jump.

'I can't see anything,' I said, pathetically. 'It's too dark.'

He laughed again. 'What is your name?' he asked.

'Sue,' I said.

'Sue, hold my arm. I will help you.'

It took two hours for us to get down that mountainside, with me clinging onto Joseph's arm every step of the way. I learnt the names of all his brothers and sisters. I learnt how he liked to walk alone every day around his mountain to enjoy some peace for himself. I also learnt my most valuable lesson: I should never again try to climb a mountain alone. I'd just have to team up with someone else when I got to Kilimanjaro. My sense of direction was so poor, I finally had to admit, I couldn't find my way down a one-way street without a map and compass.

My second close encounter was further north, when I'd pitched my tent on the sandy shores of Lake Malawi, the 580 kilometre-long freshwater lake that runs north through the entire country. I'd taken the battered old steamer overnight from Monkey Bay, sitting up most of the night on the deck watching the dark water drift by and marvelling at how so often we lost all sight of land. We could almost have been on the ocean—if it had been a spectacularly calm ocean. We docked at the beach about 2 kilometres from the small town of Nkhotakhota, a jumble of buildings swathed in masses of bright bougainvillea. The hotels were full, but I didn't mind. The beach, to me, had looked the perfect place to sleep. I marched back down the dirt track to the shore. In front of me, the wide blue of the lake lapped softly on the sand. Behind, there were a few straggly trees and mottled bursts of wild grasses. It was easy to push the tent pegs into the sand and soon I'd eaten half a can of sardines watching the lake grow dark. I crawled into my sleeping bag inside the tent, and fell asleep almost immediately.

A few hours later, however, I woke sharply from a dream about swimming across the lake to find myself lying in a pool of water. I unzipped the tent. In a glint of moonlight, I could see half my gear floating away over the lake. It just hadn't occurred to me that this lake was so vast, it was actually tidal. I shouted in alarm as I waded into the water, the night again pitch black, to see what I could rescue. A couple of men appeared from nowhere to help, and managed to gather what they could, while helping me, totally confused about which direction I should be wading in the dark, back to shore.

Laughing, they pulled my tent further up the beach and laid out everything to dry ready for the sun to come up. Then they built a little fire to try to help me dry out. By the time the sun rose, we were chatting as freely as if we were anywhere else in black Africa. 'Thanks so much,' I said to them as they prepared to go off to their own homes. 'It was so kind of you. But just hang on a second.' I ferreted through my surviving possessions to see if I had anything I could give them as a gift to show my gratitude. The only things I could think of were a couple of T-shirts. They would be easy enough to replace. Luckily, the two I had saved both had American slogans on them—one had the name of a baseball team, and the other 'Coca-Cola'. I knew that if they didn't fit, they'd be able to sell them for a decent price at the market.

I crossed into Tanzania by detouring back into Zambia, and then out again at Nakonde, intrigued by the prospect of seeing one of the few black African countries that had managed to stay independent of the west. The contrast with Zambia was stunning, and immediate. The good tar road turned to dirt on the Tanzanian side, and the first small town over the border, Tunduma, looked little more than a dusty collection of poor mud and brick houses. In the middle, there was a little café, which had nothing to offer but coffee—and not very good coffee at that. The streets were deserted of the usual food-sellers who'd routinely cluster at any border. The roads were empty because few could afford petrol.

Under one of Africa's legendary figures, Julius Nyerere, socialist, collectivist Tanzania had been a brave experiment, but one gradually undermined by problems like the rise in oil prices and the steep drop in the value of the country's staple exports of coffee and sisal hemp. The chaos was evident everywhere. In the nearest big town, Mbeya, I sat and waited for the Chinese-built TanZam railway to Tanzania's old capital Dar-es-Salaam. The atmosphere was subdued; it seemed the only thing that could be relied upon about the train was that it was always late. Mothers sat glumly on the floor nursing their babies, while the specially built wooden cribs at the station, where Chinese mums would traditionally leave their children, sat empty. And when, finally, we all piled onto the train, only for it to stop, suddenly, in the Selous Game Park, absolutely no-one seemed surprised at the eight-hour delay. It seemed eminently predictable that the train would be far more seriously damaged than the giraffe it had hit. Poor Tanzania. It seemed nothing was going its way. With the kind of run of luck it was having, you could imagine Mount Kilimanjaro erupting at any moment and covering the entire country in molten lava, in defiance of all those scientists who'd declared it extinct. But at the thought of Kilimanjaro, my spirits lifted above the turmoil all around me. It was a long-held ambition of mine to climb it. I couldn't wait.

Chugging finally into Dar-es-Salaam, I found it a derelict dustbowl of a city where men in ill-fitting suits walked to their offices alongside tall Masai warriors draped in beads and brandishing long spears. Where were they going, I wondered? Later, I found out. All the city's hotels depended on these noble tribesmen to do their guests' washing. For the Masai, it was the only entry available to them to a cash economy. Not that there was so much for them to buy. The supermarkets paraded rows of empty shelves; a breakdown at the factory that produced bottle tops meant flat beer was sold in bottles whose necks had been plugged with paper; the lack of spare parts for the country's presses prevented any newspapers from being published. But, just like any place where there were shortages, it was also a spiv's heaven. Everywhere, there were Mr Fixits who could supply anything you needed on the blackmarket. 'You want real beer?' they'd sidle up to you and hiss. 'You want a needle and thread? You want drugs? You want sex? You want ice cream?' Nothing, it seemed, was beyond them.

It was there in Dar, however, that disaster struck. Sitting in a café drinking coffee, my money belt, containing my passport and all my money, was swiped off the seat next to me where I'd stupidly left it. Devastated, I went to see the British Consul. He'd like to replace my passport, he said apologetically, but I would have to pay US$20. Yet I didn't have US$20. And without a passport, I couldn't have my traveller's cheques replaced, or more money wired over. He was sorry, he said, but rules were rules. It seemed an impenetrable circle. I'd never felt so alone.

I went back to the café. Feeling sorry for me, the manager shouted me a coffee. One of the fixers came over. If I spent the night with him, he suggested, he'd lend me twenty bucks. *Lend!* I looked down at myself. I supposed with my big, dust-caked desert boots, my baggy old faded trousers and a cotton shirt that had seen better days—a long time ago—it was understandable he didn't think a quick coupling round the back would be worth a whole $20. Anyway, I wasn't quite that desperate...yet. Later that afternoon, a couple of American backpackers drifted in. We started talking. They offered, immediately, to lend me the cash—and not even for a hand job. I'd never before been so grateful to anyone.

I went back to the Consul and applied for my replacement passport. Then, with a letter from his office, I went to the bank. Yes, they could have new traveller's cheques sent in, but they'd have to be issued in Tanzanian shillings. I was aghast. How was I going to travel around the rest of Africa on traveller's cheques in Tanzanian shillings? I could imagine Tanzanian banks being reluctant enough to redeem them, let alone presenting them over at the counter at Citibank, Nairobi, or American Express, Cairo.

'Yes, yes, I see,' said the greying manager. 'I understand that could cause problems for you,' he added grudgingly. 'How about we give you the cheques in cash?' My heart leapt.

'Yes, thank you,' I said. I could hardly believe my luck. 'That would be great.'

Only a few minutes later did it occur to me that he'd meant in Tanzanian cash rather than in US dollars. On the official rate, there was ten shillings to the dollar. On the black market, there were sixty. Shillings were worth pretty much bog-all in Tanzania itself, but as for the rest of the continent, they didn't even burn well enough to make a decent fire. The money I was going to have wired over would be worth nothing by the time it was converted into Tanzanian shillings, and less than nothing outside the country. But the biggest bank in Dar just had no hard currency. The manager's hands were tied.

I went back out to find my new American friends. Chatting to them, I suddenly stumbled on the perfect compromise. We were all heading up to Kenya but the border had recently been sealed because of an abortive coup against Kenyan president Daniel Arap Moi. The only people getting through were those with an urgent cause. If I had my money wired to Nairobi, that would hopefully be a good enough reason to let me through. I could show the customs guards the fax from the bank saying my money would be waiting for me there. It was a stroke of brilliance. And when I was there, said one of the Americans, could I telex him to say his mother was sick and was waiting for him in Nairobi? And how about I write a letter with a Nairobi postmark, said the other, saying he was due to start work teaching in a school a few days hence? I was happy to help out. My only problem was surviving the next seven days on no money until my passport was ready to be picked up.

On that, the Americans had an idea too. They were going over to the island of Zanzibar for a few days, and I should come too. I could always repay them in Nairobi. I willingly agreed. The next day, I met them at the airport. It was chaos. There were no seats allocated, so the idea was to run across the tarmac to the plane as soon as the waiting room doors were opened in the hope you'd be able to nab a seat. I ran, but not fast enough. I did the journey huddled in the aisle, squashed between squawking, flapping chickens with their legs bound together and their wings tied down, and a very large fat Arab, who shrank away from me, desperately trying not to touch skin.

Zanzibar, a maze of little streets dotted with great wooden doors into homes and courtyards, had a decidedly Arabic feel. Once a base for the slave trade for both the Portuguese and then for Muslim merchants, it was scented by both the spices that were now the chief export of the place and by the strong stench of disinfectant. I soon found out why, just as soon as I went to a shop to try to buy something to eat. Every café, restaurant and shop selling food on the island had recently been closed down, I was told, because of a cholera epidemic. The only thing to eat were the lobsters brought in by the fishermen every afternoon. After six days of boiled lobster, fried lobster and grilled lobster, I longed for something as simple as a baked bean. In fact, I've never been able to look at a lobster since. I've never been able to think of Zanzibar without a shudder, either.

On the plane back, I pushed my way on board, and grabbed a seat by the window. I was idly gazing down at the wide blue Indian Ocean when someone yelled. Immediately, there was a stampede over to the other side of the plane and everyone started shouting, 'Fire! Fire! Fire!' What? Had I heard right? The plane seemed to be tilting horribly to the right under the weight of everyone standing on the other side, jostling to look out of the window. I could see the air hostess and a man in uniform, who I assumed had been flying the plane, among them. I joined them. Yellow flames were shooting out of the engine and licking up around the wing. The hostess was yelling at us all to sit down again. There was more shouting until we'd all taken our seats. There was nothing we could do.

'Insha'allah!' a woman dressed from head to toe in black Arabic dress was crying as she knelt on the floor. If God wills it, we will all die, seemed to be the gist. We'd just have to wait and see what He wanted. The five minutes we sat and nervously anticipated erupting into a ball of fire, before exploding and getting back to earth again only in tiny, burning pieces, blighted air travel for me for years.

Yet thankfully, just as we were making our descent, the flames seemed to simply melt away. The wing was blackened, but it was still there. We wobbled as we went down, but only slightly. As we bumped down onto the runway, a cheer went up. God was praised loudly, and gratefully. When I walked down the little set of wooden steps, I noted, with satisfaction, that Tanzania had quickly mobilised its safety procedures. Four forlorn men stood watching us, holding red fire buckets filled with sand.

After recovering in Dar with an exceptionally weak cup of coffee, I headed straight for the road out to the north, towards Kenya. Almost instantly, and against all my expectations, I found a lift straight away, with the driver asking only a modest fee to put towards the cost of petrol. I agreed. He happened to be going to Moshi, passing close to the base of Kilimanjaro. As we glimpsed the mountain from the road, and its familiar snow-capped peak, my heart soared. Sadly, it wasn't going to be for me this time. My borrowed money had all but run out, and I had to get to Nairobi as soon as I could to pick up my funds. The peak seemed to mock me as I stood on the road, hoping for another lift. I wondered if Malcolm had made it.

chapter six
A LOINCLOTH THE SIZE
OF A SMALL POST-IT NOTE

destination: Lake Victoria, Kenya

My plan to retrieve money in Nairobi went without a hitch. I was waved through the Kenyan border, got a lift immediately to Nairobi and checked into a bargain basement hotel in the cheapest part of town, River Road. The next day, I picked up my money—in US dollars—and sent the letter and the telex to those nice Americans back in Dar. I felt very pleased with myself. Travelling alone was proving a bit of a cinch. Kind of. And I was in modern, sophisticated Kenya now, probably the most Western of all the African countries. What on earth could go wrong from here? Sure, I was on a tight budget and I was still having a few problems reading maps. But it wasn't as if I was facing the kind of dangers that had dogged the footsteps of others bumbling along similar routes.

I'd grown up on tales of those great explorers of Africa, men like John Hanning Speke, Richard Burton and David Livingstone, who left comfortable Victorian society to set out on brave—sometimes foolhardy—expeditions, often without any idea of what they might find on the way. While in Africa, they suffered terrible deprivations, disease and hostility. When they returned home, they were given heroes' welcomes, they were the pop stars of their era. Certainly, if I could have lived in another age, that would have been it. Sadly, I would have also needed a sex change. It would have been just my luck to have been born in the mid-1800s at the time of some of those great white explorations—and been forced to stay behind, tend the kitchen fire, and wring my hands and weep while the men disappeared off to any number of exotic adventures.

Still, I was looking forward enormously to my first glimpse of Lake Victoria, Africa's biggest expanse of water. It had captured my imagination from the first. All those terrible arguments between Speke and Burton over who was going to be the first to discover the source of the Nile, and Speke's boundless joy when he thought he'd made it first. You can sense the excitement just from his 1862 journal entry: '...it was a sight that attracted one to it for hours—the roar of the waters, the thousands of passenger-fish, leaping at the falls with all their might, the Wasoga and Waganda fishermen coming out in boats and taking post on all the rocks with rod and hook, hippopotami and crocodiles lying sleepily on the water, the ferry at work above the falls, and the cattle driven down to drink at the margin of the lake made...as interesting a picture as one could wish to see...I saw that old father Nile without any doubt rises in the Victora Nyanza, and, as I had foretold, that lake is the great source of the holy river which cradled the first expounder of our religious belief...' There was the notorious feud that developed after each claimed triumph, and the tragedy of Speke's untimely death, just as the issue was about to be resolved.

I was snapped out of my romantic reverie by a commotion back at my hotel. Everyone seemed confused that I was alone. The first night, the manager had given me a double room to myself but now that the hotel was fully booked, I would have to share. That didn't worry me, not even when the door opened that evening and a stunningly beautiful black woman in a state of half-undress walked in. We sat on my bed and chatted. I was delighted that my new room-mate was so friendly—another great plus of travelling alone, I thought to myself. At about 9pm, she said she had to go off to work. An hour later, when I was almost asleep, she returned with her boyfriend in tow. They lay down on her bed together and started kissing.

'Susie, Susie!' she called over, obviously to check whether I was still awake. I grunted, non-commitally. 'I hope we don't disturb you,' she said in a stage whisper. At that, they started to make out in her bed, and quite excessively noisily I thought. I tried hard to pretend I was fast asleep. Oh well, young passion. Afterwards, they both left.

Half-an-hour later, I heard her key in the door again. She came in, then snapped on the main light. I opened my eyes and peered blearily out from under the covers. This time, she had another man with her, and they were arguing. I couldn't make out what they were saying, but evidently it concerned me.

The man came over and nudged me. 'I pay double for the two of you—together,' he announced. 'Come on, get up. Let me see you.' Finally, the penny dropped. My new friend was doing her best to up her income by promising her punters either sex with a white onlooker or, at the top of the range, a coffee-and-cream, three-in-the-bed experience of a lifetime. Hard up as I was, I declined the offer. The next day, I moved out.

It felt good to be in Nairobi again, with an efficient public transport system, lots of cheap cafés, museums and parks. The city was still a little tense after the coup attempt, but there were few outward signs of problems.

One day, changing some money in a bank of all things, I bumped into Malcolm. He looked startled to see me. I probably looked equally surprised. He was pale.

'How have you been getting on?' he asked, in a friendly voice.

'Oh fine, fine,' I said airily. 'No problems at all. I'm having a fantastic time. And how about you?'

He grimaced. 'I've had malaria,' he said, quietly. 'I haven't been very well at all. I bought a ticket back home today. I leave tomorrow.'

Instantly, I felt terrible that I'd been so consistently mean to him, and hadn't been able to resist claiming life had been a breeze since we'd parted. It was a bit late now, however, to start trying to make amends. Too much had been said and done. We shook hands solemnly and wished each other well. I made a mental note to send him a nice postcard from somewhere along the way.

•••

It was easy to hitch rides in Kenya. Here, there was plenty of petrol and an aggressively pro-Western political and economic regime had little trouble attracting investment. The roads were good and frequently used, and public transport was fast and efficient. I took the gorgeous old train through the pale green plains of the Tsavo National Park down to Mombassa on the coast, spent a few days there, and then hitched back to Nairobi. From there, I caught a *matatu*, a small panel van or minibus into which a phenomenal number of people could be squashed, to the outskirts of town. That was always an event in itself. Accidents between two *matatu* in Kenya—and they were frequent—often ended in upwards of fifty people being killed or injured. This drive took a while. The van had run out of petrol, so the driver and his helper collected all our fares before pushing us to the nearest gas station to use that money to fill up. I was fascinated, as we drove through the outlying north-western suburbs of town, to see fields dotted with broken down stone houses, often without roofs or with entire walls missing. I assumed they were the abandoned results of an earthquake or a cyclone. I was surprised, however, to see someone come out of one small building to lay their washing out carefully on the stubbly grass to dry. Looking more closely, I could see they were all occupied. Obviously, you only left home if there were *no* walls left.

I got out of the *matatu* on a good stretch of road and started hitching. I quickly picked up a series of lifts. Along the way, I made a point of stopping off at the blue Lake Naivasha and the grey Lake Nakuru. Both looked quite different until the thousands of flamingoes at each rose en masse to turn the water bright pink with their reflections, and the shorelines white with their droppings.

It was after Nakuru, however, that I first hit a problem. I'd been picked up by an Indian driver who pulled over for a beer at the 'Suitable Hotel and Bar' and then said he had a proposition to put to me. I didn't like the sound of that at all. He knew I was eager to get to Kitale that night, but what was the hurry? I hadn't seen Lake Baringo, possibly the loveliest lake of them all. It would be a tragedy to miss it after passing so close. We could take the turn-off north to Baringo, explore the lake and then spend the night at a hotel. We'd set off early the next morning, and he'd drop me off in Kitale by 2pm.

Of course, it was very kind of him to offer to show me Baringo and yes, it was true, I would have quite liked to have completed my trifecta. On the other hand, his plan rattled with a number of unknown quantities. On my map, Baringo looked in the middle of nowhere. Probably there was a lodge, but it might well be out of my price range. Then I'd be stuck. No doubt, he'd offer to pay for me to stay but I didn't feel comfortable at the prospect of being in the debt of anyone who wore such tight trousers and a gold medallion on the *outside* of his shirt. But then was I being racist in suspecting an Indian of ulterior motives? Part of the joy of travelling alone, I'd told myself so often, was being able to take chances, throw excessive caution to the wind and see what lay just beyond the confines of my carefully constructed plans. I looked up at him. He had a dribble of Tusker beer on his chin.

'Look, that's very kind of you,' I said, finally. 'But I have to get to Kitale tonight. I've seen two lakes and I have to move on.' He didn't look pleased. 'But I do appreciate the offer,' I added lamely.

'Sure,' he replied. 'No problems.' There was a glint of gold from his mouth under the bright lights of the bar, and a frown on his forehead. 'But I think you will be sorry.' He stood up, paid for his beer and then marched to the car. I scrabbled along behind.

We sat in silence as he pulled back out onto the main road and drove the 10 kilometres up to the Baringo turn-off. My heart stopped as he slowed, twisted the steering wheel sharply to the right and set the car on course for Baringo.

'No!' I said to him sharply. 'I don't want to go. Please stop now.' He accelerated. 'No!' I shouted louder, as if there might have possibly been a way he didn't hear the first time. 'No! Please pull over!'

I marvelled that I couldn't help being polite even in such trying circumstances. He ignored me completely. I didn't know what to do. But then I did what they do in the movies: I grabbed the steering wheel and yanked it hard to the left. The car bumped up onto the bank at the side of the road, lurching straight towards an old baobab tree. Swearing and shouting at me, he applied the brakes, sharply. We skidded to a halt just a metre from the tree.

'There was no reason to do that,' he yelled shakily. 'I was only trying to help you, you silly girl.'

I looked back the way we'd come. What should I do now? I could get out and march off, but we'd probably travelled a good 5 kilometres, and I really didn't want to walk back all that way lugging my pack. And why should I? 'No, I have to go to Kitale,' I said firmly. 'Turn around and go back.'

There was a moment when I wondered whether I should have got out while I had the chance. But then he sighed, started the car and did a three-point turn. 'So,' he said finally as we started back, 'you don't want to spend time in bed with me. What is the matter with you? Do you not like sex? Or are you a racist?' I said nothing. When we reached the main road again, I said I'd get out and wait for another lift. He didn't even argue.

The next driver, a Kenyan, was a welcome relief. He was one of that old school of black Africans, who felt obliged to be painfully polite about white colonialism. As we crossed the Equator, and my spirits soared at the thought of passing such an important landmark, he stopped to let me savour the moment. 'You know, we have to be grateful to you European people,' he said when I got back in the car. 'You did leave us sheep and cows.'

I didn't make Kitale that night, nor the next. Instead, I ended up in Eldoret, a muddy little market town 150 kilometres north of the Equator. There were no hotels, so I fronted up to the local Sikh temple where guardians are obliged by the dictates of their religion to offer homeless travellers a place to rest their weary heads. They were a bit begrudging about it, I thought, but one of them did eventually lead me into a dingy courtyard and then opened off it what looked remarkably like a dungeon. It was a room, just big enough for the bed in the centre and a chair off to the side. I slept like a log.

The next day, I explored the town, which didn't take long. It was basically a motley collection of houses and shops grouped around a muddy market square, where everything from the tasteless root vegetable *manoic* to second-hand socks were being sold. One market trader took a liking to my satchel. 'Hey! You want to sell that?' he yelled, cheerily. 'I give you good price.'

I went over to him and started chatting. His name was Moseka and, despite only having had the most rudimentary of junior school educations before having to work to earn money to keep his mother and four younger siblings, he was remarkably well-informed about life beyond Eldoret. On his second-hand stall, he had dog-eared copies of the British communist daily newspaper *The Morning Star*; a strange collection of papier-mâché animals that he'd bought from a European house clearance; a few faded T-shirts; a couple of bags; some cheap children's clothes; and a book, the horrifically racist *The Essential Kaffir* by Dudley Kidd, that struck me as more than a little inappropriate. He laughed when I pointed it out. 'Probably some white man will see it and give me more for that than anything else I have here,' he said. 'You wait, you hope.'

He'd once worked as a ticket collector in a cinema and talked about the nights they'd show Kung Fu films, when he'd have to rush home afterwards to avoid being physically picked on by fired-up audiences. Disco films, like *Saturday Night Fever*, were his personal favourites. He'd often join the audience, dancing in the aisles. He was extraordinarily well-read too, being able to quote entire passages from Charles Dickens, Shakespeare, *The Communist Manifesto* and *The Essential Kaffir* with equal aplomb.

I swapped my nice, exceedingly practical satchel for a pink

plastic shopping bag that fell apart three days later. We talked some more. I asked him about his limp. He'd had polio as a child, he told me. I asked about his family. 'Come and have dinner with us tonight,' he said. 'I will show you our home, you can meet everyone and taste our Kenyan food. Where are you staying? I'll pick you up.'

I was polite in my refusal. He laughed again. 'You will be perfectly safe with me,' he said. 'When you go back home and people ask you about Kenya, what will you say? That the Sikh temple was nice and the countryside is pretty? You will be able to say nothing about how the people live.' I knew when I'd been outwitted.

At 6pm on the dot, he knocked on the door of my dungeon with a frowning Sikh standing behind him, obviously convinced we were up to no good. We then walked to the outskirts of town, which took only ten minutes, to the little ramshackle house which seemed to be home to an inordinate number of his extended family. I was welcomed like an old friend, especially when I pronounced the goat stew 'Delicious!', primarily because I had spotted not a single eyeball floating in the pot.

After dinner, we went over to the scout hall-like hut in the middle of a clearing where the town's communal TV set provided the only entertainment. Watching the extravagances of *Dallas* among the crush of fifty men, women and children who had barely enough to get by in life, was a sobering experience. Not that they seemed to have any qualms about it. They jeered every time Larry Hagman appeared on screen, and cheered Patrick Duffy.

'This J.R., he is so bad', confided Moseka's younger brother, Joseph, sitting on my left hand side, earnestly. 'He has much money, a beautiful wife and a good family but he still wants more. More money. More women. More family. Ecchh!' It was an expression of unbridled disgust. 'I have heard there are many people like this in the West.'

Moseka delivered me back to the temple by about 10pm, squeezing my hand in farewell. Soon after he'd gone, however, there was an urgent knocking at my door. I opened it a fraction, expecting to see Moseka again. Instead, it was the Sikh who'd glared at us so angrily earlier in the evening. He pushed past me, marched straight into the room and sat on the bed. 'Where have you been?' he asked. 'Have you been with that boy? You should not trust these people.'

I wanted to say, 'What the hell is it to you?' but was aware I was dependent on the Sikhs' hospitality. I didn't want to let on, either, that I felt more uneasy in his company than anyone I'd met that night. Instead, I just said, 'Thank you for the advice. He's an old friend. We just went to see his family. Now I'm very tired, so if you wouldn't mind...' I was still holding the door, so I opened it wider. He looked at me, then sprang to his feet and spat on the ground. He looked at me, hard, again, then walked back out through the door.

I closed it firmly behind him, wedged the chair under the handle and put my penknife under my pillow in a gesture that gave me some comfort, although I doubted it would ever be of much use, particularly because it had become so rusty after its time in the water in Malawi that it took me a good ten minutes to prise it open each time. I resolved to buy a padlock.

The next day, I went out early to help Moseka on his stall. My presence attracted a great deal of interest and, more importantly, a fair few extra customers. Moseka again asked me to dinner to thank me. His family seemed pleased to see me. That night, I put my new padlock on the door when I went to bed. Later, that same Sikh hammered on my door, but I wouldn't let him in. The next morning, I went into the temple early, politely thanked one of the others, made a donation to the upkeep of the temple, and dumped my pack at Moseka's stall. That night I took his mother and three brothers and sister to the only restaurant in town that stayed open beyond 5pm, then stayed the night at their house.

In the morning, I hugged them all goodbye with tears in my eyes, and took a *matatu* through the rolling hills of Kitale, dark green with tea plantations. Before I went to Lake Victoria, I wanted to take a detour up to Lake Turkana, a long, relatively narrow lake running north to south in the far north of the country, which looked stunningly beautiful in every poster of the place I'd ever seen. They must have just launched a campaign to lure more people there, as the posters of a startlingly azure stretch of shimmering water, fringed by a dazzling white beach and towering palms filled with colourful flocks of birds, seemed to adorn every bank and office wall in Nairobi. At the major petrol station in Kitale, I managed to negotiate a price for a lift to Lodwar, 250 kilometres north, in the back of an open truck leaving the next morning. I slept fitfully in a nearby hotel, worrying that I wouldn't wake up early enough in the morning.

As a result, when dawn came, I was utterly exhausted.

There were only about thirty of us in the back of the truck, so we each had enough room to sit down and just gaze out at the scenery. Gradually, the green, fertile plains of central Kenya and the great grassy slopes of Mt Elgon gave way to dusty scrub and sandy soil, dotted with spiky Acacia trees. A few women in the truck tied scarves over their eyes to protect them from the billowing sand. The day grew hotter and hotter.

A few hours in, I saw my first Turkana tribesmen, tall, stately people, their long necks adorned with row after row of beads, plugs in their lips, their bodies shiny with oil and black–brown blankets knotted over one shoulder. All of them were carrying small stools on which they'd sit for a rest or use as a remarkably uncomfortable headrest while sleeping. One man had a woman, presumably his wife, following along behind him, carrying a baby on her back, a huge bundle on her head and bags hanging off each arm. Another elderly man, striding ahead on his own, was stark naked. My fellow travellers in the truck looked away. Were they embarrassed on my account? One of them clicked her teeth. I'd already learned she was a Kikuyu, Kenya's pre-dominant tribe. 'Primitives!' she said, shaking her head.

We stopped in Lokichar, two-thirds of the way there, for a drink, and also took on a couple of extra passengers: a Turkana couple and their child. Everyone in the truck shifted round. It seemed that a few of the others were refusing to sit next to them, turning up their noses and saying they were 'dirty'. There was standing room only for their little boy. I pulled him onto my lap. He looked terrified. For one moment, I was scared he might scream. But his mother smiled, and soon he was fast asleep in my arms.

Lodwar, when we arrived, looked as if it could be a town in the middle of the Sahara. It was sandy and dusty grey and incredibly dry, with a shrivelled-up riverbed around which a few camels and donkeys hopefully grazed. I felt a tinge of disappointment. I checked into a little hotel where the only other guests seemed to be a dozen grotesquely over-sized cockroaches in the toilet. There wasn't a drop of water to be had from any of the taps in the place. I checked out early the next morning and went and sat under the shade of a big umbrella tree on the road north. I was eager to get to Kalekol, and feast my eyes on the dazzling blue of picturesque Lake Turkana.

After four hours, a truck came by, the driver stopped and we worked out a fare for the 60-kilometre ride. I sat beside him in the cab as we drove past great plains of sand, sprinkled with tight fists of coarse grass. In several places, herds of oryx, a horse-like antelope, wandered and I saw a couple of baboons scuttle away as we approached. Finally, the driver announced we'd arrived. I looked around. *Surely* this couldn't be it. No glorious expanse of water into which I could joyfully dive. No white-washed little hotels with cheery waiters rushing out to push iced drinks adorned with cocktail umbrellas into my hand. No pretty beaches with deckchairs and hammocks strung between the trees. No...nothing. There was something wrong with this vista. Indeed, Kalekol seemed to comprise nothing more than a bar and a loose smattering of untidy huts, propped up with sheets of corrugated iron with ragged straw roofs. 'Kalekol,' said the driver again, impatiently. 'Kalekol.' I jumped out of the cab, set my pack on the ground and looked all around me. A few Turkana stared, curiously.

I wandered over to the bar and asked if there was a hotel in town. The barman looked blank. 'No, no hotel here,' he said. He shook his head to emphasise the point. Then he went out the back. I sat down on a stool—there didn't seem much else to do. Finally he came back and I ordered a beer. He seemed to soften towards me. 'You want hotel?' he asked me. There were some interesting markings on his forehead and cheeks that wobbled as he spoke.

I smiled. 'Yes', I said. 'I want hotel.' I corrected myself quickly, '*an* hotel.'

He shook his head again. 'No hotel here,' he said.

I didn't trust myself to speak. I just sat, and sadly slopped my beer into my lap, not having noticed that the glass was chipped. He continued to watch me, probably wondering how I could pay good money for beer, then pour half of it away. Finally, he spoke again. 'You need place to sleep?' he asked. I nodded. 'Maybe you sleep there.' He was pointing to a reed hut 20 metres away.

I finished my beer, thanked him and wandered over. A man emerged just as I was wondering what to do next. I said I was looking for a place to sleep.

'Sleep? Sleep?' he said, excitedly. 'Sleep!' It seemed to be his only word of English. He led me into the hut and through to a little compound at the back. There stood another little room, also made of reeds but with no roof. 'Sleep!' he muttered, striding off.

I went inside and sat on the mat on the floor. Soon he came back with another man, carrying a narrow bed. He set it down and disappeared again. I got up and sat on the bed, instead. A few minutes later, he was back, this time with a pristine visitors' book. He thrust it into my hands, together with an old pencil. Mine was the first name in the book.

After a bit of a nap, I went to find him again. I was hot, dusty and sweaty. 'Shower?' I asked, hopefully, but not daring to hope too much. I made a gesture with my hands that I hoped might indicate gallons of hot water splashing down around my ears. He frowned—then his eyes lit up. He dashed off again. Ten minutes later, he reappeared and tugged on my sleeve. I followed him outside. In the blinding white light of the late afternoon sun, an elderly man was standing on a stool in the middle of the clearing holding a bucket of water in the air. I laughed. They smiled back, delightedly. I realised they were deadly serious. To hell with it. I was so uncomfortable, a shower, *any* shower, would be welcome.

I went back in and changed into my swimming costume. By the time I came out again, a small crowd had gathered to watch. Oh well, I imagined there wasn't much entertainment in these parts. I took a deep breath and stood beside the old man, still standing on his stool. He started to pour a few drops of water onto my head. He then paused while I soaped myself up. The crowd murmured at everything I did. They roared when I lifted my arm to wash underneath. I wondered why. A middle-aged woman scuttled over and motioned at me to raise my arm again. When I did, she touched it. I suddenly realised they'd never seen someone who shaved under her arms before. In fact, they probably assumed I didn't have any hair there. The hair on my head was also strangely amusing. A couple came over to touch it when I'd rinsed out the shampoo.

After the bucket had been refilled and emptied twice, I wrapped myself in my towel and returned to my room. Seven women followed me back and stood around in the room, waiting. I wondered what for, until I realised they were simply curious. So I took off my costume and got dressed again. They shrieked and nodded in turn. I was white all the way down.

The next morning, I went back to the bar and asked the man there where the lake was. It had to be somewhere close. For all I knew it could be just around the next corner, although the land here was so flat there were no corners really to obscure it. He told me it was about 2 kilometres away and pointed me in the right direction. I walked for half-an-hour under the roasting sun before I understood how foolish I'd been to start out without water. There was still no sign of the lake, and the day was only going to get hotter. I decided to walk back to my room and try again later, this time carrying a decent amount of water. I strode back and collapsed, exhausted by both the heat and the effort, onto my bed.

That afternoon, I was still lying there reading when an elderly man in a loincloth the size of a small post-it note suddenly opened the door and walked in. He crouched in the corner, his bits all fully in view, and simply stared at me. I didn't know what to do. His presence, particularly since he was pretty well naked, unnerved me, and I sat up and tried to make conversation via hand gestures. He just stared blankly back. Finally, I gave up, went back to my book and ignored him. I was clearly becoming the talk of the town; obviously these people saw few outsiders. After twenty minutes, the man made an odd noise with his tongue, stood up straight, bowed at me respectfully and left, as quietly as he'd entered. I wondered if I'd even imagined it. Later, the man who seemed to own the place barked, 'Chief, chief' at me, so I guess that's who he was.

The next day, I had another go at getting to the lake. This time, I carried a plastic jerry can of water with me. After trudging through the gritty grey sand for about 4 kilometres, I finally sighted water. But it was a crushing disappointment. The lake was little more than a series of murky, shallow puddles that joined way off in the distance into a dull steel-grey sheet, the surface interrupted only by a few flamingoes, a couple of paddling donkeys and three huge great crows diving down in the vague hope of fish. It was nothing like the posters. Wearily, I turned around and set out for home. Only later did I discover that I'd come up the wrong side of the lake. On the eastern side, where the pictures for the posters had been taken, it was fabulous. On the western side, especially at Ferguson's Gulf where I was, it was crap.

With a heavy heart and a tingling on my head and neck that I knew indicated the start of sunburn, I walked wearily away. Half-way back to town, I was waved at by an elderly woman, with a sheet around her waist. I waved back. She waved again.

I shielded my eyes against the glare of the sun and peered at her. She wasn't waving; she was beckoning me over.

I walked towards her. She looked about ninety, but probably wasn't that much older than my mum. She was all skin and bone; her ribs were poking out of her chest and her breasts were shrivelled. There was a sore on one of her lips and, when she opened her mouth, I could see only a couple of pointy teeth. Her back was hunched over and, in one boney hand, she held a long stick to lean on as she walked. She was gesturing at my jerry can of water and making a swigging motion with her hands up to her mouth. I felt panicky—if she drank out of my jerry can, that meant I wouldn't be able to afterwards. I could catch something, *anything*, from her. I pretended not to understand and merely smiled back. Her movements grew more emphatic. A one-eyed half-wit who'd lived his life in a cardboard box could have understood what she was trying to say. But I didn't want to hand her my water. I smiled again, waved merrily and went to move off. She caught my arm between her fingers. I shook her off, and walked quickly away, not looking back. It was an encounter, however, that haunted me for years. How *could* I ever have refused another human being water? And why didn't I think just to pour some into her hands?

• • •

It was time to leave Kalekol now, and try to get back to a semblance of normality. I longed too to be finally on the grassy banks of Lake Victoria which would *surely* be just how I imagined: a vast expanse of water that had once inspired awe in that flurry of courageous explorers searching tirelessly for the source of the Nile. Besides, I desperately longed for someone to talk to. I hadn't spoken to anyone in days. That morning, I'd looked at myself, in horror as if from afar, chatting to my own image in my little make-up mirror. Even worse, I realised I was actually enjoying the conversation.

Those explorers may have survived, and admirably too, with only themselves to talk to at times, but they were made of far sterner stuff. And I bet they'd never begrudged sharing their water. Oh well. I had the long journey south back to Kitale, then on to Kisumu and then west to the lake at Usenge to go. Hopefully, somewhere along the way, would be a person who spoke English. I was desperate for a friendly conversation and to find a way of redeeming myself as a half-decent person. It was all very well travelling alone but sometimes, just sometimes, you had to admit when you were standing on the brink of insanity.

chapter seven
MAYBE NOW WE SHOOT YOU
destination: Kampala, Uganda

The revolver spun round and round on the table between us, clattering to a halt to point straight at me.

'Ah yes,' drawled the soldier with a triumphant sneer. 'Maybe now we shoot you.'

I felt my blood turn to ice, an aching cold that spread slowly from the top of my head, all the way down to my feet. I opened my mouth to speak, but nothing came out. This was it. This time, there was no way out. What a miserable, bloody way to finish up.

'We have been watching you,' the soldier continued, picking at his nails with a penknife. 'We know you are alone. Nobody will know that you die here. You will not be the first.'

It's the moment any lone traveller dreads. No-one knows your whereabouts. No-one will come looking for you if you don't turn up in the next town within twenty-four hours. No way out. It's just you, your wits and a dogged faith in the essential compassion of the human spirit—and a creeping, uneasy fear you might have been wrong on that one too.

•••

Uganda in 1982 was a country in political turmoil, economically bankrupt, ugly and desperate, with generations of corrupt government dragging the country down into a mire of poverty, anarchy and fear. In the three years since the brutal tyrant Idi Amin had been overthrown and had fled to Libya, the military had stumbled from being his personally indulged, much-feared elite, to an armed rabble who were unpaid, hungry and out of control. After Amin's disappearance, the presidency had gone back to Milton Obote, the man whom Amin had originally deposed. Many claimed that the election had been rigged. Some said he was just as bad as Amin, and there were at least two guerilla groups active against him. The place was in a state of civil war. Tourists were warned not to enter. And certainly not alone. I, of course, had been confident I could sail right on through untouched by the chaos around me. Now I finally realised that it's one thing travelling alone with a certain degree of self-assurance. It's quite another to do so blinded by pig-ignorant stupidity.

But the thing was, I'd been eager to visit Kampala ever since reading about the fascinating independent kingdoms that had made up Uganda before the British arrived. Kampala had been the seat of the kings of Buganda before Amin forced the last one into exile. I wanted to see Kabaka's Palace. I also wanted to see the capital of the country once dubbed the 'Pearl of Africa', described as one of the most beautiful countries on the continent, with magnificent game parks, stunningly lush scenery, an incredibly rich history and a population said to be among the friendliest, kindest and most generous on earth.

I was eager to meet them. I was sure they'd get to like me too when they met me. Besides, the rainy season had blocked the only other route northwards—the desert track between northern Kenya and Sudan. If only I could just get to Kampala, I was convinced the route north would be simple. And, hey! you'd have to be pretty unlucky to run into any *real* trouble.

Just to be on the safe side, however, I'd tried to keep a low profile as I'd left the cheerful familiarity of Kenya through its quiet border town of Mlaba. These days, a *mzungu* passing through was a rarity, and a white woman on her own a particular novelty. At Kenya's border post, the guards had flirted, laughed and joked with me. But as I hiked over the stony scrubland of its border with Uganda, the atmosphere had darkened. At Uganda's border, immigration officials looked at me grimly, said barely a word and waved me on without ceremony.

Standing at the railway station on the outskirts of the nearby little town of Tororo, the mood had been tense. Little knots of locals huddled together at the back of the exposed platform waiting for the train to the Ugandan capital, Kampala. They all seemed to be trying to merge into the shadows. No-one wanted to attract attention. The place was simply too dangerous. I'd smiled at a little family standing crouched at the foot of a nearby tree as I'd passed, and they'd all shrunk away. No-one wanted any association with a white woman who stood out so starkly. I could mean trouble—and lots of it.

Two hours later, however, I could feel the hostility towards me starting to melt. The train was late. The sun was white hot. We were all buying warm fizzy drinks from a seller who'd wandered by with a tray on his head. One young man asked me where I was going to. Another asked me where I was coming from. Both answers seemed to be bleeding obvious as we stood on that dusty platform in the middle of nowhere, but I was grateful for the human contact.

Suddenly, there was a sharp cry, the two men looked around fearfully and I saw, out of the corner of my eye, the little family by the tree beckoning at me urgently to move away. I turned back to the two men to see only their figures disappearing into the distance. 'Hide! Hide!' hissed the drinks seller as he sloped off into the shadows. I understood too late. Two soldiers, their uniforms dirty and torn, machine guns slung over their shoulders, a revolver each tucked into their pants, were striding straight towards me. It was too late to move. I stood my ground and, as I felt my knees turn to liquid, I fixed a welcoming smile on my lips and a nonplussed look on my face.

But these guys meant business. They looked me up and down, very slowly, then told me to come with them for a passport check. 'Let's do it here,' I suggested brightly. The taller one shook his head and barked something at the other. He picked up my backpack, and the taller man grabbed my shoulder and pushed me, hard, in the direction he wanted me to go. The little family by the tree called over to the soldiers to leave me alone. They were silenced by a glance. As I was marched roughly past them, they avoided my eyes.

We walked and walked across the dry dusty plain, stubbled with rocks, the odd patch of wiry dark grass and the occasional stark, leafless thorn tree. We walked away from the relative safety of the by now crowded platform and away from the direction of the border post. We walked, in that blinding white sunlight, away from anyone—I knew with a sick knot in my stomach—who might be able to help me.

Finally, about a kilometre away from the station, we neared a little corrugated iron shed, smeared with the dark red of rust. The door was hanging open on only its top hinges. It was windowless and looked pitch black inside. I was half-pushed, half-dragged into the darkness.

One man snapped on the light, while the other closed and bolted the door. They propped their machine guns in a corner and then sat down on one side of a worn desk, motioning at me to sit down on the other. This wasn't looking good. The army throughout Uganda hadn't been paid for three months, with soldiers living off the cash they terrorised locals into giving, and off the food they stole from nearby farms. At best, they'd want money from me; it would just be a question of how much, how smoothly the whole process could go, and how quickly I could get out of there. At worst...it didn't bear thinking about.

'Could I make a contribution to your funds?' I asked, hoping they'd take the wobble in my voice to be my accent. 'How much?' They looked at each other. Obviously, they'd dragged me here without discussing what exactly for. And now they didn't know what to do with me.

There was a short, awkward silence. In the harsh light from the bare bulb I could see the taller man had a long, livid scar on his left cheek. It looked quite fresh. The other had appalling acne and two front teeth missing. Neither could be much more than twenty. I wondered idly if their mothers knew what they did for fun.

There was a coughing and scraping of chairs. 'A thousand American dollars,' said Scarface, suddenly, obviously plucking a random figure from the air. A thousand US dollars? It could just as easily have been 10 000, a million or even 100. Tucked into a little pocket in my pants, I had just US$50 in cash. But that would present another problem: I hadn't declared that money to customs. If I offered it to them now, and they asked to look at my entry documents that stated I was carrying no foreign cash, they could get me. And, this time, they would be quite within the law to do so.

I took out a wad of local currency the size of an average house brick from my pack and slammed it on the table between us. They didn't look impressed. And to be honest, I couldn't blame them. Ugandan shillings were worthless outside the country and almost as bad inside. With a rate of inflation galloping so fast that bus conductors wound their little ticket machines around ten times to produce a ticket longer even than the journey you were undertaking, that much money probably wasn't worth the cost of the paper it was printed on. I'd heard it had become a common sight in Kampala to see the servants of wealthy Ugandans pushing wheelbarrows of money down the street to cement business deals. I could believe it. I knew that massive bankroll sitting on the table might be worth tomorrow only three-quarters of what it was worth today, and that wasn't much at all to begin with.

The soldiers looked angry. I felt beaten. From the sour smell of the breath of the one who'd been pushing me along, they'd obviously been drinking the homemade maize beer that made so many soldiers' lives bearable. Stuck out in the hot scrub, away from their families, unpaid, unfed, despised by the government they protected, hated by the locals they scavenged off, life had little value. Deserters were shot on sight. Those who stayed had to manage as best they could. They were as trapped as I was and, for once, it was they who held the initiative. It was a taste of the kind of power they used to have. They felt mean.

The pile of money was shoved back towards me. 'We want dollars,' shouted Scarface. He stood up and jerked his face close to mine. 'Dollars! Dollars! You understand?'

I shook my head. 'I'm sorry, I don't have any,' I said. 'How about...' and I paused, weighing up the situation, 'traveller's cheques?'

His fist smashed down on the table and his eyes glittered with rage. The mood turned ugly. I instantly regretted mentioning the traveller's cheques. These men weren't stupid—they knew cheques would be worthless to them—but now they could see I thought they were dumb. And they were furious.

'You know, we can rape you,' said the shorter, quieter one, taking over from his partner. I wondered which one was in charge. 'Then we shoot you,' he added, taking out his revolver from his waistband. He held it up, then put it on the table between us. 'But first we play a little game. If it points at you, we do anything we want.'

He spun the revolver. I held my breath as the gun wobbled around, then came to a rest pointing towards the door. He grabbed it, and spun again. This time, it fell off the table and the pair jumped, in panic, back out of the way in case, presumably, it went off. The third time, I was left looking straight down the barrel.

I looked up at the men. They hadn't exactly said they could have three goes at this. But at the triumphant look on their faces, I decided to keep quiet. Scarface licked his lips. I felt an icy-cold dread seep through my entire body. My stomach contracted and there was a sharp jab of pain in my head. These men looked deadly serious. And, in a country like this, torn apart by civil war, where life and death were so cheap, you could never afford to assume they were kidding. Two weeks before, a tourist had disappeared in Uganda. He was last seen crossing the border I had just passed. Three months before, a nun had gone missing. Her body was later found, beaten and violated, in bushes not too far from the railway station. These men were for real—and they knew I was on my own.

At first, I sat stone still as my mouth tried to form words that never came. But I knew that would do no good. I took a deep, slow breath and tried to get a grip. I had to think how to get out of this—I had to find out where their weak spot lay. It would be a question of trying every trick in the book and hoping, just hoping, that one would work.

'But I am not alone,' I said finally, trying to exude an air of a confidence I did not feel. 'My husband is crossing the border after me and will be looking for me.' Even to me, it sounded unconvincing. Scarface laughed and looked deliberately at the bare wedding ring finger of my left hand.

I moved up a scale. There was also a friend, who worked with the government, expecting me in Kampala the next day. He would be suspicious if I didn't arrive. A bad move.

'The government?' said the one in urgent need of a tub of Clearasil. 'The government?' He spat noisily on the floor, narrowly missing my pack. 'That is what we think of the government.'

Dumb, dumb, dumb.

I looked at the wall next to me. There was a thin spear of sunlight on the ground from a gash in the corrugated sheet. Next to it was a dark patch of something that had been spilt. Coca-Cola? Beer? *Blood*? I looked away and back at my two captors. 'Where is your passport?' asked Scarface. I pulled it out of my money-belt. He snatched it from me and flicked to the front page. 'Ah haa,' he said, triumphantly. 'This is out of date. You are under arrest.'

My mouth went dry. I leaned forward to try and see what he was looking at. He was showing his mate the page. They both nodded sagely. 'How you explain this?' The passport was flashed in front of me. A dirty, cracked fingernail was pointing to the date of issue. I tried to tell him he was looking at the wrong point on the page. They weren't listening.

'Look,' I said, finally, 'I am here because I want to help. I am a teacher. I have come here to help the children. You have had a difficult time in Uganda. We are trying to make things better.'

They looked at me blankly. The acne-scarred one gave a short, bitter laugh. 'You want to help?' he mocked. 'Then you are wasting your time with the men we have in charge.'

Beginning now to feel real despair well up inside me, I summoned all my strength. I sat up straighter in the chair and fixed them with what I hoped might convey resolution, confidence, authority. 'Look, I'm fed up with this,' I said, sternly. 'I'm going.' I moved my feet ready to stand up.

Scarface fingered his own revolver, still tucked into his trousers. 'No,' he said, sharply. 'You stay here.'

I knew I was fast running out of options. Desperately, I tried another tack. I thought of how alone and helpless I was. I thought of my parents back home weeping when, after months of fruitless searching, the Embassy delivered the news that I had disappeared without trace. I imagined a slow and painful death. I considered how unfair the whole situation was. It wasn't long before it had the desired effect. I wiped my nose on my sleeve and crumbled into tears.

Yet, as I snivelled and sobbed, I felt that, somehow, this just wasn't having the desired effect. I'd hoped it might soften their hearts. They'd be touched. They'd be sorry. Instead, I could sense their contempt growing. It was bad enough I was a weak white woman, let alone an hysterical one.

After perhaps five minutes of crying, I shut up and gave up. The three of us sat in silence. There was nothing more I could do. I had to leave it to fate now. The short one nursed the revolver still on the table between us. The silence grew deeper.

Scarface picked his nose. 'Okay,' he said, eventually, examining his finger. 'We take this money. We let you go—but only if you tell nobody what has happened.'

I felt my heart leap into my throat. 'No, no,' I faltered. 'Of course not. No, nobody.'

'And one more thing,' he added. I felt my heart sink. 'You send us a postcard from your home.'

Maybe I had been lucky that it was still early in the day, when the grog hadn't made them so reckless with others' lives. Maybe one of the tactics had worked. Or maybe they'd simply realised that indeed I had no thousand dollars, no hundred dollars, not even ten. If they'd had it, any person in their right mind would have handed it over.

This game of nerves was finished. They had their money, they'd had their fun, and they'd been able to exercise what little power they'd ever had over anyone. Scarface clamped his hand over the wad of Ugandan shillings and pulled them towards him. The shorter one stood up and unlocked the door of the shed. 'Go,' he hissed through the gap in his teeth. 'Go now.'

I stood up shakily, slung my pack onto my back and, bizarrely, saw myself hold out my hand to the two men. They each shook it gravely. I then turned to the door and walked out into the blinding sunlight, back in the direction of the station, not daring to look behind me. Suddenly, a single shot rang out. They'd fired over my head. It turned my weak knees hard again and I started to run.

As I panted up to the platform, a babble of excited voices sprang up. The family who had watched me being taken away came over and took turns to hug me. 'When we heard the shot,' the father said, 'we thought they had taken you. You are not harmed? You are all right? What did they do to you?' He drew me towards a large crowd of people watching us, and they opened their ranks and closed behind us. 'You will be safer here,' said the man. 'These people will help you.'

I looked around me: a sea of smiling faces. I was now one of them. We were facing a common enemy. I smiled back, grateful to be back on the platform, among friendly people. Alive. 'Ahh,' said a man who looked ancient but was probably only about forty-five (it was no doubt what the stress of living in a place like this could do for your complexion). We all waited for him to continue his sentence. 'They don't kill tourists so much any more,' he added, finally. 'We just kill each other.'

There was a quiet moment, there on platform one, but the spell was broken by a woman carrying three huge shopping bags. 'Keep down,' she muttered. 'They might come back.' I imme-diately fell to the floor, horrified by the thought. The crowd pressed in. A cloth was thrown over me and bags piled on my shoulders. My knees ached, it was hard to breathe and I was in urgent need of a pee, but I was determined not to move.

About an hour later, I heard the scream of a train in the distance, and a buzz of relief from around me. The noise of the train grew louder until it wheezed onto the platform. 'Slowly, slowly,' someone whispered to me, as I was half-pushed, half-carried towards the train, still buried under cloth and bags. At the steps, I was shoved up and eager hands reached out to pull me into a sleeping compartment. The top bench was pulled down, I was hoisted roughly up and blankets were piled on top of me. 'Stay there, quiet,' hissed a woman's voice. 'They are back. They are looking for you.'

My heart was pounding as I lay under the blankets, my face pressed into the leather, my rucksack hidden under the seats by boxes of fruit, crates of chickens and piles of pots and pans. I felt exhausted and scared. Why were they coming back? They'd obviously decided they'd let me off too easily the first time. This time...who knew what they'd do?

The passengers in my compartment were tense and silent. I felt inordinately grateful to them. If I was discovered, they'd all be implicated in having helped me to hide and, while these soldiers might be tough on me, I had little doubt they'd be even tougher on them. It amazed me how willingly people would put their own lives on the line to help a stranger. So many Africans across the continent live in daily fear of the police, the army and corrupt government officials. For the first time, I'd really tasted that fear and understood exactly how paralysing it could be; how sick you feel every time anyone in authority looks at you the wrong way; how powerless you know you are; how helpless. What on earth would it be like to live under that kind of pressure constantly? I only hoped I'd be a quarter as courageous as those Ugandans if ever I had the chance to make a difference. Mind you, I had been the one who had refused to share even her water with a woman in need.

Compartment doors were being slid open and I could hear the angry bark of the soldiers. The heavy footsteps were coming closer; they were opening the compartment next door. There was the sound of raised voices. The door slammed shut; our door was opened. A question was shouted in. Everyone murmured back. There was a silence that seemed to stretch forever as I waited for a hand to reach up and pull back the blankets. But then the door slammed shut.

Twenty minutes later, there was the shrill scream of a whistle, the train pulled away, and the compartment exploded into excited chatter underneath me. I stayed on that top bunk, sweating and unmoving, under the blankets. I wondered how many hours to Kampala, and whether my legs would support me when I finally climbed down to go for that pee.

chapter eight
DO YOU HAVE CHICKENS IN YOUR COUNTRY?

destination: Juba, Sudan

The edge had somehow been taken off my appetite for exploring Uganda after the battle to get to Kampala. That had provided enough excitement for a lifetime, I thought. Why tempt fate any more? Sure, poverty-stricken Sudan was having troubles of its own, with renewed tensions between the Muslim Arabs of the north and the traditional, Nilotic people of the south—plus a flood of war-weary refugees from Uganda to contend with—but it had to be safer, calmer and more peaceful. I was eager to get moving north.

Besides, my gratitude at being permitted to stay at Kampala's Sikh Temple, the only place in the city recommended as being safe for foreigners to stay, was wearing a little thin. Just the day after my arrival, I was walking along a corridor that wound around the complex when I noticed one of the Sikhs walking towards me. As I smiled and readied myself to wish him peace, *'Assalam alaikum'*, he bent down, took the hem of his gown in two hands and lifted it up past his waist. He wore nothing underneath. Stunned at such an unexpected development, I carried on walking, my greeting frozen at the first word in the air between us.

I hoped he was simply a visitor to the temple. He wasn't. The next morning, he did it again, and again that afternoon. The trouble was, with all the Sikhs dressed identically in their gowns and turbans in those murky corridors, and because they tended to avoid much contact with their overseas guests, I was never able to work out in advance which one it was. Sometimes I'd walk past, with downcast eyes in silence, only to have one of the residents cheerily greet me, so I'd end up feeling terribly rude. I found the whole experience incredibly unnerving. As I was the only woman staying in the temple, I'd obviously become something of a target. He never seemed to behave like that when there were any of the male foreigners around. My natural anger was, however, tempered by commonsense. Although I fantasised about giving him a good, hard kick in the area he so enjoyed exposing, or coming out with some crushing retort—although it would have to be in Arabic for maximum effect, I supposed—I was always far too afraid he might, in fact, be in charge, and I'd end up thrown out onto the streets to take my chances after the 7pm curfew.

After the first day, I never went to the toilet at night without first waking one of the men from the little group of backpackers in the room next door to accompany me. They were fine about it, and very sympathetic. For me, it was bad enough being flashed during the day; at night it would be so much more threatening. All day, I'd avoid drinking too much water in the hope of not having to disturb anyone else's sleep at night. All evening, during curfew, when the streets outside would echo with the chatter of machine guns, the sharp bang of rifle shot, screaming, the sounds of people running and intermittent explosions, I'd try and limit my liquid intake to one small coffee. At night, I'd put my own padlock on my door.

I was also growing tired of the deserted, potholed streets of Kampala, the empty shells of burnt-out buildings, the constant lack of water, the food shortages, the big shoe shops with only six pairs of shoes to sell inside, the supermarket with nothing but the occasional shelf of floor polish, canned milk, bread and scouring pads for sale. Those night-time bursts of machine-gun fire and distant explosions also played hell with sleep.

It was depressing too to chat to Ugandans on the street. 'What do they say about Uganda in your country?' a man dressed startlingly in a bright orange-and-yellow checked suit asked me one day in the supermarket, when I was staring at the scouring pads wondering why supplies of everything but those had dried up. 'Do they say it's a shambles?' I didn't have the heart to tell him that Uganda was rarely, if ever, a topic of conversation.

My departure from the country was, however, being held up by the Sudan Embassy. It would take a few days for my visa to come through, I was told. Only then would I be able to strike out north towards Juba, the capital of southern Sudan. In the meantime, there seemed nothing for it but to explore Uganda while I waited. But that was easier said than done. Jaunts out of Kampala were difficult as the army had set up roadblocks on every route out, ostensibly to safeguard security, but in reality to raise extra cash for themselves. At every stop, there was a queue of disconsolate Ugandans counting out their money, and a gaggle of soldiers clutching fistfuls of notes. It was heart-breaking.

Much easier, then, to try the train. The line west from Kampala ran all the way to Kasese just by the stunningly beautiful Mountains of the Moon on the border with Zaire. I'd wanted to see them from the east, having seen them the year before from the west. Just by there, too, was Lake Idi Amin (since renamed Lake Kivu) with all its gruesome connotations of a man who became one of the world's most evil dictators, presiding over a brutal reign under which so many people died. Then there was the Queen Elizabeth National Park, a place, it is said, that once boasted the richest variety of wildlife in the whole of Africa.

Kasese turned out to be a scruffy little town of low cream buildings, stained with red earth, which it seemed few outsiders these days deigned to visit. Everywhere I went, people stared. Others, rather less courteously, yelled, 'Mzungu!' at the top of their lungs whenever they saw me. Was it a warning to others that an outsider was on the prowl, or a spontaneous expression of delighted surprise that someone was visiting? I could never quite make up my mind. The one saving grace of the place was the Sunshine Cinema. I hadn't seen a movie for an age, so when night fell, I couldn't resist going. I took one of the tattered red seats at the front and waited to be enthralled by the 1979 prison drama, *Escape from Alcatraz*. Unfortunately, it started a little late and, after the penultimate reel, the lights suddenly came up and the usher strode to the front. It seemed there was not going to be time to show the last reel before the cinema's closing time. We'd have to come back the next night to see whether Clint Eastwood ever succeeded in his attempt to tunnel himself out with his nail clippers. I decided I really didn't care enough to stay on an extra day.

For there was little else in the town to keep me there. The local café had neither tea nor coffee to serve, but it did have three very keen young waiters. When I asked for coffee, they each shook their heads in turn. They then went off to confer. When they came back, they asked me for money to go out and buy a can of coffee. I handed it over and they came back proudly with a tin of Brazilian blend, never considering, I'm sure, the irony of making it in a country that once boasted the finest coffee in the world. It was quite probably still the best, but production had long since come to a stop, with no means to distribute the finished product.

• • •

Down by Mweya, on the green, bushy shores of Lake Idi Amin, I saw my first dead body. It was a man, probably only about twenty years old. He'd caught on some reeds on the bank and lay bobbing on his back in the water, swollen and grey. His eyes were staring straight up. I was standing, frozen with horror, when a soldier walked by. I immediately averted my eyes and pretended to be looking at the view.

'Did you see the dead man?' the soldier asked me.

'No,' I said, anxious to avoid any possible problems. 'No, I haven't seen anything.' I was shocked to realise how quickly

do you have chickens in your country? / 133

I'd adapted to this way of life of denial and desperation to keep a low profile. He frowned at me, and walked on.

Over at the Queen Elizabeth National Park, a short bus ride away, there was an equally gloomy atmosphere. Even the weather was dull and overcast. The park itself was a great, gently undulating expanse of grass, with trees, banks and watering holes. The lodge, designed, no doubt, for weekenders and holidaying rich foreigners was a magnificent old mansion with high ceilings, dusty chandeliers, overstuffed red leather armchairs and the heads of various game mounted on wood on the walls. In the restaurant, the tables were each laid with snowy cloths and shiny silver cutlery. Bizarrely, however, I was the only guest there—and I was only half there, at best. I'd arranged to sleep on the floor of the kitchen, courtesy of the cook, for a small fee as the room rates were completely beyond me.

Sitting down at a table after 'checking in', feeling I ought to show willing at least to spend a bit of money while I was there, I was immediately surrounded by waiters. One presented me with a grand, oversized menu. One poured me a glass of water. One tucked the napkin carefully into the neck of my T-shirt. One flicked at the table with his tea towel. A fifth hovered. I sat back in the chair, luxuriating in the surrounds and the thought of a good meal, and perused the menu. The fish sounded nice.

'Sorry, no fish,' said one of the waiters when I pointed to the dish. There was a vegetable lasagne. Or not. 'Sorry, that is not available today.'

'How about the chicken?'

'No, no chicken.'

'The chips, then?'

'No.' The waiters were shuffling their feet about in embarrassment.

I decided to try a different tack. 'Well, how about you tell me what you do have?' I asked.

There was a pause. The one who'd handed me the menu with such a flourish took a breath. 'Well, madam,' he said, slowly. 'We have an egg.'

'Aha!' I said. 'I think I'll have the egg then.' They looked pleased. Twenty minutes later, it appeared in front of me, soft boiled and sitting piteously alone on a large silver platter.

The next day, I persuaded one of the park rangers, for a small fee, to drive me around in his truck to take a look at the game. It didn't take long to see why he'd been so reluctant. After all, a game park with no game...you wouldn't want that to get out to too many potential visitors. The ranger, a young bloke called Archer in his early twenties, looked sad. Some said that everything had been killed by Amin's trigger-happy soldiers, he told me. Others held that the animals were slain and eaten by Tanzanian troops on their way back from deposing Amin and securing the country. He had only been there a year. He didn't know who was responsible. Whoever it had been, however, had sure done a pretty thorough job.

In the evening, I wandered down to the little village within the park, made up of the families of the people who were employed there. It was a Friday, and Archer had told me that Friday was disco night. He also said I'd be very welcome to come along. These days, no-one had too much to do. After all, there were no animals and very few guests. A visitor would be a welcome diversion.

The venue for the disco was a little wooden hall in the middle of the village. I could hear it before I could see it. The door was open, and I walked straight in. It was stifling. There were about twenty people packed inside, all bouncing boister- ously around to very loud music, and obviously fuelled by the local banana wine that was quite possibly the cheapest liquor on the planet. Archer emerged from the gloom to grab me by the hand and try to introduce me to some of the others. I smiled at them, noticing one of the waiters from the night before, but could hear nothing. The music was deafening. It seemed much easier simply to pull Archer into the middle of the room and join in the dancing. Everyone seemed delighted that I had, taking turns to hand me cups of wine and be my dancing partner. It was fun. Indeed, the only problem was the music. It took me only a few minutes to grasp the reason—the Friday night disco only had two records. One was Shauri Yako, a popular hit from a Zairois group, that I'd become familiar with all over central Africa. The other was a catchy little ditty from Jim Reeves. *Jim Reeves!* Taking a break from the dance floor, I asked why Jim Reeves happened to be so popular, and was stunned by the answer.

'He is wonderful,' shouted the young waiter, jogging around in time to the music. 'We all love him. He is a very famous black American.' *Black?* I didn't have the heart to enlighten them. After all, it wouldn't be much fun getting together week after week, month after month, year after year, with just one record in their proud collection.

•••

I chose the train back to Kampala over a free lift offered by a truckful of raucously loud and mystifyingly exuberant soldiers. As they drove off, after I'd very politely—and effusive with gratitude for their kindness—explained why I just *had* to catch the train, I saw the crates of bottles of home-made gin stacked up behind them. Another great escape.

By now, I was even more eager to get out of Uganda and into Sudan. I felt like I was living on borrowed time. The place had the air of imminent eruption. I didn't want to be there when that happened. Arriving back in Kampala, I picked up my Sudan visa and slept one more fitful night at the Sikh Temple. As I was packing my rucksack early in the morning, ready for the off, another backpacker arrived. His shirt was ripped and he had a deep cut just under his eye and grazes on his cheek and forehead. He'd been beaten up at a roadblock coming into town from the north, he explained in a heavy German accent. 'Be careful,' he warned me. 'Try to get through in the morning, before the soldiers have the chance to drink much. And make sure you have some small monies to give them.'

I took another look at the map. The only alternative to the direct road north to the border, via Murchison Falls and Gulu, was the longer route east and north. 'You could get the train to Tororo on the border with Kenya and then go north from there,' said the man, helpfully. 'But I do not think that road is very good.' For me, that wasn't even an option.

There was no way on earth I'd return within a hundred kilo-metres of that border post. I thanked him for his help, but said I'd take my chances with the Gulu road. He shook my hand gravely. 'Good luck,' he said. 'May God be with you.' I flashed him a grin I hoped looked terribly brave and cheery both at once, hoisted my pack onto my back and marched out of the temple, hoping my legs wouldn't buckle before I was out of his sight.

It was still early and I walked slowly, keeping a careful lookout for soldiers buoyed up from the previous night's shooting. I kept close to walls, peering around corners before darting across the deserted roads towards the bus station. There was a bus to Masindi, halfway to Gulu, due to leave at 6.30am. I arrived at 6am, only to be told by a tired-looking ticket seller that the bus had been cancelled because of a lack of petrol. He was obviously getting little sleep too. 'Maybe another bus,' he said, helpfully. I walked cautiously to the offices of the rival bus company who were said to have a bus leaving at 8am. It wasn't there yet, the manager said. I'd have to wait. I sat on the floor of the office and started on a new book I'd swapped one of mine for with one of the back-packers at the temple, George Eliot's *The Mill on the Floss*. It was an odd one to be reading in Africa, but I suppose this was escapism at its most sublime. At 9am, the manager came over to me, kicked my leg to get my attention and said the bus was still on its way to Kampala from Masindi and would be a good few hours yet.

I walked back to the first station. At midday, a Masindi-bound public bus arrived and I hopped on and offered the fare. The conductor wound his little ticket machine round and round. The final ticket was more than 3 metres long. He looked embarrassed as he handed it over. I laughed, then he joined in. 'Inflation,' he said, with a shrug. 'It is terrible. We use so much paper now.' Sitting on the bus, I examined it closely. Evidently the fare used to be 12 Ugandan shillings. It was now 400.

Finally, with eighty people squashed into a bus designed to take fifty, we pulled away and a cheer went up. As we roared through the suburbs of Kampala, the mood lifted. On the outskirts, however, the bus slowed down and there was a collective groan. We stopped at our first roadblock. The driver got up from his seat, opened the doors and slowly climbed down the steps to the soldiers outside. He came back a few moments later and waved us all out. We filed out steadily. As one of the soldiers caught sight of me, he pointed and shouted gleefully, 'Ah! *Mzungu*!' As I came down the steps, I was surrounded by five camouflaged young men, none of whom could have been any older than twenty, each slung with a variety of weapons ranging from AK-47s to heavy, finned bazookas. I felt uneasy. Then the first one went to speak and I steeled myself for the worst. 'Give me a dollar,' he said. 'Give me a dollar.'

It was a request immediately taken up by the others. 'Give me a dollar, give me a dollar,' they chanted, just like the little kids in Zaire who had begged for pens. I gave them each five shillings, and they nodded and smiled happily. I slunk away across to the other passengers. Eventually, we were all ordered back into the bus. As I walked down the aisles, the rest of the passengers were smiling at me. I'd obviously taken the heat off them.

We were stopped at three more roadblocks in quick succession. At some, I gave money; at some, I was ignored. There seemed to be no rhyme or reason to the soldiers' actions. They'd single out one person and push them around, sometimes taking money, sometimes rifling around in their bags to see if they had anything worth stealing. At each place, everyone who wasn't being harassed, me included, would stand with our heads down, avoiding the soldiers' eyes. I'm sure we were all going through the same torment. It felt terrible to be standing by doing nothing when someone was picked on. But, honestly, what could any of us do? They had the guns, they had the upper hand. Yet if things got really nasty, I wondered, would the rest of us try and stand up for their victim?

After the fourth roadblock, we drove on for four hours without interruption. The mood, however, was sober. Many of the villages we passed, little clearings of brown dirt and huts in the middle of lush greenery, looked empty and deserted. The middle-aged man sitting next to me said their inhabitants had probably been driven away by soldiers or by bandits. Here and there would be an upturned bucket, a stool lying on its side outside a hut, a stray goat mewing piteously. Evidently, everyone had been in a hurry.

'How is the situation in your country?' my neighbour asked me. I said it was very different. He nodded, sagely. He had once met someone from Sudan, he informed me, gravely. Their country was very different too. I nodded, as if not surprised to hear it.

He was in the mood for talking. 'So, in your country, do you have chickens?' he asked me.

'Yes,' I said, gravely. 'We do have chickens. Lots of them.'

'Ahhh!' he said, delighted by our new bond. 'And in your country, do you have *ugali*?' I explained we did, but we called it 'cornmeal' and had never discovered the delights of boiling it up in water and eating it with nearly every meal.

'Ahhh!' he said, clearly perplexed by my answer. 'I see.' He plainly didn't. 'And in your country...' He was obviously now searching for another important indicator of our mores. I sighed. I'd grown inexplicably tired of this conversation. But I turned to look at him again politely. 'In your country,' he repeated, 'do you have trees?'

About 50 kilometres before Masindi, just as we'd all started relaxing, believing we were now very nearly home and hosed, we were flagged down by a soldier in a beret. The driver got out to speak to him. Then the soldier stepped in. 'There is trouble,' he announced formally. 'Guerillas ahead.'

The effect on the bus was immediate. Women began wailing and the men dived down, fiddling in their socks and the lining of their jackets to pull out rolled up wads of money. They started stuffing them instead into their breast pockets. 'Why?' I asked my neighbour, feverishly shoving my cash down my knickers.

He placed a hand on my arm. 'Sister,' he said solemnly, 'better your money than your life.' I was struck by the quiet wisdom of his words. I stopped immediately.

All the passengers in the aisle then crouched down, while those who had seats scrambled to crawl down into the gaps between their seats and the ones in front. My old friend and I crunched heads each trying vainly to squeeze into the space in front. 'Ready?' shouted the driver. He then revved up the engines rather flamboyantly, I felt, in a demonstration of reassuring bravado, and pulled away with a roar. The bus bounced and jolted at top speed over potholes, and veered up on to the banks at the sides of the road and then bumped back down again in a tactic I couldn't quite understand. We all were thrown against the walls of the bus, banging against each other and helping each other keep down to avoid any gunfire. We travelled about 30 kilometres like that, in a strange, deathly silence. My neighbour held my hand. I wasn't sure who was comforting whom.

Finally, the bus slowed and the driver yelled something. Everyone began screaming. My heart gave a jolt, until I realised they were screaming with *pleasure*. Evidently, we were past the danger. A group of women at the back started singing a hymn and a crowd of the men at the front joined in. A few people in the middle punctuated it with the shout, 'Thanks be to God!' The knowledge that He'd allowed such problems to happen in the first place seemed to make little difference. Half-an-hour later, we arrived safely, and exhausted, in Masindi. I shook my neighbour's hand warmly and went off to find an hotel.

• • •

The next day, I took a bus further north and spent a few days at the Murchison Falls National Park, where I bumped into a crowd of holidaying UN workers who allowed me to tag along on their game drives. The best was a night drive, gazing at the hippos and waterbucks at astonishingly close quarters, before finally tearing myself away to continue on. I got lucky again and hitched a lift with a group of American missionaries who were going all the way to Gulu, the last big town before the border with Sudan. There, I checked into a little hotel and wandered down to the truck park to find out if anyone was driving to Juba.

It took me five days to eventually find a lift on a huge articulated truck travelling north as part of an eight-vehicle convoy. Everyone was nervous of guerilla activity near Atiak, close to the border, so no-one was willing to drive alone. The journey was, however, tortuously slow. The rainy season was well under way and the road was muddy and slippery. Every time one of the trucks became bogged in the mud, another would have to overtake it to pull it out. Often that one would get stuck too, so a third would have to power over more mud, even further from the main tracks, in the hope of pulling out both.

The truck drivers made up a disparate community of mostly Kenyans, Somalis and one Ethiopian. I'd paid for a lift with the Kenyan, Jean, and his helper, Moses. I soon discovered it was an uneasy coalition with a very firm pecking order. Jean was of the Luo tribe, the natural leaders of East Africa, he explained, gravely. Moses was a Kikuyu, and Jean treated him like dirt. Both, in turn, looked down on the Somalis and the Ethiopian. 'Savages,' Jean would mutter, making sure he was safely out of earshot first.

It was Moses' job to cook Jean his meal every night, clean up after him, wash his clothes and do any work that needed to be done on the truck. Jean, by contrast, only drove. Every evening, he'd sit back in a chair Moses lowered down for him from the back of the cab, smoke, eat and tell stories, while Moses scurried around. The first evening, I found my place in the order of things. I ate stew with them—my food was included in the fare I'd paid—and then went to help Moses wash up. Moses looked at me fearfully, shaking his head. I didn't understand. He tried to take the metal dishes back off me. I resisted. Then Jean walked around to our side of the truck. 'No! No!' he yelled. 'That is his job. You do not do that. It is not right.' I protested, but was silenced by the angry look in Jean's eyes. It became my role, then, to sit and listen dutifully to Jean's stories while Moses worked.

The trouble was, Jean's stories were boring and I didn't much like him. He was a good-looking young man, but he was also unbearably arrogant and vain. The way he liked to parade me in front of the Somalis was, I think, a determined attempt to try and impress them with the fact that he had a white woman on board. I was in little doubt that he'd told them I was sleeping with him too. Yet I was in a bind. I needed this lift to Juba and I certainly didn't want to provoke him into chucking me out in the middle of guerilla country. Of course, I could then have got a lift with the Somali drivers, but I really didn't like the look of them, either. Every night, they'd drink themselves blind and push around the two stunningly beautiful, tall Ethiopian women they had with them. Any time I strayed near their camps, they'd yell out to me, and I was in little doubt as to the gist of what they were saying.

Moses was lovely, but he was too frightened of Jean to spend much time with me. He did become a valuable ally, though. While he spoke hardly any English, I was sure he understood the politics of the situation as well as I. Every night I'd unroll my sleeping bag and lay it out on any dry piece of mud I could find under the truck, close to where Moses would sleep. Every night, Jean would yell down from his sleeping position on the roof of the truck for me to come up and join him. I'd decline, but always he'd insist. Eventually, I'd climb up and lay down at the furthest point I could from him.

The first night, he stood up and walked over to where I lay, bringing his sleeping mat with him. He sat up and told another of his interminable stories, absent-mindedly stroking my shoulder. I wriggled further into my bag, and pretended to fall asleep. After a while, I heard him sigh and lay down himself. A few minutes later, I felt a hand steal into my bag. I pretended to continue sleeping while I rolled over, forcing Jean to withdraw it before I twisted his wrist. It began a pattern. Every night, the same thing happened. I began always to make sure I slept on the zip of my sleeping bag, so he wouldn't be able to undo it. It was horribly uncomfortable, but absolutely necessary, I told myself, as night after night he'd stroke my shoulder, then move his fingers around to try and search for the zip. Gradually, he began to bring up the subject of the night to come during the day. 'I am a good looking man,' he'd say, glancing up at me from the wheel. 'I give my wife great satisfaction. I will make you very happy.' I just smiled and apologised for my reticence, dreading the coming darkness. At night, Moses would smile at me sympathetically when Jean called for me to come and join him.

The days stretched on and on. The road became more treacherous as the rainy season set in hard. Most of each day would be spent sitting on a muddy bank, waiting for various trucks to pull each other out, and avoiding the Somalis. Burying my head in *The Mill on the Floss* wasn't much of a distraction. It was hard to be completely absorbed in Tom's worries over which school to attend, or Maggie's agony about which beau to choose when the struggles every day against the mud and every night against Jean seemed so much more real.

Every so often, there'd be a fresh rumour that there were guerillas waiting up ahead. Going back, however, was never a possibility. Sitting hunched in the truck at those times, hoping for the best but fearing the worst, I tasted again what it must be like to live in fear every day. It was just exhausting.

It took us an interminable six days to travel the 106 kilometres to the Sudanese border, and just ten minutes to get through. It was as much as I could do to stop myself kissing the ground. The next 174 kilometres to Juba took only two days. I just couldn't wait to get there. And when I saw the road sign announcing that we were almost there, I even hugged Jean. He looked angry. It was a bit late now to decide I had wanted him after all.

chapter nine
SEVEN YEARS! SEVEN YEARS!
destination: Khartoum, Sudan

We all lay like sardines on the cramped lower deck, end to end, side by side, as the dark waters of the Nile flowed silently past. I hadn't quite envisaged this when I was told that the boat was the best way to travel north from Juba. The person who'd described it, back in Kampala, had waxed lyrical about a slick, modern boat with groovy little cabins, motoring swiftly along the Nile to Kosti, en route to Sudan's capital, Khartoum. Too late I found out that I'd bought a ticket on one of the old, slow boats, little more than a collection of old barges strapped together, with the nearest thing to a mod con two stinking holes in the bottom deck, with doors to the outside that didn't lock. Still, the ticket had been cheap and the boat was obviously popular. I joked with the German backpacker lying next to me that if someone turned over suddenly in their sleep, we'd all be forced to turn over, and the one nearest the side would tumble overboard and disappear beneath the murky waters. 'Why do you say that?' he asked, puzzled. I started to try to explain. By the time he understood, I really wished I hadn't bothered.

But I was determined that nothing was going to dampen my mood. I was well away from Uganda, guerillas, army roadblocks and lecherous truck drivers. I was safe, secure and in another land. Of course, Sudan wasn't *that* secure but, relatively speaking, it felt it. I had no idea that, in only a few months' time, the country would plunge headlong back into the civil war that had devastated the country for seventeen years after independence in 1956, when President Muhammad Gaafar al-Nimeiry finally tried to impose Muslim law on the rebellious south. For now, however, all was at peace, and I had nothing more to do than sit on the deck and watch the world slip by. This was going to be sight-seeing at its easiest—there'd be villagers to gaze at as they went about their daily lives on the banks of the Nile, there'd be fabulous scenery, animals, birds and maybe even the odd croc, and there'd be the chance to view the Sudanese at close quarters as we all slept, washed, ate, drank and, let's face it, defecated together.

It was a romantic notion, but by this stage of my travels, I'd learned life rarely worked out quite as I imagined. That day, however, was happy. I'd seen three other backpackers buying tickets for the same boat, so knew I'd have some Western company. I'd bought a little charcoal stove on which I could cook food and boil water which, in Juba, had always been served straight from the Nile. I had a good stash of food, including bread, sardines and a bag of oranges. I had my *Mill on the Floss* to finish, I had plenty of letters to write, and I'd just paid A$5 for what I'd imagined would be a little twist of grass to smoke, but had been handed a bag the size of a small pillow slip. Oh, well, what the hell. Everyone seemed extremely easy-going about the whole thing, and I could always throw the rest away afterwards.

As we were told to board the steamer, however, I'd nearly lost my nerve. Hundreds of people had suddenly turned up just half-an-hour before we were set to get on, all heavily laden with bags, boxes, drums of oil and fuel, children, goats and chickens. At the captain's word, they'd all surged forward en masse, leaving us backpackers trying gamely to dart out of their way to avoid being crushed. By the time we'd got on board, it looked as if every available space had been taken up. The four of us squeezed ourselves into a little gap close to the toilets. Handy, we laughed. Horrific, we later discovered.

Kathy was a cheery Australian, and her boyfriend, Tim, an easy-going New Zealander. The pair had met in London and were now travelling to Sydney with a side trip through Sudan and Egypt. Stefan was the German, on his way back to Europe after a period spent in Juba working for an aid organisation. I wasn't so keen on him. It wasn't simply that he didn't laugh at my jokes; it was more that he seemed utterly devoid of any sense of humour at all. That first evening, after we finally got going in the late afternoon, we ate a couple of oranges, chatted, watched the Ugandans, Sudanese and Kenyans around us expertly establish their space in family groups, gazed at the vivid sunset, sniffed the myriad smells of a couple of dozen meals being cooked up around us—none of us felt like bothering to cook that first night—and then lay down in our sleeping bags. The area we'd marked out for ourselves, however, seemed to be shrinking with each new body that lay down for the night. I ended up sandwiched between Stefan and Edward, a friendly Ugandan from Kasese going to Khartoum to find work.

I fell asleep quickly, dreaming of sardines, but was woken around midnight by a loud bang at the front of the boat, a grinding and a shuddering. That's how the boat stopped every night, I had been warned. It had no lights, so carried on until it simply hit a river bank, and would start up again in the morning, when the captain could once again see where he was going. At 2am, I woke again to feel the deck around me shaking and hearing someone panting. I realised, with a sinking heart, that Edward was masturbating.

At 4am I woke once more with a terrible stench in my nose. It made me want to retch. I realised it was coming from the toilets nearby. We'd have to move, I thought. This smell would only get worse. By 6am, I'd crawled out of my sleeping bag and moved as far away as I could. The fumes were so pungently acidic, I thought they were going to melt my brain.

Very quickly, life established itself into an easy pattern. As soon as it was light, I'd get up, boil some water for coffee on my little burner, and put some sardines and a slice of onion on a hunk of bread. Then I'd haul up some water from the river to try to clean all the charcoal smears off my hands and face. After my breakfast, I'd simply gaze out towards the river banks. At times, the Nile was so wide, you could barely see the other side. At others, it narrowed, became clogged with weeds or lapped serenely on little islands in the middle. Sometimes, our boat hugged one of the banks closely as it throbbed and strained its way upstream. Everything was so close, you could wave at the people doing their washing, hanging out clothes, cooking on fires outside their huts, fishing and bathing in the river while their children swam. Usually, they waved right back. Little kids in their own small boats would drift up and hang on to the sides of our motley collection of barges, trying to sell fresh fish, bananas or wooden carvings to the passengers.

The boat itself erupted into a hive of activity at around 6am each morning. People dragged buckets of water from the river and showered each other, cooked meals, talked and laughed. The men crouched down on the side of the boat, their gowns spread to keep their dignity intact, while the women cursed and muttered about the state of the toilets, the only place where they could keep theirs. In the afternoons, when the sun grew so strong everything was bathed in a blinding white light, everyone went down to the lower decks and slept for a couple of hours. As the late afternoon grew cooler, there was another mass migration to the upper deck, where everyone would sit and smoke marijuana and watch the glorious red sunsets. They smoked dope quite openly, even the two policemen and five soldiers on board, and very soon I relaxed and did so too, although my three backpacking friends didn't seem interested.

We'd found another little spot to sleep well away from the toilets, even though it meant none of us had the room to lie out straight. We all had to curl, to keep within our space between two families of Jubans visiting relatives further north. We'd bought that area by presenting those families with small gifts of Australian flag pins and pens. It was still infinitely better, however, than our previous location. Stefan had washed his sleeping bag three times to try and rid it of the stench from an unfortunate overflow of urine that first morning. The only smell near us now was from a nearby huge netted mountain of dried, salted fish that was due to be delivered upriver. At first, we found it difficult to stomach. After a few hours, we barely noticed.

On the third morning, there was a commotion from upstairs. We all sat up, bleary-eyed in our sleeping bags. A young black man in T-shirt and shorts was running towards us, yelling and waving his hands in the air. 'Hey, you gotta help me!' he shouted in a broad American accent. 'I don't know what I'm gonna do.' He was a New Yorker called Mark. He'd been in Africa two months—which he described as the worst two months of his life. He'd joined this boat to ride along to Khartoum from where he was planning to catch the first flight home. But, sleeping on the top deck, he'd woken that morning and shaken his sleeping bag over the side. Too late, just as he heard the plop in the water, he remembered he'd stashed his money-belt with all his cash, traveller's cheques, papers and passport, in the bottom of his sleeping bag. He'd tried to explain to the captain, but he didn't seem to understand the gravity of the situation. Stranded in Africa, without cash or papers, he just couldn't imagine ever getting out again. He put his head in his hands and tears welled up in his eyes. 'I can't bear the thought of it,' he whispered. 'I've got to get out of this place. I can't stand any more.' I put my arm around him, hugged him and tried to calm him down, then offered to go back up with him to see the captain.

We climbed up to the captain's little wheelhouse and I greeted him politely. I then explained the situation again. This time, inexplicably, he seemed to listen. He nodded, solemnly. 'What can we do?' I asked him. 'Is there a hook'—and I made the gesture of someone fishing in the water with a long boathook—'or any good swimmers who don't mind going in?' He thought a moment, then shouted to someone else. He motioned at us to stay where we were, while he went outside to talk to them.

Mark was silent. I found out later that he'd managed to antagonise many of the Africans on the boat, and presumably most of those he'd met along his journey, merely by his colour. At that stage, few black Americans had travelled on the cheap in Africa. Most Africans had never seen one and, indeed, seemed to assume most foreigners were white. So, he was a complete mystery. In some down-beat suburb of Nairobi, he had been beaten up by a gang at night outside a bar who couldn't understand why he didn't speak their language. They'd shouted at him and shouted at him, yet still he seemed to be pretending not to understand. Eventually, enraged, they attacked. Elsewhere, he'd had similar experiences. He was black, yet insisted he was a foreigner. His clothes, nice quality US gear, also invariably invited suspicion. It appeared that locals had assumed he was trying to play tricks on them. As a white in Africa, even a cheapskate backpacking white, certain privileges are conferred on you merely by dint of your colour.

But being black, yet not knowing the ways of the African, meant you were either stupid, or up to something underhand, or both.

The captain came back and, I noticed, totally ignored Mark to speak to me. They would try to help me, he said. He had stopped the boat and someone had volunteered to enter the water for a small fee. We climbed down to the bottom deck, where a crowd had already gathered. There was a man flailing around in the river, disappearing every few minutes under the water, and someone else was poking hopefully around with a pole. Neither were having much luck. The water was so murky, the swimmer could see little. Of course, without a mask or fins, it looked a task well nigh impossible, but both men tried for half-an-hour, no doubt mindful of their fee, before finally giving up. I was effusive with my thanks, slipping them each a couple of Sudanese pounds. Mark just hung his head dolefully. The captain gave me a little bow and went back.

I caught Mark's arm and led him up to our corner. The others made him coffee and reassured him that the US consulate in Khartoum would be able to help. He looked unconvinced. 'This is the arsehole of the world,' he declared, unhelpfully. 'I never want to set eyes on this fucking continent again.'

I tried to change the subject. 'But how come you never said "hi" to us at all?' I asked him. 'We didn't know there was another foreigner on board.'

That was easy, he said. He'd had no intention of speaking to us. In fact, he'd quite despised us for sleeping and eating together. He had been determined to live with the locals. What was the point of travelling if you merely mixed with your own sort? I could feel the warmth we'd been feeling towards him cool.

That evening, the four of us went up as usual on the top deck to watch the sunset. Mark said he'd join us later. I rolled a joint, lit it and took a drag. I then offered it to Kathy and Tim who both shook their heads. Stefan hesitated. 'Oh, OK,' he said, reaching out. No sooner had he taken it between his fingers, however, then two policemen marched up to us, shouting. They made me jump, but I thought they were playing a joke. I smiled at them. They glowered back. As I watched, I could see dozens of locals, as well as a couple of the soldiers, leap to their feet and throw their burning joints over the side of the boat into the water. Suddenly, I realised this could be trouble.

The policemen yanked both Stefan and I to our feet. They snatched the joint from Stefan and rubbed the burning tip to put it out. 'What's the matter?' I asked, trying to stay calm. 'Sorry. I...I didn't realise we were doing anything wrong.' Their faces, however, were set. They marched us up to the captain's wheelhouse. The captain was standing with his back to the door. When he turned, his expression was grim. There was no sign of the earlier friendliness. This time, I knew we'd had it.

'You are arrested,' one of the policemen was saying. 'You must hand over your passports.' My heart sank and I looked over at Stefan. He was glaring at me. I could hardly blame him. 'We go now and search your bags,' the officer added.

The pair walked closely behind us as we went down to our deck, to our little space on the boat. The crowds waiting outside the captain's room to see what would happen parted for us as we moved through. This was more excitement than anyone had ever bargained for on this trip. But I could also sense sympathy. 'There but for the Grace of God', seemed to be the sombre mood. We pointed out our packs, and the policemen slowly took everything out. They flicked through my books, cooed over Stefan's little radio and looked completely perplexed by my tampons. They examined everything minutely. It didn't take them long, however, before they pulled the bag of grass out of the lining of my pack. Suddenly, seeing it through their eyes, it looked huge. They gave a little whoop of victory and put our passports into their pockets.

'What will happen now?' I asked gloomily.

'We will see at Malakal,' said the policeman, who seemed to be the spokesman for the pair.

'Can we pay a fine now?' I said hopefully. 'Maybe ten pounds...' I began to lose confidence when I saw him scowl.

'Are you offering me a bribe?' he said grimly.

'No, no,' I protested. 'I just thought...' The two left to go back to see the captain.

I looked over miserably at Stefan. If looks could kill, I'd have been lying dead, and quite possibly disembowelled too, at his feet. 'You are to blame for this,' he was spitting. 'It is nothing to do with me. Why did you give me that ...that...*thing*?'

I apologised, over and over. I'd obviously never dreamt it could lead to anything like this. I realised it was all my fault, he had nothing to do with it, and I was so very, very sorry. Of course, I was sorry we both now looked to be in so much trouble, but I wasn't really so sorry he'd been arrested too. I didn't want to be in this on my own. Sure, I felt bad. But not *that* bad.

That night, I couldn't sleep. Stefan had gone, in disgust, to bed down on the other side of the boat, away from me. Kathy and Tim had been sympathetic. They were sure nothing would come of it. Probably tomorrow they'd ask for some money, and that would be the end of the matter. They'd just want us to sweat on it a while. I hoped they were right. Mark was too tied up in his own problems to offer much consolation. I felt a bit miffed at him. After all, I'd really done my best to help him out, hadn't I? At least he could offer me a shoulder to cry on. But I didn't want to push it. He'd probably only tell me we were all doomed.

The next day, Stefan and I decided to go and see the captain. He was obviously the kingpin on the vessel. His word probably carried a great deal of weight, but he gave us a remarkably cool reception. 'No, there is nothing I can do,' he said. 'The police say they saw you with drugs. They will interview you today. And then they will take you off the boat at the next stop, Malakal.' Malakal! I looked it up on the map. It looked like a tiny town in the middle of nowhere. Surrounded by desert. The only feature nearby looked like a swamp. Great!

We went back to our camp on the deck. I tried to read *The Mill on the Floss*, but I still couldn't concentrate on Maggie's piddling problems. Stefan fretted. 'I cannot believe something like this has happened to me,' he was muttering. 'I am not to blame. I have done nothing wrong.' I could see he wasn't going to be much comfort.

At midday, the two policemen came to see us and took us back up to the captain's wheelhouse. They unlocked a safe in the corner and pulled out our passports. At least they were taking care of them, I noted grimly to myself. They carefully copied down our names from the passports in a big notepad, then wrote down our addresses. They then delved back in the safe and hauled out the bag of grass. They held it up. 'This is yours?' the first policeman said to Stefan.

I thought Stefan was going to choke. 'No! No! No!' he exclaimed. 'It belongs to her!' he jerked his thumb in my direction.

The policeman looked unconvinced. 'No, this is yours,' he said. 'Women do not do this. That does not happen.'

For one fleeting moment, just one you understand, I was tempted. It would have been oh-so easy to have burst into tears and said, 'Yes, yes, it is his. He *made* me put it in my pack.' I'd be home and dry, away and safe, and, besides, I'd never much liked Stefan anyway. I banished the thought. Apart from anything else, I could never really live with myself if I went through with it. It was bad enough that I'd refused an old woman water.

Stefan was looking daggers at me, waiting for me to speak. I took a deep breath. 'No, it is mine,' I said, wearily. 'I bought that. I was smoking it. He did not smoke any. It is my fault. I am very sorry.' Why was I talking so strangely? It must be Stefan's influence. The policemen looked at each other and shrugged. I could see the relief on Stefan's face, but he still looked at me with undisguised hatred. One of the officers wrote something on his notepad and then put the bag back in the safe and locked it. 'What happens now?' I asked.

'We will get off the boat at Malakal and talk to the police there,' said the policeman who did all the talking. 'We will arrive tomorrow. You go now.'

Dismissed, we wandered back through the boat. A couple of people tutted as we passed. Most, however, shot us sad, commiserating glances. I went and got my book, and read it determinedly all afternoon. Mark came down and sat with me for a while later on. 'You know what everyone's saying on the boat, don't you?' he asked. I shook my head. 'Apparently, the penalty for pushing drugs is seven years in jail. Everyone's saying you're going to be locked up for seven years.'

I looked at him. He was deadly serious. I wished I'd never befriended him. What was wrong with this guy? I could see why he'd made so many enemies. 'Oh, well, we can only wait and see,' I said, in a show of bravado that reached no further than my tongue. 'If you don't mind, I'd like to be alone now.'

He mooched off, hands in his pockets. Thanks Mark, I thought. Nice of you to let me in on the gossip. Push drugs? I'd only had a couple of joints to smoke. Stefan hadn't even inhaled. Mark was obviously in the frame of mind where he loved bad news, enjoyed embroidering it and then adored delivering it. I hoped he'd have to spend the rest of his life on this boat, going up and down the Nile, dreaming of home in the US, having Africans laugh at him when he insisted he wasn't from Africa. There could be no way I was facing seven years in jail. The idea was ridiculous. I told myself that at Malakal we'd be marched off the boat, taken in to see the police, ticked off sternly, and then delivered back onto the boat to continue up the Nile. It made perfect sense.

The next day, we docked at Malakal at about 11am. There were a couple of policemen standing on the wharf, and a small crowd around them. I wondered if they were new passengers, but they didn't move when the gangplank went down. They were obviously our welcoming party. The police officers on the boat came to collect us and, unexpectedly, told us to make sure to take our packs with us. My heart sank. Stefan swore. I said a fond farewell to Kathy and Tim, reminding them to alert the consul at Khartoum, and a rather cool goodbye to Mark. Then Stefan and I were marched off the boat and up the dusty path towards the centre of town.

'Seven years!' I could hear a couple of people mutter in a loud voice, obviously directed at us, as we all straggled towards town. I looked over at them and frowned. 'Seven years!' they repeated again, encouraged, and shouted something to the rest of the crowd. Very soon, the words had caught on among everyone else, even though I felt sure few of them would normally speak English. It just seemed they'd been briefed at what a huge joke it would be to taunt us so. The chant grew louder as more people joined in and others came and walked with us to the centre of town. By the time we arrived at the local jail, there must have been a couple of hundred people following us, shouting various permutations of 'Seven years!'

We were ushered straight in to see a man I assumed was in charge. He was wearing a dark blue uniform and a natty black beret. Our police saluted, handed over our passports and pulled out the grass from a kit bag. I gasped. It was *half* the size it had been when the police confiscated it. I went to say something, but thought better of it. Those police either smoked it with the captain one night, or sold it to other passengers on board. The hypocrisy of the situation! We were obviously here to be made an example of.

The man in charge stood up and frowned at us. 'Do you know what the penalty is for this offence?' he asked. We were silent. I shook my head. 'It is seven years in prison,' he said. I suddenly felt faint. 'You will stay here until your trial.' Our trial! This was getting out of hand.

Stefan elbowed me in the ribs, hard. I ignored him. 'We're very sorry,' I ventured. 'Very sorry. We didn't realise there was a problem. So many other people on the boat were smoking too...'

He silenced me with a look. 'And if they had been caught,' he said sharply in a tone that would brook no nonsense, 'they would be here too. Now wait outside.'

We walked outside and stood quietly. They were evidently working out where to put us. After a few minutes, the two local policemen came out and pushed us down the hallway to an open air courtyard. On one side sat a kind of cave with bars all along the front. A couple of ragged men emerged from the gloom inside to come to the bars to look out at what was happening. They were in leg chains and there was a strong smell of sweat and dirt. Stefan blanched. The gate was opened and he was shoved inside. I could hear him shouting his innocence as I was led away. Once again, as a woman, I had drawn the long straw. I was taken to a small office inside the main building, and then had the door locked on me from the outside. I felt relieved. I'd have hated to have been where Stefan was being kept. Once again, I felt a terrible surge of guilt, tempered, however, by relief that I wasn't about to go through this alone.

The office had only one small window high up on one wall, and was bare except for a few straw mats in the corner. I dragged one to the centre of the room and sat down. What now? I guessed we'd have to wait and see. We'd left our backpacks in the main office. I hoped they'd bring them to us, later.

Afternoon slowly dragged into evening. Evening became night. No-one came to see me. Nothing to eat. Nothing to drink. I lay down and tried to sleep. A couple of hours later, the door swung open and a guard walked in, carrying a glass of water. He introduced himself as Isaac. We shook hands in a bizarre little ritual of politeness, then I thanked him and drank it thirstily, never thinking to ask if it had been boiled or purified. What was the use?

Isaac sat down on the edge of my mat and started to talk. Everyone was very sorry I was there, he said. They were sure that other man had put me up to it. If I only said I'd be a witness against him, he was positive it would be better for me. Adamant, I said no. 'But it is seven years,' he said, not terribly helpfully, I felt. 'Seven years. Seven years is a very long time.'

I didn't really need him to point that out. Seven years, at the moment, sounded like a lifetime—two lifetimes.

But, he said, he had a plan. I smiled, encouragingly. He had been working in this jail for six years now, he said. He was well respected by everyone. One day, he would take over from the Mr Njmena at the top. Everyone knew that. I shifted impatiently. He noticed and got right to the point. 'I can help you,' he said. 'I will make sure you are not punished.' I smiled at him again, more warmly this time. 'Yes, I will help you,' he said, 'if you have sex with me.'

I froze. Maybe, if he'd offered a better guarantee of help, or he was at least equal to or over Mr Njmena, I might have thought about it. Maybe. But as the situation stood, with the case sounding as if it had already been tabled for court, I failed to see how anyone in his position could help. Politely, I thanked him for his interest, but said my imaginary husband would be very angry. I'd take my chances with the court.

He looked crestfallen, but he was gracious. 'Well, good luck,' he said, as he edged out of the door. 'I hope you don't get the full seven years. And you won't tell Mr Njmena about this, will you?' I shook my head reassuringly. I was in enough shit as it was, without getting the guards offside.

The next morning, I was sitting waiting for the sky to brighten outside my little window to the outside world well before the sun actually rose. I hadn't been able to sleep much at all. 'Seven years!' was echoing around the inside of my head like a mantra. Surely they wouldn't keep me in prison for all that time, however? I had my qualification certificates in my pack, including an extra, doctored one, saying I was also a qualified teacher. What if I offered to teach in the local school for seven years instead? It'd be a much better solution all round. Hopefully, they'd be able to see that too. In the meantime, I'd write home and tell people I'd got an aid job. Then, when I stayed seven years, everyone would just think I was having too good a time with it to come back. But what if anyone suggested visiting? My mind was racing. At the same time, my stomach was complaining. I'd not eaten since the morning before.

A guard came round about 11am to check I was all right. I was fine, I explained, but I was so hungry. He looked perplexed and went away. A short time later, Mr Njmena himself arrived at my door. 'In our prisons,' he explained, 'people are fed by their families and friends. They visit them and bring them food. I can see in your case this isn't possible.' I shook my head sadly, and apologised for causing him even more trouble. 'We have thought about this, and we are willing to allow you into town to eat. But you must promise not to try to escape.' I felt enormously cheered. A jaunt into town! And as for escaping, where on earth would we escape *to*? There was nothing around here for miles.

I nodded solemnly. 'Thank you, sir,' I said.

An hour later, four guards came to the office to pick me up. They obviously thought I might be a handful. I smiled. They marched me down to the ghastly cave where Stefan was being held. They called his name and clanged open the door. I felt like hugging him, but his expression stopped me in my tracks.

'They're letting us out to eat,' I said instead, cheerily, noting that he'd assumed that communal cave pong.

Two guards marched ahead of us, and two behind, to town. We soon gathered another crowd along the way. They chattered brightly among themselves. It was easy to pick out, however, one phrase. 'Seven years!' people yelled to each other. 'Drugs! Seven years! Ganja, ganja!' I was surprised to hear it being called that, but smiled to hear the strange pronunciation.

We came to a stop outside a little café and the throng followed us in. We ordered two plates of the national dish, a soapy red bean stew called *foul* but, with rather less accuracy I felt, pronounced 'fool'. Everyone crushed inside the café was extraordinarily friendly. They asked our names, where we were from, where we were going, why we were in Malakal, if we were big drug pushers. Evidently, not much happened in Malakal. We answered all the questions and said, no, we hoped we would not be here for seven years. At that, they laughed, and slapped hands with each other and then with us. I smiled, but failed to see the joke.

Meal over, we were marched back. That evening, there were more footsteps at my office door and we were walked out again, back to that same café. This time, the crowd was shouting out our names, every step of the way, for all the world as if we were movie stars. I noted one disturbing development, however. Before, the crowd had been whispering, 'Ganja'. That had been replaced by the words, 'Hashish, hashish.' Now there were a couple of voices, 'Cocaine, cocaine.' I hoped our trial came soon, before we were charged with peddling three hundred weight of high-grade heroin to schoolchildren.

The days soon melded one into the next. We were given our packs, and I read *The Mill on the Floss* three times. I got to quite like Maggie. At night, I dreamt of Khartoum and how wonderful it would be if we ever, eventually, got there. I vowed to kiss the ground if we did.

We'd gradually got to know most of the townsfolk. A startling number had never even been on one of the big boats on the Nile, let alone visited Juba, or Khartoum. The furthest most dreamt of going was to Tongo, 27 kilometres downstream. They were still nervous of the Muslims in the north, they said. They wanted to take over the entire country, and kill everyone who wasn't one of them. What did we think of their *foul*?

At the café, we became valued customers. A couple of days they even treated us to a little watercress on top of the *foul*, and on another memorable occasion we had some crumbled goat's cheese. Nothing had ever tasted as good. Stefan was still pretty inconsolable, though. Some days, he ignored me completely. Other days, he was almost friendly. Almost. Still, I suppose I couldn't really blame him for still being so angry. After all, he did live in that cave.

After five days at the prison, we received some disturbing news. Our trial was set for the next day. I asked permission to cut Stefan's and my hair for the occasion. We'd do our best to look respectable, at least. I lent him my trousers to wear in place of his loud, floral pair. I put on my best, and only, dress. We still looked like refugees.

Marched out across town to the court by our regular guards, my heart sank when I saw the courthouse. I'd been expecting, I suppose, some higgledy-piggledy little house. This was a big colonial building with ten steps up to the front, and great stone columns. It looked terrifying. Inside, it was hardly less intimidating. We stood in a real dock, while the judge wore a white wig and spoke as if he'd just popped over from Cambridge.

A lawyer read out the charge, and brought out the exhibits. One was my bag of dope. I hardly recognised it. It was *minuscule*. No wonder the guards at jail had seemed so jocular. We were asked if we wanted to say anything in our defence. Stefan hung his head, so I thought I'd better. 'I'm very sorry sir,' I said to the judge, 'but I thought this was legal in Sudan.'

He looked down on me through half-moon glasses. 'Tell me,' he said finally, 'who was Sudan colonised by?'

I bit my lip. 'Britain and Egypt, sir,' I said.

'Right!' he replied. 'And is it legal in Britain and Egypt?' I felt most of the fight drain out of me.

'No, sir,' I said. 'But then there were a lot of other people smoking on the boat,' I added.

'Yes?' said the judge, 'what were their names?'

'I don't know,' I replied. It seemed like it was all over. Would it be seven years after all?

The judge summed up the case, and then said it was imperative that foreigners didn't start thinking they could come to Sudan and take drugs with impunity. He crashed his gravel on the bench. 'I sentence you both,' he pronounced, finally, 'to two years in prison...suspended for two years.' I looked at

Stefan in bewilderment. Had I heard right? *Suspended*?

The judge smiled. 'You are free to go,' he said.

I stepped shakily out of the dock and the guards all pressed around to shake hands. They walked with us to the doors of the court. We stepped out into the sunlight, in front of a massive waiting crowd. Someone shouted something to the guards and one of them called back the verdict. A deafening cheer went up, and we were hoisted onto shoulders and carried on a lap of honour around the town. Everyone was clapping us on the back, shaking both our hands and offering to put us up. 'You want to buy drugs?' asked one person from the crowd, to great hilarity all round. I forced a smile.

All I wanted to do was get the hell out of Malakal, but there wasn't another boat due for two days. We accepted someone's kind offer of hospitality and went back to the jail, again shaking hands all around, to pick up our rucksacks. We dropped them back at our new home and went inside to drinks of cold goat's yoghurt from a fridge in the middle of the lounge room. Our new hosts couldn't do enough for us, and every time we stepped out of their door, we were treated like local heroes.

The next day, an official arrived from the consulate to enquire if we needed representation at court. He was a little late, but we thanked him for the thought. Indeed, the only jarring moment in our two days free in Malakal came when one of men in whose home we were staying asked if we wanted him to go and get drugs for us. This time it wasn't a joke.

Finally, a cargo boat arrived and we offered them whatever fare they wanted to take us north to Kosti. We waved the assembled townsfolk goodbye and breathed a huge sigh of relief to be at last leaving Malakal. The name of that town, I felt sure, would be forever engraved on my soul.

After a few days, we reached Kosti and stumbled back off the boat. Stefan turned to me—he'd hardly spoken two words since the court case—and held out his hand. 'I go now,' he said, shaking my hand. 'Goodbye.' He then turned quickly away and marched off into the distance. I shrugged. I hadn't been overly keen on him, either. Anyway, Khartoum was only an eight-hour express bus ride away. I couldn't wait to get there. I was looking forward to kissing the ground.

chapter ten
A WHITE WHORE AFTER ONE THING

destination: The Pyramids of Ancient Egypt

On the day I left Khartoum, all ready to triumphantly enter the land of the Pharaohs, I was shocked to discover my urine had turned bright red. I'd just gone to the loo before boarding the train up to the border with Egypt at Wadi Halfa. It was going to be a thirty-five hour journey and no doubt the toilets on the train, if there were any, would be terrible. I was doing my best to make sure I'd have to use them as little as possible.

It was going to be a fabulous train ride, too, through the dusty Obayuda Desert, past the sandy plateau of Jebel Abyad and up into the stony, inhospitable Nubian Desert. I imagined spotting camels racing in the distance, past the soft yellow dunes, with be-robed Lawrence of Arabias on their backs, their blinding white robes billowing out behind them. The first part of the journey would follow the Nile north as far as Anu Hamed, then strike out through the desert alone, while the river meandered back south and west before joining the main route north. We'd also be passing plenty of temples on the way, and I planned to follow the map closely so I'd know when to hang out of the window in the hope of a glimpse.

My red urine, however, eclipsed my excitement. Suddenly, I was struck with terror about the state of my health. I'd got this far without any real problems; maybe now was the pay-back. Blood in the urine was always a symptom of something seriously wrong, I knew that much at least. And if you fell ill, there was nowhere worse to fall ill than far from home, all on your own. I knew it from bitter experience from my trip last time. Surely I couldn't be so unlucky as for this one to end the same way? I took my seat on the train, gazed out of the window at some of the most astoundingly barren scenery anywhere in the world, and fretted.

Several hours (and several trips to the toilet to monitor my state of health) later, I decided to seek help. I could well be sitting there dying for all I knew. I might not even make this last part of the trip. And that would be a damn shame. I couldn't bear the thought of falling at the last hurdle. I only had this train trip to finish up to Wadi Halfa, Sudan's final frontier town, and then I'd be in Egypt, the last country of my journey, with the sight of those incredible pyramids outside Cairo to mark the symbolic end of a monumental trip. I was looking forward to it immensely.

Yet now I'd come to the conclusion that I'd better get some advice, and fast, if I was to live to see them. I wandered up through the carriages until I came across a train guard. 'Doctor?' I asked him. 'Doctor?'

He nodded and led me back through a couple of carriages until we came across an elderly well-dressed man with a briefcase. 'Doctor!' shouted the guard, embarrassingly loudly, and shoved me towards him.

The doctor, happily, spoke impeccable English. I was terribly apologetic about interrupting his journey, but he looked pleased to have someone to talk to. Incredibly barren scenery can be interesting at first for its lack of anything to look at, but after a few hours, it does tend to lose its appeal somewhat. We had a polite conversation—where are you from, where are you going, what are you doing, why aren't you married?—before I got enough confidence to broach the subject that was clouding my day.

'Doctor,' I said hesitantly, 'I wonder if you might be able to give me some advice?' He looked interested. 'Well,' I said, not knowing quite how to put it, 'my urine has gone bright red.' He looked startled.

'Bright red?' he echoed.

'Yes,' I replied. 'Bright, bright red.'

He asked me if it looked spotted with blood, or mucus at all. I said no. He sat and thought a moment. 'You've just left Khartoum, haven't you?' he asked.

'Yes.'

'Did you drink many fresh juices there?'

'Yes,' I said, puzzled, 'loads.'

'And which was your favourite?'

I wondered where he was going with this. I cast my mind back to happy afternoons sitting outside the fruit juice vans that dotted the main centres of Khartoum. 'Pomegranate juice,' I said finally. 'That was fantastic.'

The doctor beamed and clapped his hands together in delight. 'That's your problem,' he said. 'Too much pomegranate juice. That will turn urine red every time.'

I felt my face flush with embarrassment. Here I'd been, planning the arrangements for my funeral, and all that was wrong was an overdose of pomegranate juice. I made my excuses and left him to his laughter as soon as I decently could.

The rest of the train ride passed quickly, now I was no longer trying to live each minute as if it might be my last. I was able to look out the window and savour the scenery, rather than just anxiously seek, in the reflection of my complexion, any signs of my impending demise. Mind you, there wasn't much to savour: flat, dusty scrubland punctuated by the odd rocky outcrop. Occasionally, there were signs of life. A lone man herded a group of camels God knows where, a few ragged people wandered past in the distance and, close to the tracks, a little family sat in the sand under the shade of a tent made of an animal skin, with a pot, a knife and a few scraps of clothing—presumably all their earthly possessions. I wondered if they lived there, or were simply moving house. Either way, how could they survive in such emptiness? But the two little children I could see were laughing and waving at the train as we trundled past. I couldn't get that image of joy plucked from the midst of nothing out of my mind for a very long time.

We arrived late in the evening at Wadi Halfa, the empty little border town with Egypt. Apart from some etchings dating back to Egypt's fifth dynasty and the cemetery where the head of the legendary Sudanese warrior-leader, the Mahdi, was hastily buried (after an outcry in Britain, when it became known that victorious Lord Kitchener had severed the head from the body and planned to bring it home to use as an inkstand or a cup), there wasn't much else to commend it. I didn't have time to wander around, anyway. Mindful that the steamer from this point up the Nile and over Lake Nasser would be waiting for the train to arrive, I rushed through the paperwork. I didn't want to miss the boat; I didn't want to spend any longer in one-horse Sudanese towns in the middle of the desert than I had already. But the steamer was still there, sitting patiently on the water, by the time I'd finished and I quickly bought a ticket and boarded. It was already packed. Evidently, everyone else on the train knew of a shortcut, possibly bypassing the border, to the dock. Still, I just enjoyed seeing water again after so much desert. As I feasted my eyes, I caught a glimpse of my doctor also hurrying aboard. I was careful not to catch his eye.

I rushed to stake out a space on the deck, noting, not without some pleasure, that this steamer looked new, and in far better condition than the one I'd caught earlier further south. There was even a little restaurant. That might be handy, as my stocks of sardines were running a bit low for a two-day trip. It'd be quite nice to have a break from them anyway for a couple of meals. My mouth watered at the thought.

It turned out to be a beautiful ride. The boat was extremely comfortable, and the atmosphere very relaxed. The scenery slipped past quietly, often just craggy sandy moonscapes, some-times adorned with astonishing temples looming up out of nowhere. My only regret, really, was that there was no stop at Abu Simbel, the majestic monument of ancient Nubia, which was relocated to higher ground in the 1960s to stop it being flooded by the rising waters of Lake Nasser after the new dam at Aswan, further north, was built. From the water, the temple looked incredible. It was possible to take a flight there from Aswan for a one-day excursion, but I didn't have much cash left. It would have to wait until another time.

Aswan, when we finally arrived, was glorious. The southern-most city of Egypt was a clean, bright, modern town, with big wide streets, a bustling market and even ice-cream stalls. Along the banks, the Nile swept past several pretty green islands, and became dotted with *feluccas*, the traditional sailing boats of the area, with white sails fluttering in the breeze. On the other side, the West Bank loomed bare and forbidding. Sandy mountains from the edge of the desert made it look like a completely different world. It was the perfect base for a few days 'R and R'.

• • •

The modern train up to Luxor took only five hours but travelled centuries as it passed close to the ancient city of Thebes and the Valley of the Kings. Taking a few days there to explore, I found all the temples and tombs quite startling in different ways—some with great columns reaching to the sky, others adorned not only with perfect hieroglyphics, but the graffiti of centuries. The gorgeous paintings on the walls of tombs, telling stories of revered kings and gods, love affairs, treachery, enslavement and acts of generosity, were still as delicately coloured as I imagined they were in their original state.

I even had a ride on a camel, although I really had little choice in the matter. Its owner kept leading it in front of me to cut me off as I tried to pass, shouting, 'You ride! You ride! Nice camel!' He even tongue-kissed it to demonstrate how attractive his camel indeed was. Since I've always had a healthy regard for the way camels can bite when provoked, I was nervous of trying to squeeze out of its way, and finally agreed to a short ride. It couldn't be over quickly enough for me, however. Being tossed around on a camel's back as its evil owner slaps it into running down a hillside, knowing it's going to fold up like a concertina at the bottom and try and jettison you off headfirst, wasn't anything like my idea of fun.

From there, it was only another thirteen hours by train to Cairo, my final destination before I flew back home. As I stepped out of the central station, blanching at the clamour of taxi drivers, street-sellers and car horns, and the stench of one of the most polluted cities on earth, I smiled happily in triumph. But this enormous, crumbling city of more than sixteen million people was a massive culture shock. Somehow, it didn't feel too welcoming, either. I checked into the cheapest hotel I could find, since my funds were almost gone and I didn't want to start eating into the money I'd saved for my ticket back home. It did nothing to warm me to the city. Sure, it was cheap, but it was also filthy. If I got bored, I mused to myself, looking at the room I was going to share with five others, I could always train the cockroaches to race. They might do well. After all, there were enough of them for a real competition.

My room-mates hardly cheered me, either. Two of them were American men who'd been staying in the same room for three months. I wondered how they'd managed to stay sane. I found the answer on the third day: money or, rather, the dream of lots of it. They were in the business of buying local drums, they confided the first day, and shipping them back to the US to sell at curio markets. It was only when I walked back into the room in the middle of the afternoon on the second day when they obviously weren't expecting to be disturbed, that I discovered the real point of the drums. Yes, they were sending the drums back—but packed with high quality marijuana resin, stuffed inside a lining of silver paper that they reckoned would withstand the most powerful of customs X-rays. I wondered if the weight of the drums wouldn't give them away, but thought better of mentioning it.

The other two in the room were a French couple who had been planning to do the reverse of the trip I'd just done, and travel from Cairo to Cape Town. Somehow, however, they'd got stuck in Cairo. They'd been there for a month and showed no sign of leaving. Every day, they'd wander out in their old cheesecloth shirts and pants, barefoot, talking about today being the day when they'd buy a train ticket south. Every day, they'd return without one. They just seemed incredibly easily distracted. One day, they'd come back having spent the afternoon both having their hair meticulously plaited by locals. Another day, they'd confess to sitting in a coffee bar for five hours, drinking tiny cups of thick, dark coffee and smoking bongs, the big old water pipes which were meant to cool the tobacco before it reached your mouth. Another day, they said they just couldn't find the station. At first, I encouraged them to get out and get on. After a while, I realised they were never going to leave Cairo before they'd run out of money and were forced to return to Paris, dining out for weeks, no doubt, on their fabulous African adventure. Maybe they'd lost their nerve somewhere on the plane between the two countries.

I had no intention of staying there for long. I still hadn't got over my initial distrust of Cairo. Yes, of course, it had its charms, but I felt they were few and far between. I wandered around, seeing the highlights, but also unintentionally discovering the lowlights. Sure, the Egyptian Museum was fabulous with its magnificent collection of mummies and their sarcophogi and the dazzling treasures of Tutankhamen, discovered by British archaeologist Howard Carter in 1922, who re-activated the ancient curse of the Pharaohs against anyone who broke the tomb's seal. Of course, the tiny streets crammed with market stalls were also fascinating. But there were plenty of other sights I did not want to see: the deformed beggars; the grid-locked streets filled with traffic; the slums everywhere.

There was another attraction I decided to avoid. People said the Camel Market was a marvellous spectacle, but to hell with that. Three days after I arrived in Cairo, my groin had become terribly itchy. I spent a day or so trying to scratch discreetly, but then it simply got too bad to bear. Finally, I found a woman doctor in the city and visited her surgery. 'Goodness!' she

exclaimed, after she'd examined me. She handed me her micro-
scope. On the glass, I could see a tiny little crab clinging to a
pubic hair. Yes, I'd caught them off that horrible camel—
or whoever had been on it before me. The Camel Market?
No chance. I'd had enough of those horrible animals to last
me a lifetime.

But, most of all, after the easy-going Africans of the southern
part of the continent, I found many Egyptians difficult. It was
impossible to visit any of the tourist sights without feeling a
sly hand rubbing my bottom. Even at the museum, I found
myself cornered by a man who had followed me all the way
through and seemed intent on having a crafty feel. And then,
from others, there was naked hostility. One stinking hot day
in Cairo's busiest street market, Khan-al-Khalili, finished off
the charm of the place for me.

A man was selling cans of Coca-Cola. They stood winking
at me from a crate of rapidly melting ice. 'The Coke,' I said,
pointing idiotically to the cans, as if he had a whole miscellany
of goods to choose from, 'how much?'

He smiled, a mouthful of gold glinting in the bright sun,
then carefully picked a can out of his crate, rolled it enticingly
over his forehead and named some bizarrely inflated price.

I chuckled good-naturedly and, like all dab hands at market
shopping, offered him roughly half the figure. A growl came
from somewhere near the back of his throat. 'No!' he barked,
and repeated the original price.

I was surprised. 'No,' I repeated, 'I'll pay you...'

He tossed the can back into its ice and spat on the floor.

'You don't pay the price,' he said, 'you fuck off.'

My mind was made up on the fifth day, when a terrible, chilling scream came from the room next door at about four in the morning. We all sat up in our beds, instantly awake. The manager knocked a few minutes later saying the police were on their way. Apparently, a young German woman next door had committed suicide in the night, and her body had only just been discovered.

I'd been saving the pyramids until last, ready to savour that inevitably emotional, awe-struck moment, and now I felt this was pretty much time. Located only 9 kilometres from the centre of Cairo, it'd be easy—and cheap—to catch a bus there, so I wouldn't have to follow another bunch of tourists around on some tightly planned tour itinerary. I wanted to have plenty of time to gaze on the mighty Sphinx and pyramids scattered in the desert, and truly appreciate the magnificence of one of the seven wonders of the ancient world. After that, I could dive inside the cool of the largest one, the Pyramid of Cheops, to climb into the funerary chamber.

As I found the bus stop for the No. 900, the sun was already high in the sky, but I felt my spirits soar. This was going to be a truly incredible ending to my trip. This was my last journey in Africa, and one that millions of tourists had done before me. Not much could go wrong now. The bus trundled up and I pushed my way in. It was packed, and it felt like an oven. Standing room only—but only just. I was crushed in the middle of a group of men, all sweating heavily. The only other women on the bus were all nicely ensconced in the seats, I noticed. Maybe I should have gone to the bus station and caught it earlier? That way I might have stood a better chance of a place. But it was too late now.

The bus lurched through the busy Cairo streets, as we all stood, swaying, inside. We careened round a couple of corners and I was swung to my left, then to the right. It was hard to keep on my feet. But, then again, it would have been even harder to fall, so jam-packed was the bus with bodies. Not that it seemed to worry anyone. At every stop, we picked up more and more people.

And then I felt it. A body, somewhere behind me, was rubbing slowly, deliberately, against mine. Maybe I'd imagined it. I'd been in Cairo a week now and had become so used to being touched and grabbed and poked and fondled at every opportunity, perhaps I was just getting paranoid about it. The body behind might be similarly being thrown around and the owner couldn't help the friction between us. I tried to inch myself forwards. The body followed. There was another session of rubbing. I moved to the side. So did he. There was more rubbing. And then more. Finally, I could stand it no longer. This was deliberate, I was sure of it. What was wrong with these bloody men that they just couldn't control themselves? Why pick on me just because I was white and on my own? Why couldn't they just sodding well leave me alone? I snapped. Months of feeling alone and vulnerable welled to the surface; months of frustration at being singled out for the colour of my skin and my sex rushed to my head. I turned around as best I could, looked straight into the grinning face of a middle-aged, overweight

Egyptian man and slapped him hard, straight around the face.

The bus went quiet and there was what felt like a full minute of silence. The man looked dazed, and then it came. He lifted his hand and slapped me straight back around the face. It stung so sharply, it brought tears to my eyes but, more than that, it stunned me. I had never expected that. I'd completely misjudged the situation. I'd expected him to take the punishment and to slink away in shame. Everyone else on the bus, I'd imagined, would guess what had happened and be indignant at the way I'd been treated. I'd be overwhelmed by their sympathy. Someone might even give me a seat. But no. No, not at all.

'Whore!' spat my antagonist in my face. 'White whore!'

One of his friends joined in the refrain. Someone shouted something in Arabic from the front of the bus that didn't sound so friendly. A man growled from just behind me, 'You white women come here wanting one thing. And then you can't take it at all.'

I looked over in desperation at the women sitting in rows just in front. Some had averted their eyes. Others were looking over with similar contempt in their faces. It took a couple of minutes to sink in that nobody was going to see my side of the argument. I was a white woman, alone on a bus. I wasn't respectable, obviously, otherwise where was my husband? I deserved whatever was going to be dished out. More people started shouting at me in Arabic and a couple of men, just in my field of vision to the side, started shaking their fists. Everyone, it seemed, felt just as strongly as the man who had hit me. I suddenly felt afraid, and very alone.

The driver of the bus pulled over to the side, stopped and pushed the button that made the doors slide open. He got up and pushed his way slowly down the back, towards me. Ah, help at last. His face, however, was like thunder. 'You!' he said, pointing to me. 'You! Off! OFF!' He was now pointing to the exit. It looked pointless to argue, but my legs didn't seem to be moving. He came closer, seized my arm and led me off the bus. There was a round of applause. Outside the bus, he leaned close, 'It is better,' he said, gently. 'It might not be safe. I cannot guarantee that.' With that, he strode off towards the front of the bus, then went back inside, sat behind the wheel, closed the doors and pulled away. A couple of men leaned out of the windows and spat in my general direction.

I watched the bus disappear in a cloud of dust and stood, horrified by what had just happened. I felt angry, I felt upset, I felt terribly hard done by. Most of all, I felt extremely sorry for myself. I felt tears well up in my eyes—I had never imagined this.

But I couldn't stand here much longer. The sun was blazing down, it was hot, and I wasn't carrying any water with me. The road stretched out in front of me. I reckoned we'd travelled about 5 kilometres, so there'd still be about another 4 kilometres to go. I wiped my eyes, sniffed and started walking. There was nothing else I could do. After so long travelling the length of Africa, I wasn't going to give in now. I hadn't exactly conquered Africa, but it hadn't quite beaten me yet. This was the very last bit of my journey. I was going to make those damned pyramids even if I had to crawl.

chapter eleven
WAILING ABOUT THE WALL

destination: The Great Wall of China, Badaling

I looked down at the bowl in front of me, and then back up to see everyone else looking at me. I smiled. There'd been something nightmarish in that bowl. I shuddered to think what it was. But no-one returned the smile. Every single passenger in the dining car of the No. 320 train from Xian in central China to its capital Beijing in the north was simply staring at me—a long, hard, blank stare, rich with absolute, total and utter incomprehension.

That stare was an old friend. It had followed me all the way from Guangzhou in the south-east, China's gateway city from Hong Kong, through each village, town and city I visited. I'd encountered it on every street corner, in every hotel dormitory, at every public monument. Even when I was standing, lost in awe, in front of Xian's incredible 2200-year-old army of life-size terracotta warriors, I'd turned round to find a crowd of fifty-odd Chinese gazing in wonder at me, the way I might stare at an alien from outer space. But, in the China of 1985, I *was* that creature from another galaxy. Foreigners, particularly on their own, were a novel sight and remnants of the xenophobia encouraged by the Cultural Revolution of 1966 to 1970 lingered on. Even the word by which the Chinese knew us, *gwelo*, meant 'foreign devil'. And while Chinese leader Deng Xiaoping had acted to normalise diplomatic relations with the outside world in 1979, most ordinary people were still nervous and fearful of outsiders. Occasionally, they were openly hostile.

I winked at one of the young men staring at me, a particularly unattractive youth with sallow, pitted skin and his mouth hanging open to display a half-masticated mouthful of the same disgusting sight I'd seen in my bowl. His gaze didn't flinch. 'Hi!' I called over to a couple dressed identically in green army overcoats and blue Chairman Mao peaked caps. They continued staring, unblinking. One man at the table furthest away from me climbed onto his seat to get a better view.

For weeks, I'd been searching for ways to crack those stares. Talking to people didn't help. It was as if they couldn't hear the strange noises coming from my mouth. Waving at them and winking was hardly any better. Once, in frustration, I'd even taken a step towards a little crowd who'd gathered to stare at me in a street in Changsha, and roared like a lion to see what might happen. They didn't flinch.

Today, though, I was feeling tired, fed-up, cold and, above all, hungry. I couldn't be bothered trying any more to elicit a response. I went back to my bowl. At the bottom, I could see some boiled rice, but it was what was lying on top that bothered me. It was a long, plump, pallid slug-like creature. I lifted up the bowl and sniffed it. It smelt like a cross between congealed fat and old prawns. I put it down again, took a deep breath, picked up my chopsticks and turned it over. It was horribly squishy and slippery, and looked pretty much the same on the other side. I fumbled around in the rice for a while, eating some of that, delaying the moment. And then I pounced.

I managed to juggle the chopsticks to gingerly place them either side of The Thing. I firmed my grip. It was terribly slimy. I lifted it delicately to my mouth. The best way to do this was obviously to hold it up with the chopsticks and then bite bits off. I moved my face towards the slug, opened my mouth and closed my eyes. And then I felt the chopsticks come together with a snap and opened my eyes to see the slug flying through the air to come to a rest on the corridor floor. I looked at my audience: not a flicker of a reaction. I wasn't sure what to do next. I didn't want to touch that Thing on the ground with my fingers. I clearly couldn't eat it now. I quickly shovelled the rest of the rice into my mouth, not looking up again from my bowl. Then I stood up, buttoned my heavy People's Liberation Army overcoat, pulled my furry hat back on my head, wrapped my scarf around my neck, grabbed my bag and inched my way out between the table and the seat. As I stepped out, however, I promptly slid on the slug, coming crashing to the ground. There was still silence in the dining car. I picked myself up and, with tears stinging my eyes, made my way through the thick fog of cigarette smoke, back to the cheap, hard seat section.

There was only another ten hours to go of this journey to Beijing and I was eager to get it over with. I was looking forward immensely to arriving at the country's capital. Of course, there was that wonder of the world I'd come here to see: the 5000 kilometre-long Great Wall of China that snakes its way across the mountaintops from the east coast to the Gobi Desert. But I also hoped there might be decent restaurants, a comfortable hotel, a good public transport system around the city, music, coffee and, joy of joys, other foreigners to talk to.

For I'd never imagined just how lonely travelling around China alone might be. I'd met no-one so far who spoke English, nor understood a word of the few Cantonese and Mandarin phrases I'd painfully learned in preparation for this trip. I hadn't realised before I read it in a guide book, a couple of weeks into China, that they're tonal languages, so every word has a different meaning according to almost imperceptible nuances of sound. And that universal backstop, sign language, was of absolutely no help either. Everywhere else in the world, people would realise you wanted a place to sleep if you put your hands together as if in prayer then rested your head on them, while looking quizzically about. In every other corner of the world, if you cradled your arms and then rocked them, they'd see you were talking about their baby. But, in China, they'd simply look back at you, blankly, or even peer into your arms as if you might be holding something they just couldn't see.

I knew there was at least one other foreigner on this train. We'd noticed each other on the platform and both smiled to see another Western face amongst the sea of Chinese. Then he'd been swallowed up by the crowds. I hoped we might bump into each other again, and a few hours later, we did.

He'd come in search for me, he said, desperate to speak to another Westerner. I sympathised. He was a Mexican called Emilio, spending a few weeks travelling around China. He wasn't, however, having a good time. Between sniffs and vigorous nose blows, he told me he'd caught a terrible cold a few days before, and was steadily feeling worse and worse.

'Ah, Suzannah,' he sighed (I wondered where the Suzannah came from). 'This country...' he shrugged his shoulders in despair, 'is so difficult. I have been here a week and that is enough, I think. I am ready to go home.' After twenty minutes, he'd had to make a dash back to his own seat in search of more toilet paper for his nose.

We bumped into each other again as we were both getting off the train in Beijing. The temperature was well below zero and late November snow lay thickly on the ground. He had the name of a cheap local hotel that accepted foreigners—most tourists were expected to stay in astonishingly expensive foreigner-only hotels—and asked me if I wanted to share his horse and carriage there. It was going to be slow, and cold, but there was a couple standing waiting for passengers at the station, and it was the best offer I'd had for weeks. As we crunched our way along the white roads, through aisles of bare trees and along wide avenues bereft of any other traffic, I started to quite enjoy myself. This was more like it. Emilio obviously wasn't, however. I could see his face was looking extremely grey, and his eyes bloodshot. I gave him my furry hat to help him keep his head warm, and my scarf for his neck. I could see his nose dripping onto it immediately.

When we arrived at the hotel, I checked into the women-only dorm, and he into the men's dorm. We said we'd meet up the next day to have a look around town together. The next morning, however, there was no sign of him. That afternoon he didn't show, either. I began to worry. Being sick when you're overseas, completely alone, is a truly miserable experience. And, besides, he had my hat and scarf. I asked at the reception where he might be. Since he was the only other foreigner there, it was pretty easy to describe him.

'Ah, Mexico!' the woman at the desk said. 'No, Mexico is not here. He gone.'

'Gone?' I echoed stupidly. 'Gone where?'

'Ah,' she said. 'Hospital. He very sick.'

It took me six hours to find the hospital. There were so many in Beijing and it was firstly a question of even locating them all. In a chemist shop which was allegedly close to one hospital, I tried to get the staff to give me directions. When I drew a red cross on a piece of paper, they shook their heads and tutted, thinking I meant a church. When I went through an elaborate charade of pretending to be ill—fainting and clutching my stomach—to indicate a hospital, they rushed to fetch me a chair, and wipe my forehead. I couldn't help laughing; sometimes it was the only thing to do. Even when I'd found those damned hospitals, however, it was only the first round of the battle won. Then I had to find Emilio. Invariably I'd just be directed to a foreigner's bedside—*any* foreigner's bedside.

When I finally found Emilio around midnight that same day, it appeared to have been worth the struggle. He was so happy to see me, he said, gripping my hand as I sat down by his bed. 'Thank you so much for coming, Suzannah. I am so terrible, terrible. I think I die here.' He explained he'd felt so bad that first morning in the hotel, he'd contacted the Mexican Consul who'd picked him up and taken him to hospital himself. It turned out he'd contracted pneumonia. He'd be staying at the hospital for a week before being flown back home. I visited him every day, bringing him food and drink since both seemed to be provided only sporadically in his ward. I also regularly alerted the nurse when his drip neared empty, just as he began to panic about air bubbles in his bloodstream. He wasn't the best of patients, but I couldn't really blame him. I didn't mind putting up with his moods and it was nice and warm in the hospital, compared to the freezing temperatures outside. Besides, one day, someone might do the same for me.

During the days when I wasn't in the hospital—listening to Emilio complain about the lack of food, the medical care, the bright lights (even at night), the transistor music other patients played at top volume, the hard bed, the fear of air bubbles and the state of Mexican politics—I explored the city.

It was a mammoth task. The city itself, it's said, is the size of the entire country of Belgium, and after slogging it by foot around the place, I could well believe it. I tried catching the occasional taxi, sure enough, but found it not worth the effort. One day, asking for the main train station, I ended up at the airport, 25 kilometres away. Another day, I spent hours watching taxis slow as they approached me to get a good look, then speed off again when they'd sated their curiosity. Someone told me taxi drivers were paid a fixed wage, so it didn't matter whether or not they actually ever carried passengers. I could believe it. I also tried the underground system, but found it horrendously complicated and almost impossible to work out. A simple trip across town, that should have taken twenty minutes, took two-and-a-half hours when I stumbled from station to station, having no idea of the correct line I should be taking, or the junction to change at, let alone the right place to get off. The problem always came down to language. With everything written in pictograph script, you had to memorise the way your destination was written, and hope like hell you'd recognise it again later. That made everything a battle—from the basics like finding a hotel (when only the posh foreigner-only places had the word 'Hotel' anywhere near them) and restaurants, to monuments and public toilets.

I also found the people hard-going. They were just so incredibly different to Westerners and, with communication so difficult, I was often close to tears of frustration, exhaustion and despair. All around China, at the cheap hotels that took both Chinese people and foreigners, the managers would usually tell you the place was full, even while locals would continue to arrive and be signed in. It was an elaborate waiting game, with rules that seemed to be made up on the spot. If you had the staying power to sit there for two, three, sometimes four hours, you'd more often than not be rewarded, finally, with a bed. That was no guarantee of sleep, however. Your dormitory mates would happily indulge in the national pastime of noisily gathering in their throat every speck of mucus in their body, gargling with it for a few minutes, and then spitting with enormous gusto onto the floor—even in the middle of the night, from bed. In my Beijing hotel, it seemed even worse. With such freezing weather, so many people had colds and not only spat at night, but also sniffed, snorted and blew their nose vigorously with their fingers onto the floor between us.

Still, it was interesting to live so differently. It was also an education to be such an obvious outsider and to get a sense of how minorities across the world feel. As a white Westerner, you tend to live such a privileged life. In China, you were instantly a second, maybe even third-class citizen. In shops, you'd always be served last, when there was absolutely no alternative to dealing with you. At train stations, you'd often queue for a couple of hours, only to have the ticket seller slamming closed the shutter on his counter when he saw you, presumably knowing the exchange to come would be so difficult. Everyone else would then rush over to another counter, leaving you at the back of a new queue. It made you suddenly realise what it must be like for other nationalities who are often treated so badly in the West. Then, of course, there were the crowds to contend with. Walking along a street, sitting down in a café or stopping to gaze at a sight, people would halt, turn and stare every time. If I hesitated even for a moment at a street corner to check something on the map, within seconds I'd be surrounded by a crowd of interested people. Mothers would snatch up their children at the sight of me, toddlers would scream and cling to their mothers' skirts. At every shop, my fascinated entourage would step right in with me. I don't think I'll ever quite get over the experience of having a pee in the open-plan female public toilets near the fabulous Forbidden City, only to look up and see dozens of women's eyes curiously peering through the open doorway.

One day, I had a brainwave and hired a Flying Pigeon pushbike to join the throngs of Chinese pedalling around the city. Surely it would be a great way of avoiding being stared at all the time, I told myself hopefully, as I looked at the sad rust bucket against the wall. It would also be far better than slogging around the sights on foot and getting trampled as the crowds heaved into buses at every stop.

I pulled my cap tightly down over my head to hide my blonde hair, swung my leg womanfully over the crossbar and was soon swept off into the hurly-burly of the bicycle rush hour towards Tiananmen Square in the centre of the city. One national magazine I'd read reported there were around 500 million bicycles in China. It felt like I was right in the middle of half of them.

For the first ten minutes, it was a joy, but then came problems. As cyclists whizzed past me, they slowed up in front and turned to stare. They shouted over to other cyclists in the crowd and they turned to look at me too. Cyclists behind tried to ride up beside me to get a closer viewpoint. As more pedalled in front and then looked behind, the more and more worried I became—and I was right. One moment, there were a few hundred of us cycling in a tight group along Dongchang'an Jie, the next, one man swerved into another man as he looked over his shoulder, that man bumped into another, his bike became entangled in the first, someone ploughed into the back of him, he was torpedoed into someone else and suddenly the whole pack of us came crashing down to the ground.

I was helped up out of the tangle by a student who had learnt English at university. I could have hugged him. 'Bicycles are dangerous,' he told me gravely. 'Better you go on tour bus. There are plenty, plenty. Where you come from?' We sat down on a low wall nearby as I got my breath back. He had lots of questions: Was this my first time in China? Where was my tour group? Where was my husband? Why wasn't I married? Why was I on my own?

As I answered, I knew he wouldn't understand. The Chinese, perhaps traditionally, perhaps by virtue of the communist revolution, perhaps even because there was over one billion of them living on small farms in the countryside, crushed into towns, or sharing small spaces in the cities (often with family and extended family all living together), didn't seem to have any notion of the Western idea of 'space to oneself'. That was a luxury here few could afford. Still, we talked on. He wanted to practise his English, he said. How about he show me the Summer Palace the next day? I jumped at the chance. We arranged to meet at the same point on the wall the following morning. I then jumped courageously back on my bike and pedalled away. That evening, I handed it back to the shop. I was covered in bruises from prangs all day. Travelling by bike was just too dangerous for me.

It seemed to cheer Emilio immensely that I'd had such a tough time on my bike. 'This place is not good for people like you and me,' he said, after admiring my bruises. 'It is not

civilised. You must come to Mexico one day. You will love it.'
His eyes grew misty at the thought. He had only two days left
to go before his plane. 'I am pleased to be going home,' he
said. 'China...no, it is full of barbarians.' It was little wonder
he'd had such a bad time with that point of view.

And yes, while I was finding the place tough going, it had
its bright spots. That afternoon, when my bicycle chain had
come off and I'd been thrown—yet again—to the ground,
another cyclist had dusted me off and lifted me back to my
feet. The day before on a bus in the city, when I'd been
bowled over by people pushing to get off, the conductress
had snapped the doors closed again and ordered the other
passengers to help me back up before she'd let them off. Later
that afternoon, I'd had a brainwave when, sitting on the edge
of a fountain resting my feet after another long walk, a crowd
gathered just to watch me. I noticed one young girl staring
at my gold signet ring so I took it off and passed it to her.
She examined it minutely and passed it to her mum. The
ring made its way all around the crowd. At one point, I lost
track of it entirely and felt a stab of worry about whether
I'd ever see it again. But, sure enough, it appeared again
fifteen minutes later, with the crowd applauding me as if I'd
just performed a double somersault, with twist, on the roadside. But it was a nice moment to feel I'd communicated,
after a fashion, with people.

It was in cafés that I had the most problems. The majority
of them were great, noisy, functional places full of Chinese
families or groups of workmates sitting around big tables

shovelling down food as fast as they could. Because they were geared up to a number of people eating together, I presented a real problem. Once, I ordered chicken, and was presented with a huge red washing up bowl piled with rice, and three chickens on a platter. When I tried to get the point across that I couldn't possibly eat that much, I realised they simply weren't used to catering for lone customers. I'd order tea and get beer. I'd ask for rice and get more meat. I'd ask for vegetables, any vegetables, since they seemed in such short supply in northern China, and I'd get a bun with a chicken's foot inside.

On one memorable occasion I sat down and pointed to a dish someone else was eating, asking to have the same. When it arrived, it smelt odd, but I was hungry. A few mouthfuls of the dark, strong-tasting meat later, I had to give up. I tried to ask what it was. The café owner tried to explain, but neither of us understood the other. At last, inspired, he beckoned me through to the kitchen to show me. There, hanging up on giant hooks, were the bodies of ten skinned dogs. He pointed to them and beamed. I fled from the place, overcome with nausea. He rushed after me to ask anxiously if there was anything wrong, but I couldn't think of any way of explaining, so just smiled and thanked him and shook his hand. It didn't matter now that there was something wrong—even though I blanched to think about it—it was the thought that counted.

•••

In my new friend Han's company, Beijing suddenly seemed a completely different city. It was a place full of good food, since he knew a couple of nice places to eat, efficient public transport, and wonderful sights. We caught a bus to the Summer Palace, and spent hours wandering around the lake, the buildings, the gardens and the bronzes. We went and ate a delicious meal in a canteen back in Beijing, and I was amazed at the huge range of tastes. We took another bus over to the university, and he showed me through the grounds. In the evening, we went to see the famous Beijing Opera. To my untrained ears, it seemed like everyone just stood on the stage and screamed in as high a pitch as they could manage, but it was an education. The audience simply carried on talking, eating and spitting while the performance went on in front of them. One man had even brought along his transistor radio, which he turned up when the talking about him grew too loud. None of our Western reverence for those on stage. This was real life that continued to throb on, regardless of the surroundings. At first I was enthralled, but after an hour-and-a-half the novelty had worn off and it all got too much. I made my excuses to Han and left with a splitting headache.

Emilio left the next day. He said a tearful goodbye and took my photo, advising me to get out of the place as soon as I could. He waved forlornly from the ambulance, taking him to the airport. 'Don't forget, Suzannah,' he cried. 'Visit Mexico! You won't ever want to go anywhere again after that! This place is...is shit compared to Mexico.' When they closed the doors on him, I couldn't help feeling a stab of relief. I went straight to the train station and bought a ticket for the next day to Badaling, the easiest place to see the Great Wall.

It was a long, slow journey—I hadn't realised it was so far.

But when I finally arrived, I was shocked to find the platform near deserted. Somehow, I'd expected throngs of people to get off with me, all marching to the Wall. Yet there was nobody. Even worse, when I left the station I had no idea where to go. The Wall might well be the only man-made structure on earth that can be seen from the moon by the naked eye, but I sure as hell couldn't see it, standing, no doubt, only a couple of kilometres away. I wandered around for an hour or so in a desultory fashion before I arrived back at the station. There was a guard standing there. 'The Wall?' I asked. 'The Great Wall? Where is it?' I waved my arms around to indicate a wall, and pointed north, south, east and west with what I hoped was a quizzical expression. He shrugged, turned around and scurried away.

I'd thought out my approach a bit more thoroughly by the time I saw someone else, outside the station. I had my guide-book open to a photo of the wall and pounced on an elderly man carrying a bag of eggs. 'Look!' I said, pointing to the photo. 'Where?' I looked around me in a mime of searching for something.

He seemed bewildered. 'No English! No English!' he said and retreated fearfully into a nearby house.

I was getting desperate. This was a ridiculous situation. I'd come so far to see this bloody wall, and I sure as hell wasn't going back home without seeing it. If Genghis Khan could find it after riding over hundreds of kilometres of desert and mountains, I should really be able to too, after getting off a train at the nearest station. I spotted another man in the distance. He was going into the station. I waited, and followed him in. Then I approached and pushed my book at him.

'Wall, wall!' I said. 'Where, where?' His eyes grew wide with alarm and he started as if to flee. I couldn't bear it. 'No, no!' I yelled, and grabbed the collar of his coat. I thrust the photo of the Wall in front of his eyes. He struggled, but I wasn't going to let go for anything. He finally looked at the picture, then looked about him wildly. He pointed towards the train that had just pulled up. 'No, no,' I said. 'The *Wall*.' He pointed again, more urgently this time. I looked more closely—he was waving at a couple of elderly men getting out of the train. They'd stepped down onto the platform, then scrambled down onto the tracks, and were walking back up them. I understood, I hoped, and let go of the man's collar. He dusted himself down and darted off to the train. I felt bad about having been so mean to him, and shocked at how quickly I might resort to force to get my own way. China, I thought, has that effect on people.

Then, I jumped down onto the tracks, and raced off after the two men in front. They seemed to know where they were going; I just hoped it was the Wall, and not their village somewhere out in the sticks. They trotted through a couple of railway tunnels and scrambled up and down banks of grass.

I grew more uneasy—surely it couldn't be this hard? But I continued following. We crossed a patch of wasteland, and then a yard. Finally, we turned a corner and I reeled back in shock. There, just in front, were hundreds of buses disgorging thousands of tourists onto a steep stretch of misty grey wall. I walked up closer and there it was—if only I could push my way through all these crowds to get there.

chapter twelve
SOUTH AMERICA IS NO PLACE FOR A WOMAN
destination: San Lorenzo, Ecuador

The station master scribbled a strange approximation of my name on a crumpled cigarette packet and grinned. The paperwork was now all completed, he assured me, to guarantee a place on the Ecuadorean Railways' express to the northern Pacific port of San Lorenzo, 193 kilometres away. I smiled, uneasily. He smiled back, brimming with confidence. I'd just have to arrive the next day, perhaps five hours before the train was due, and pick up my ticket. We shook hands warmly. It all seemed so simple.

Feeling cheered at that point by the apparent efficacy of the system, I wandered off to find a hotel. I'd just arrived in Ibarra, a busy little market town in the north of Ecuador, and so far so good. It felt far friendlier, in any case, than the capital Quito where I'd landed five days before to start my one-year trip around Latin America.

'Hey *gringa* (white woman)!' bellowed a man in a string vest and tatty trousers with a broken zip, from the doorway of a white-washed building nearby. 'You want hotel? Here! You stay here!'

I wandered over. My backpack was heavy, and I was only staying one night, after all. The room was little more than a box with a window too high to see out of, but you couldn't really demand much more for a dollar. I paid, checked in and sat on the communal balcony to read my book *Teach Yourself Spanish* that I'd not quite had time to master before I'd left—beyond useful phrases like 'Open that window!' and 'I have a pencil!' and 'Pass me the ruler!'.

It was only a few minutes before the owner came over, drew up a chair and pressed his knee against mine. 'This town is very dangerous,' was his opening gambit. 'You do not trust anyone.' I wondered what this was leading to. 'You need a man friend to look after you.' Ah, there. I decided to be polite. After all, in his eyes, he was probably doing me a favour.

'Thank you,' I said, moving my knee out of range. 'But I am married, my husband might not like that.' I fluttered my right hand with, on my third finger, its gold wedding ring I'd borrowed from my grandmother for just such occasions.

'Ahh! You might be married, but obviously not happily,' he said. 'Otherwise your husband would be with you.' He grinned and poked his tongue through a gap in his front teeth.

'No, my husband is arriving tomorrow,' I said calmly.

'Ah ha!' he yelled, triumphantly. 'That gives us twenty-four hours!'

I couldn't win at that game. I shook my head firmly and retreated back into my book, in the hope he might get bored and go away. No such luck, he was persistent. He asked me about my family; my home; my husband's performance in bed. He talked about my book; the problems of communication in Spanish; his willingness to teach me the Indian language, Quechua. It took two hours before he finally announced he had things to do, but then promised he'd be back at 7pm to keep me company. At 6pm, as I showered in the communal room down the corridor, I was horrified to suddenly notice an eyeball pressed to a crack in the door. As I locked on to it, it vanished and I plugged the gap with soap. At 7pm, he came back to my room and I called through the door that I was too tired to talk. At 11pm, I ignored the drunken banging at the door, hoping he might think I'd gone out to find a friend elsewhere.

The next morning, at 5.30am, I crept downstairs to the gate. Damn! It was locked. He slid out of the shadows. 'What's the hurry, *gringa*?' he asked. 'Where are you going?'

'San Lorenzo,' I replied. 'Please open the gate.' He hesitated a minute, then shrugged, before sliding a key into the lock. By the time I'd pushed the gate opened, he'd disappeared without a word.

I didn't care. I was off to San Lorenzo in my pre-booked seat. I rounded the last corner towards the station, and stopped in surprise. There were hundreds of people clustered around the ticket office, and the clamour was deafening. A few stragglers had formed a semblance of a queue at the back and, brimming over with optimism, I joined the end. By 7am, the crowd pushing towards the ticket window had grown and I was much further back than when I'd started.

So, finally, I decided to join everyone else and threw myself into the melee, fighting for a ticket with all the other would-be passengers squeezed into a row between the wall of the ticket office window and iron railings running alongside. Two hours of relentless pushing later, I managed to get to the front. A booking? No, no sign of one of those. But I could buy a ticket and just try my luck. I did, but then my problems really began.

Turning away from the window, the crowd surged forward to take my place. I tried to step out of the way and push back through the passageway, but there were more than 200 people behind me fighting desperately to get to the ticket window. Weighed down and pushed and twisted by my rucksack, I'd become wedged between the wall and the railings. People shouted at me to get out of the way, but I could move neither backwards nor forwards. They lunged at me to heave me out while another group shoved, just as hard, in the other direction.

The only escape looked to be under them, so I ducked down and crawled on all fours through the legs of the seething crowd. But they just kept on pushing, and I could feel the breath being steadily squeezed out of me as I became jammed in the tangled crush of legs, all pressing forward. I began screaming in panic. People had started stepping on my back to gain height in the struggle for tickets. Their weight was excruciating and my back felt like it might snap at any minute. I was being slowly suffocated.

The image from the movie *Suddenly Last Summer* of the raised, outstretched hand slowly disappearing into a group of hungry, scrabbling locals flashed into my mind. I felt my back give and my hands being pulverised under kicking shoes. Summoning every ounce of breath left in my body, I screamed as loudly as I could. I clawed at people's feet. I tore at their legs. I swore at them in Spanish. I knew I wouldn't have long before I collapsed under all those people and I'd be stomped to death. Suddenly, I heard a commotion and felt hands grab me and pull me up. A small knot of people, watching my lack of progress from the edge of the crowd, had darted in and pulled me clear...but partly so they could take up my space.

I crawled away from the crowd and eased myself painfully into a sitting position on the floor of the platform, trying to catch my breath. I watched as the locals battled furiously and bitterly for tickets. Two hours later, the office slammed its window shut. Everyone had tickets. The fight had been utterly pointless. A neat and orderly queue would have worked much less painfully. But now everyone was grinning—maybe it was simply sport in a place where precious else ever seemed to happen. *Maybe*.

Now I was more eager than ever to get to San Lorenzo. Apart from travelling one of the last of the spectacular railway journeys left in South America, it was meant to be a splendid place, a town made up almost exclusively of people of African descent, with houses on stilts, pretty creeks, dusty mangrove swamps and a thriving contraband industry up to Columbia.

It would be nice to get further westwards, too, away from the devastation caused by a massive earthquake in Ecuador's eastern jungle lowlands the week before, in March 1987. The flooding and mudslides in its wake were now known to have claimed 1000 lives and left 30 000 people homeless. In addition, it had destroyed a great stretch of the country's trans-Andean oil pipeline running to the Pacific port of Balao. The knock-on effects were immediate. The government said it expected lost oil sales to cost around US$1 billion—in a country whose total GDP added up to only US$1.8 billion, that was devastating. They immediately raised the prices of gas, fuel and public transport but froze the prices of basic foodstuffs.

Angry student demonstrators had clashed with police in the capital Quito on a march through the city centre a few nights before. I'd been strolling through and watched the rows and rows of students march past as they demanded the resignation of right-wing conservative president Leon Febres Cordero. I'd stepped inside a café when, suddenly, there was an abrupt lull in their chanting. Then, there was the sound of running, screaming, explosions and clouds of smoke: the police had tried to break up the demonstration with tear gas. People rushed into the café, their eyes red and weeping, dragging behind them small howling children. The doors were locked against the police and bowls of water were brought out for their victims to drink and bathe their eyes in. The students had simply run away when they saw the police coming. The police had hurled tear gas at their fleeing backs and caught passers-by who hadn't seen the danger in time.

Later that evening, I'd thought it wise to catch a taxi back to my hotel. Too late, I discovered that cabs in Quito rarely know where they're going. We drove endlessly through darkening streets, as we passed increasingly familiar landmarks over and over. I was naturally hoping the driver would say at some point, 'Here! This is where you want!' He was obviously hoping I'd say, 'Here! This is it!' Men generally, in my experience, don't like to ask for directions. Latin American men, I began to suspect, would rather die than say they didn't know the way. Eventually, I got out, paid the fare on both meters—the supplementary for increased petrol prices—and wandered around asking passers-by for the way. Eventually, a woman took my elbow and waved down a bus, and got on it with me. I was overwhelmed by her kindness. No, no, she insisted, she was going to a place nearby anyway. I was interested too to see she didn't pay. Only later, I realised I'd paid for us both.

All that was now far behind me as I stood on the platform of Ibarra station, waiting for the train. Suddenly, there was a commotion on the platform that wrested my attention back to the tracks. A little metal coach with the words 'The Silver Bullet' proudly emblazoned on the front wobbled its way up the tracks to stop in front of the station. Everyone immediately flung themselves at the doorway, and kicked, punched and scratched their way in. As the coach filled, it pulled away with a tight knot of people still trying to clamber through the doors and windows, and as it picked up speed, people fell off the sides onto the tracks. I stood, mesmerised, and watched it disappear. Was that it? Was that the train that I'd just missed? Would I have to return to that awful bloody hotel and go through that entire rigmarole for a room again?

But people were still standing around, so I waited too. Then two more coaches—little more than converted school buses mounted on train wheels—appeared. Again, there was the same mad fight for the doors. I gritted my teeth and pushed my way on to one—only to be told when I was on, that my seat was on the other. But if we had all been allocated seats, why all the fighting? It was beyond me. But I pushed my way off and on to the next, where I was given a seat at the front next to a fat jolly-looking man, near a woman who crossed herself continually.

We finally chugged off. The woman's genuflections were making me nervous—I'd heard the train was often derailed—but the views from that thin little line were magnificent. We pushed and pulled around green and dusty mountains, rattled across rickety wooden bridges with girders missing and swayed violently over rivers swirling far below. Sudden black tunnels echoed the chugging and clanging and the shrieking of the whistle. I thought about a bus in central Ecuador that had plunged off a bridge a few days before, killing all 100 passengers. I pictured the coach sliding off its tracks and rolling down the mountainside.

But the mountains soon levelled out and thick greenery dripped down tunnels of forest. Bright bouganvillea, orange blossoms and orchids fractured the green and hosts of butterflies fluttered helplessly through the carriage as they were sucked inside. Banana trees heavy with clumps of green fruit flapped in the breeze, pawpaw and coconut trees formed a roof above and red dust swirled in the air. Groups of children, some wearing old torn T-shirts and patched shorts, ran out of mud and wattle houses to wave. Some were Indian; others were black with short curly African hair.

My neighbour's thigh pushing into mine was becoming impossible to ignore. Every time I coughed and moved away, he took up more of my space. Short of clambering out of the window, there was nowhere further to go. I didn't much care for his conversation, either. 'San Lorenzo,' he'd started off lovingly, 'is a very dangerous town. Don't trust the people. They will try and cheat you. Many people are tricked there. Very dangerous. Many thieves. Too many smugglers. People disappear.'

It was a theme he was anxious to explore in more depth. Ecuador as a whole was exceedingly dangerous, he claimed. Many Ecuadorean men—himself excepted, of course—were dangerous for *gringitas* alone. I was in dire need of a man friend to be my protector. This all sounded familiar, somehow. I sighed. I was a captive audience.

Three hours later we stopped at a station. Its platform was covered by wooden tables and women were ladling out piles of rice, fried bananas, slivers of curled meat and dark red cabbage from huge cauldrons onto plastic plates. Children sold oranges, tomatoes, Coca-Cola and glasses of red jelly. We spent half-an-hour clustered around the tables, eating and drinking, as I tried gamely to avoid my neighbour whenever he approached.

Back on the train, it was stiflingly hot and sweaty from the blazing sun pouring through the open windows. We had been riding for seven hours. The journey was meant to last eight, so I slipped into a reverie about cold showers, icy beers and starched white sheets. But the coach suddenly shuddered to a halt. A derailed train from the day before lay across the tracks somewhere ahead. We were told it would be four hours before the rails would be clear. This made perfect sense. I'd read that successive governments' failure to maintain the 1957 line had indeed cost the area its livelihood when plywood factories moved away, because of the increasing unreliability of the town's main link to the rest of the country.

We all left the three carriages and wandered along the tracks until a clearing opened out into a little village of ten dusty wooden houses with washing hanging over the verandahs and strung around the banana trees beside. Plants in old margarine tubs withered in the heat. A shed stood in the middle of the line, which turned out to be a store selling torches, soap, clothes, rice, salt and bottled drinks from a fridge that no longer worked. I bought a bottle of water and watched barefoot children coming in on errands for parents and buying gob stoppers with the change. They looked at me wide-eyed, smiled shyly and bolted off when I said hello. Two mangy dogs slunk around the store, and sniffed around the children, now throwing *sucres* at bottle tops before an audience of disgruntled passengers.

After four hours, everyone piled back into the coaches standing patiently on the tracks. There was a buzz of excitement. We could still reach San Lorenzo before nightfall. But the buzz stuttered and died as our driver held up his hands and announced we wouldn't be starting again until the next day. Dismay. We all piled off again.

A man dressed in a business suit approached me and said he'd been told there was a boat that could take us downriver to the next village. He'd rounded up a few more of the wealthier-looking passengers, and a Scottish backpacker I hadn't noticed before in the other coach. I gave him a friendly smile.

'What are you doing here?' he asked, abruptly.

Taken aback, I said warily, 'The same as you, I guess. Trying to get to San Lorenzo.'

He looked around me. 'Are you on your own?' he asked.

'Yes,' I said, rather proudly, I must admit.

He shook his head in disgust. 'It must be so easy for a girl travelling on her own,' he said, as if to himself. 'It'd be so easy to meet people. You must have men following you everywhere.' He said it as if being stalked and hounded and harassed at every turn was a wonderful perk. He had no idea. If I could have been bothered I would have put him straight, but there was no point. He probably wouldn't understand, anyway. I moved away from him in disgust, and went and sat with the business suit. We crouched on the ground and waited expectantly. Nothing. Finally, a young black man came up to a knot of passengers and said he would take us on his raft for 300 *sucres*. I, and a number of the others, agreed eagerly—perhaps too eagerly. We handed over our money and he disappeared.

An hour later, just as we'd started muttering about having been taken for a ride—without the ride—he reappeared. He was pushing two small trolleys along the tracks, little more than wooden platforms with a wheel at each corner. These were obviously the rafts he'd been talking about which, rather than taking us down the river, would be staying firmly on the tracks. They looked dodgy. Very dodgy. But we had no choice. Six of us piled on each one, throwing our luggage in the middle and sitting on the outside with our legs dangling down.

Men from the village jumped onto each corner and started punting the platforms along with long wooden poles. It felt bizarre (imagine Venice surrounded by thick green jungle). I clung to the arm of a man sitting next to me as the thing lurched and jumped along the tracks.

After half-an-hour, they slowed to stop as we reached the derailed train. It lay on its side, wheels buckled and twisted, but with no sign of any attempts to move it. We jumped off, picked up our luggage and stumbled past in the mud and rough ground beside the train. Three carriages had been derailed and it would take weeks, rather than hours or days, to clear the wreckage. When we had passed, we climbed back on our chariots and set off.

Travelling downhill now, they soon picked up speed. We hurtled around and down at a terrifying pace. Darkness fell and we were still whipping on. I was sitting on the back of the first raft and had to hold up my legs to stop them dragging on the tracks. Now and then, the second raft would come dangerously close to crashing into ours and crushing my legs. The chief gondolier of each would whistle to the other continually to signal their position.

But the two platforms were travelling faster and faster and I began to get nervous. The thing was completely out of control.

If we hit a bump in the tracks or a wheel fell off, we would be thrown off down the mountainside. We wouldn't stand a chance at that speed. Everyone started screaming. One of the drivers pushed his pole to the ground to try and slow it. I felt a knee in my back as his pole got caught in the undergrowth and he somersaulted off sideways. We couldn't stop to see if he was still alive.

I held for dear life on to the little Ecuadorean beside me. Through my terror I could hear him asking, in a calm shy little voice, 'Are you married? Are you lonely? Would you like a special friend?' I was incredulous at his composure and through gritted teeth assured him I was not, I sometimes was and I might well later—just in case, if I put him off entirely, he wouldn't let me hold his arm any more.

Four hours later, we rolled along an uphill stretch towards a few lights that I took to be the end of the line in San Lorenzo. I shakily got off the raft and thanked the drivers who were squabbling over their share of the fares. But the second raft was nowhere to be seen. We stood around, waiting. Twenty minutes later, a small knot of people carrying luggage walked towards us. An axle had snapped just as they were approaching the town. One man, who thought he had broken his leg, was being supported by two others. The Scot marched up to me, grinning. 'That was quite an adventure,' he said. 'I was quite nervous there. You must have been terrified. South America is no place for a woman.'

I smiled back through gritted teeth. It was a pity he hadn't been the one to break a leg. But he seemed to be totally oblivious to the waves of hostility pulsing towards him. 'Do you want to share a room in a hotel here?' he asked. 'It'd be cheaper.'

I paused, desperately casting around for some devastatingly cutting remark that would chop him down to size. South America no place for a woman, indeed! 'Um, no thanks,' I finally replied. 'I couldn't think of anything more unpleasant.' It wasn't all that cutting, but it was the best I could do. As I turned to walk into town I noted, with some satisfaction, that he looked totally taken aback.

San Lorenzo, as I approached, looked like heaven. Its name suggested a dusty cowboy town, full of wooden bars with slatted doors. On first sight, it looked exactly that: tall, creaking wooden buildings lined either side of a wide dusty road, a raised wooden platform running along the front of each building; a few skinny dogs sniffing at the open sewers running beside the road; and a few bars from which could be heard drunken singing. It looked like a ghost town. I expected John Wayne to appear at the end of the road, point a pistol at me at any moment and ask if I was married. I was so happy to be there, still in one piece, I would have said, 'No,' and 'What are you doing tonight?'

chapter thirteen
UP, UP AND THEN UP SOME MORE

destination: Machu Picchu, Peru

A tourist walking down a street in Lima one day suddenly had a baby tossed at him by its mother. Shocked, he reached out his hands, caught the child and held it close. Just at that moment, a man came up from behind, cut his rucksack straps and carried his pack away. In his confusion, he clung to the baby until its mother started screaming she'd call the police unless he hand back her precious son.

Then there was the one about the couple in Cuzco who had shampoo poured on their shoulders in a crowded bus. When they took off their jumpers to wipe it off, their bags disappeared from under their feet. And that's not to mention the man in Puno pelted with stones and held up at knifepoint by thieves who took everything but his underpants.

All these tales were sworn to be true by people who'd just returned from Peru, and with quite distressing gusto. 'Look at us,' said a middle-aged Dutch woman I met on the border who'd been travelling in Peru for a month with her husband and two children. 'We've had everything of ours stolen at least twice over. We've been robbed by small children slithering under tables to get to our bags in restaurants, we've had bags razored from our shoulders, I've had my earrings wrenched from my ears—twice—and we've all actually had rings pulled off our fingers.' I grimaced. She laughed. 'We even put our money in our little girl's daypack, but she put it down somewhere and forgot to pick it up again, so we lost that too. We've just learnt to treat it like a game.' A game! It really didn't sound much fun to me at all. I wondered if I should play safe and cross back into Ecuador while I still had the chance.

But I desperately wanted to see Machu Picchu, the legendary sixteenth century Inca city built in one of the most inaccessible parts of the mighty Andes to elude the ransacking Spanish invaders. The last of the Inca emperors, Tupac Amaru, is known to have lived there, along with around 1000 people, in the white granite refuge which lay hidden from the rest of the world until 1911. These days, you can reach it by bus, but I had my heart set on the Inca trail, the long walk through the mountains passing the remains of other ruined settlements on the way.

Maybe everyone else had just been unlucky, I told myself sternly. I had learnt to be careful with my possessions, and in places where people were so poor, could you really begrudge them a little of your wealth? I cleared customs into Peru, and started to feel a little happier. Only then did I realise my hat had vanished from its loop on the back of my pack.

My next experience wasn't long in coming. I'd taken the bus south to Trujillo, half-way along the coast road to the capital, Lima. One of my neighbours on the thirteen-hour ride, a middle-aged woman dressed all in black, suggested we share a taxi to town from the bus stop. I readily agreed. As she bartered with the taxi drivers over the fare, however, she suddenly gave out a high-pitched scream. Her two suitcases had disappeared from between our feet. She ran off, leaving me feeling faint-headed with the speed and skill of the operation, huddling over my rucksack and her handbag. She returned ten minutes later with the bus driver, each carrying a case. They'd evidently been heavy enough to impede the thief's hasty getaway. She snatched her handbag from me and jumped back in the bus with the driver. I called weakly up through the window to see if she still wanted to share a taxi. 'No, my brother will pick me up in his car,' she replied. And then she closed the window. I took the first taxi I saw, paid double the price I should have and checked into a far too expensive hotel.

The next day, I caught a bus nervously to Chan Chan, the ruins of the largest adobe city in the world. Set in the middle of what felt like a vaguely threatening, bleak, deserted lunar landscape, there was a series of walls, some as high as 9 metres, enclosing the old city spread out over 25 kilometres. Inside, you could make out the grainstore, workshops and homes. There was an eerie atmosphere, and my guidebook didn't help by warning that these days robbers often hid behind the crumbly old walls to pounce on unwary visitors. I was ready, tense and on my guard. A guide ambled over and offered gloomily to show me around for free since I was the first tourist he'd seen for days. I relaxed. 'But where is your camera?' he asked. It felt suddenly silly that I'd been too nervous to bring it in case I was mugged. But before I could explain that, he hung his head low and apologised for his compatriots who'd obviously stolen it.

Lima hardly felt much safer. On the way in, through the infamous slums of corrugated iron and straw matting, with roofs of sheet metal held down with bricks and rubbish, people threw stones at the bus. The city itself was an astounding contrast between old and new with modern skyscrapers, elegant old colonial buildings, child beggars and Indian women ladling out home-made alcohol from buckets in the streets. Rumours were flying about an impending coup by the military, who were enraged that President Alan Garcia had put forward a bill for a united defence ministry. Already, there was an 11pm to 5am curfew to help police to control the activities of the Maoist *Sendero Luminoso* (Shining Path) guerillas working at night, often targeting the banks. Visitors out after curfew were advised to walk down the middle of the road waving a white handkerchief to avoid getting shot. One evening, I was strolling the streets when all the streetlights went off and we were plunged into darkness. People stood absolutely stock still. 'It always means a bomb is about to go off somewhere near,' said a woman nearby, helpfully. 'We are not close to a bank here, so we should not be in danger.' Sure enough, five minutes later, the lights all flickered back on. The bustle of the city, suspended briefly, began again.

That kind of bunker spirit made people pretty friendly. Sure, there were some simply trying it on, like the man who sat next to me on a bus to Trujillo for a time and pretended to be sleeping, only to fling his arms around me as if he was turning over in bed. He was furious when I nudged him hard in the ribs and told him to keep his hands to himself. In Trujillo, the hotel porter let himself into my room in the dead of night and only woke me when he sat on the bed, presumably in preparation for climbing in with me. He'd been ready for this eventuality, however.

'No, no, you are wrong,' he said when I snapped the light on and said I'd scream if he didn't leave. 'I came to wish you Happy Birthday.' He fished a bottle of lemonade from his bag on the floor. 'I saw on your passport in reception, it is your birthday today.' I screamed. He left. I drank the lemonade, and used my own padlock to lock the bolt behind him.

• • •

Others, however, were genuinely friendly, even if it was tinged with bewilderment at the strange behaviour of foreigners.

One day, I took the journey to Huancayo, a 420-kilometre train ride from Lima up one of the highest stretches of rails in the world, at one point reaching 4782 metres above sea level. I was chatting to an English backpacker sitting opposite when he suddenly went white and fell face-first into his bright yellow lunch of saffron chicken and rice. My reaction surprised me: I simply couldn't stop laughing. Other passengers, however, were suitably alarmed. They shouted for a doctor. The man who'd been cooking the meals rushed in, swapping his greasy yellow apron for a white coat as he approached our seats. He brought with him a big cushion with a nozzle attached, which he pushed at the backpacker's nose while squeezing the cushion under his arm, rather like bagpipes. It contained pure oxygen and he soon came round. When he eventually sat up, his face yellow from the meal, I couldn't contain my hysteria. Everyone else looked at me oddly and then, finally, joined in. I laughed, however, long after they'd stopped.

It was the same later when a snapped pipe hanging down over the line from coal slagheaps by the side of the track poured filthy water through an open window onto a couple holding hands. And not even the sight of a collapsed woman on the other side of the aisle having a heart massage to revive her could stop tears of mirth pouring down my face. If someone had died, I could have been in real trouble. It was a salutary lesson on how thin air at altitude affected me. After that, whenever I was climbing high, I readied myself mentally for an attack of hysteria.

In the town of Huancayo itself, people seemed eager to meet and welcome visitors. A cold, wet commercial centre, totally without charm, was made far more welcoming by the policeman who insisted on escorting me to the cathedral when I asked him the way. A fellow diner in a café looked mournfully at the spoon he was given to eat his two fried eggs. 'It wouldn't be like this where you are from,' he said. 'Today we don't get a knife. Tomorrow maybe we don't get a spoon.'

Then there was the passer-by who, asking if I was a tourist, said he would show me a great sight that wouldn't be in any of the guidebooks. After a ten minute walk up and down the greasy streets, we reached a bridge hanging over a river on the outskirts. He told me to close my eyes. I steeled myself against a kiss, but was led by the hand to the end of the bridge and then told to look down. Below was the slaughter yard. 'We have the biggest bulls in the whole of Peru,' he told me proudly. 'Look what fine meat they are making.' A man was swinging an axe at a bull standing with all four legs tethered, another was hacking at a carcass, and a woman was walking past with a great steaming tray of calves' heads held aloft, while another huge platter held a shivering mound of entrails. 'Not many tourists see this,' said my friend, licking his lips. 'It is a big honour for you.' I made my excuses and left.

•••

Back in Lima, I caught the bus to Nazca to see the famous lines etched into the sandy plains in a bewildering array of patterns over a vast area. Erich von Danniken, in his best-selling book *Chariots of the Gods*, put forward his theory that the perfectly drawn designs were the calling cards of alien visitors. Most experts today believe they're simply massive representations of the agricultural calendar or the constellation of the stars, drawn on such a grand scale to please the ancient gods. I went up in a little plane to look, since their size and scale can only really be appreciated from the air. I found it a wondrous, breath-taking sight, despite my stomach being left somewhere behind as we swooped and dived to examine the different shapes and pictures.

I then flew from Arequipa to Cuzco, the old capital of the Inca empire, and the starting point for the Inca Trail. As I arrived in the little town, nestling in the Andes, I felt my mood lift. Amid the maze of open cafés and market stalls, my first sight in the square was an Indian woman, fully dressed in the traditional wide skirt, embroidered blouse and felt hat, holding a llama by a rope. I was enchanted. Ah! This was the *real* Peru. I stopped to take a photo but she held up her hand and demanded her fee of ten *intes* first.

I meandered through Cuzco, a charming little town that was beginning to feel more and more like the Kathmandu of South America. Beyond the wide boulevards of the financial sector and the long shopping streets was the huge sprawling market, filled mostly with Indians and a few European hippies ambling around—white women often on the arms of beautiful, long-haired Indian men, trying to earn a living selling earrings and cocaine. My main task in the town was to find someone with whom I could walk the trail to Machu Picchu. I had been warned not to do it alone—guerilla activity and robberies along the way were common, I was told. More importantly, I knew my appalling sense of direction could doom me to wandering around the mountaintops for the rest of my potentially short life.

I put up a few notices at tourist haunts around the place, asking if anyone was planning the walk soon, and was approached that afternoon by two Australian women, Robin and Sue. They were leaving the next day. Much to their surprise, I was eager to go with them.

'Are you sure you'll be able to cope?' asked Robin. 'You're meant to get used to the altitude for a few days first.' I hesitated but knew the sooner I set out, the less chance I would have to talk with weary, footsore people who had just returned. If I heard too many tales of hardship, I knew my resolve would weaken and could well dissolve all together.

'No, no, I'll be fine,' I said resolutely. 'Tomorrow would be ideal.' I was excited to be so close to Machu Picchu, and anxious to press on. History felt so very near. After all, it was only in 1911 that the American archaeologist Hiram Bingham finally discovered the legendary Inca sanctuary that the Spanish were never able to locate.

I spent the rest of the afternoon running from shop to shop to hire a tent, buy food and fight for a train ticket from the station to the start of the trail. Halfway through buying a couple of avocados in the busy market, someone pushed me from behind and, as I lost my balance, snatched my purse. I stood there stupidly, waiting for my change, then gave chase. I asked a couple of shoeshine boys where the man had run to. They both giggled and pointed in opposite directions. My purse hadn't had much cash—they were welcome to that—but it did have my ticket to various tourist attractions. I went to the tourist police office, specially set up to deal with assaults on foreigners, to report it so I could claim a replacement.

The office was crammed with gloomy tourists, holding slashed handbags and wearing trousers with pockets cut open. Two even had something that looked suspiciously like shampoo on the shoulders of their T-shirts. We compared our losses. The harassed police officer on duty put a photograph album on the counter and told us all to have a look through. It held fifty hazy photographs of jail escapees, standing against a wall with their faces all in shade, their aliases written carefully by hand underneath. We protested that all we'd seen of our assailants had been their fleeing backs or the results of their handiwork.

The officer grew annoyed. 'How can we fight crime if you refuse to help us?' he asked. He had a point, so we flipped obediently through the pages, gazing at Juan Fuentes who also went by the name of 'Fingers Fuentes' or 'Shifty Eyes'; a fat Indian woman who shoplifted by concealing goods under her traditional rows of skirts; an elderly bent man who had murdered his wife; a smartly-dressed *mestizo* (a person of mixed Spanish and Indian race) who had sold his car to five people at the same time... I shook my head and went, instead, through the painfully slow process of making a statement in Spanish which the officer carefully wrote down, asking me what I was wearing at the time, what I had been doing all day, and who I had spoken to since the morning.

After an early night, I was up at 3.45am, walking through the dark streets to the station. I immediately got lost and wandered around disconsolately until I saw a little knot of backpackers walking purposefully in one direction. I followed them to the station, feeling relieved I wasn't going to be tramping through the mountains alone, relying only on my map and wits. I met up with Robin and Sue and the train eventually pulled away at 5.30am. Almost immediately there was shouting from the first-class carriage next door. Three men in guard uniforms had informed the passengers they'd have to change compartments, then helped them with their luggage—and leapt off the train with it. The rest of us thanked our lucky stars it hadn't been us.

The train shunted backwards and forwards four times during

the journey as it zig-zagged up the side of the mountain range, the fields of crops and grazing animals gradually giving way to grey peaks and steaming sulphur ponds. At each station, crowds of brightly-dressed Indians and their children waited to board the train, greet relatives or sell oranges, fizzy drinks and bread. The children often knocked on the windows, holding out their hands to plead for money or food, or to ask for either in exchange for a photo. The train then charged through the towering, snow-capped Andes, rutted with Inca terraces. Finally, we reached the peak of the 3000 metre-high mountain, Picchu, and the vast plateau of Anta unfolded before us. The canyon of Pomatales opened its jaws below and its river traced our journey.

Inside the train, Indians with fat hessian sacks, trays and buckets walked through the carriages, calling their wares. They were selling onions, mint, coriander, sweets, cigarettes and toilet rolls. On trays, they carried piles of *choclos* (roast cobs of corn), greasy pieces of roast suckling pig, *tamales* of meat wrapped in maize and boiled, and *picarones*, fried egg and flour fritters. Hot strong coffee or cinnamon tea was slopping in their buckets. Little Indian girls dragged huge sacks three times their size, tied at the top with string and presumably containing food and clothing.

At Kilometre 88, a field where the trail began, the train stopped and there was a flurry of rucksacks. The train pulled away as people were still queuing to jump off. Luckily, we three had been among the first to jump. As the train picked up speed behind us, I glanced back and felt terribly sorry for those looking disconsolately after us.

'Why did they do that?' I asked Sue.

She shrugged. 'Good sport, I suppose, for those on board who *didn't* want to get off there.'

We tore ourselves away from the lines, and strode cheerfully over the bridge and into a meadow with thick clumps of bright yellow flowered bushes either side of the track. So far, so good. The sun was hot and the air felt invigorating. This trek could turn out to be a piece of cake, but it didn't take long for my feeling of wellbeing to evaporate. The trail started climbing steeply up a hillside, and from then on it was ever upward. We tramped up and up. Finally, the trail levelled out through a pine forest and it began to drizzle steadily. Our pace slowed. Other walkers started overtaking us. An organised group marched solidly past, the men all in green plastic coats and the women all in pink. They looked silly, but I dearly wished I had one. I had pulled on my kagoule but was now soaked with sweat from the inside. My rucksack grew heavier and I grew short of breath. We clumped through dense forests with darting hummingbirds and bright red, yellow and pink wild flowers. We jumped from stone to stone to avoid getting sucked into the increasingly sticky mud of the trail. Every now and again, the trees would clear to show a mountaintop standing chillingly tall before us.

I was exhausted, and breathing hard. I started urging myself on with short, achievable goals. If I could just reach that stone; that part of the track I could see a few hundred yards away; that tall tree over there; I could reward myself with a rest. The goals got nearer and easier as I became more tired and my pack dug deeper into my aching shoulders. What wouldn't I give for a warm bath, I mused.

It felt like we were in the middle of nowhere. The trail was deserted and we hadn't seen anyone for a while. The only sound was the steady dripping of rain from the trees. Even the birds were silent. Rounding a tight bend, however, we were suddenly shocked to see a big wooden sign with 'Fanta' written on it, and a house selling soft drinks over a windowsill for triple the normal price. It was hard to believe that anyone would possibly haul crates of Fanta up that steep, punishing path just to make a few bucks. I bought one in admiration.

Three hours later, we came to a clearing in the forest. 'This must be the first campsite,' said Robin, examining the map.

'Great!' I said, feeling exhilarated. We had made the first milestone! Flushed with a renewed spurt of confidence, I suggested we walk on and camp at the next. The others looked unsure. 'Oh, come on!' I said. 'It's probably not that far, and it's still early.' They looked uncertain, but nodded and trudged off once more. It couldn't be far.

We walked and walked and walked, on and on and on, growing more and more snappy with each other with each passing kilometre. Finally, we all fell silent and each retreated into our own private gloom. We met an Indian leading a horse down the steep path as we were struggling up.

'How far is the next campsite?' I asked him.

He looked vague. 'About an hour,' he said. My spirits soared but plummeted again as he jogged away. An hour at his pace meant three hours at ours.

Robin gallantly tried to comfort me. 'He probably didn't understand campsite and meant the first pass,' she said. Then she urged us on, encouraging us as we climbed each crag.

An hour later, we came to a tiny clearing in the dripping woods. Could this be it? We weren't sure. The map wasn't clear. Robin walked on ahead to check what was there and yelled at us to follow. A few hundred metres away, she'd found a much larger clearing. This must be it. Robin and Sue pitched their tent in the mud, while I struggled to put up the one I'd hired. We ate sardines and bread in the dark, then each huddled into our sleeping bags, chatting through the tent walls.

Robin, small, dark and wiry, was emerging as the best walker and the strongest character, rallying Sue and I whenever we faltered. She had a tough, quiet strength, but would sometimes become sad and withdrawn. Sue was fair and plump, jolly and funny, jockeying Robin out of her morose periods. The two had shared a flat together in Melbourne, working in women's theatre. I liked them both tremendously. It was so good to be in the company of women again.

'We did have our doubts about you,' Sue yelled to my tent, 'on that first stretch when you raced away up the hillside. We thought we'd never be able to keep up. We thought you'd been lying when you said you hadn't done much walking.'

'But we liked you a lot more when you suddenly flagged and slowed down,' Robin joined in. 'Sleep well!'

Fat chance. My tent had no fly-sheet, which I hadn't noticed in my hurry to get out of the hire place, and dipped low at the opening so the roof of the tent lay right over me. It poured with rain all night, so the tent steadily sagged lower and lower under the weight of pooled water, soaking my sleeping bag. I spent the night shivering with cold and wet. At the first sign of dawn I was up, desperately trying to rub feeling back into my limbs.

We set off early, and the trail continued to weave up and up the mountainside, as I daydreamed of having someone to carry my pack for me. A tiny Indian woman who passed us actually offered to carry our packs for a fee. Just as I was on the point of ripping off my pack for any price, the other two refused politely. I couldn't believe my ears. 'No, we'd always feel as if we cheated if someone else carries them for us,' said Sue. 'Wouldn't you?'

No—but I nodded my head sadly. The woman told us it was about an hour to the first pass. I wondered idly if the Indians who lived here knew only the Spanish words for 'about an hour'.

We dragged ourselves uphill for another two hours until we saw a peak teasing us above. This must be the first pass, and reputedly the hardest. I was stopping now every three paces to get my breath. The air was so thin, I couldn't stop gasping, wheezing and panting loudly. After what seemed an age, we reached the top—only to see another, higher, peak further on. I almost wept. We set off again and struggled through mud which oozed over the top of my shoes. As we neared the peak, I crouched down on all fours to climb as the others, ahead, yelled encouragement. I couldn't breathe. I couldn't move another inch further. The next inch would be my last. They yelled again. Another inch, another, and, finally, I was there. We hugged each other and broke open a celebration bar of chocolate to mark the defeat of the first pass, Warmiwanuska, 4200 metres over the Wulluchapampa mountains. We were over the worst now, but there was still a long way to go.

We scrambled down the other steep side of the pass, climbing over rocks on our hands and knees to avoid the stream flowing swiftly between them. We decided to keep going until we reached the Runcurakay Inca ruins, but once we'd looked around the site we examined the map to see how far we were from the top of the second pass. It looked as if we were already about three-quarters of the way there, so we agreed to keep going to try and cross two in the day. But as we climbed over the top, we looked aghast at a steep rocky path leading upwards ahead. The mountains seemed as if they'd been carved out deliberately to mock climbers.

A thick mist descended. There were two other paths to each side, so we trudged along each in turn, hoping we'd be able to find some way of avoiding the steep climb. We walked along the first, hardly able to see a foot in front of us. Robin suddenly yelled and we all stopped dead. The path led straight into a lake. It lapped just ten inches before us. We followed the path back and took the second. That trickled off into the thick, dripping forest. There was no way out. We went back, and hauled ourselves slowly and painfully up the steep middle path to the top of the Runcurakay pass, 3800 metres high. There was little reward for our climb. The peak was completely shrouded in mist, drifting away only momentarily in the chill wind to show us tantalising glimpses of snow-capped peaks and what must, in normal weather, be fabulous views.

We were each shivering, so we agreed to make for the Sayajmarca ruins, just 3500 metres high, where surely the mist would be lighter. As we descended, the rain started falling in long, miserable streaks. We reached the ruins and wandered round them, cheering at the sight of the lovely old stone walls huddling on the hillside. They overlooked snowy mountains and forests looking like clumps of broccoli far below. But the thought of a damp night in the clearing by the walls sobered us again. We started to pitch our tents, mine still sodden from the night before. As we peeled open another can of sardines, a group of three Israeli men arrived. They laughed at my tent, hanging limply under puddles which had already started forming on the roof and dripping their way slowly through. They offered me a piece of plastic sheeting they had brought with them and I gratefully heaved it over the tent. They then unpacked a box of dry firewood, lit a roaring fire and sat happily around it while their soup and coffee warmed up. When it became obvious they weren't going to offer us any, we three poor relations crawled into our tents and tried to sleep.

The rain fell harder and harder during the night. It thudded onto my plastic sheet, trickled into the tent over the sides and rose up from the ground. I was soon soaked, cold and thoroughly miserable. It was impossible to sleep and I spent the night cursing and fantasising I was some place else, far, far away. In the morning, I crawled out of the tent, pulling back the plastic sheet and receiving a flood of water that had been caught in its folds right over my head. The men, already cooking porridge, laughed when they saw me. I tried to smile back. I took down my tent and laid it out to dry as I wandered away from the smell of hot oats filtering around the ruins.

A man, probably about forty, appeared on the pathway alongside, dressed in just shorts, a T-shirt and trainers. He too was walking the Inca trail, but rather more briskly than us. He believed in travelling light and had brought only a plastic bin liner to sleep in. As a consequence he had spent most of the night doing exercises to keep warm. He tried to start a fire with those pages of Hiram Bingham's *Lost City of the Incas* he'd already read, but as he couldn't see in the dark he'd mistakenly torn up pages from the back of the book instead of from the front, so didn't even have the ending to look forward to.

Robin, Sue and I packed our bags and set off again. We walked through a dark stone tunnel, chiselled through the grey rock face, and inched around a two-inch ledge along sheer cliffs. We held hands to cross shaky bridges made of rotting tree trunks over dizzying drops; if one went, we decided, we would all rather go. Finally we came to the Puyopatamarca ruins, spread over a large hill with an intact acquaduct system, fed by the river, and baths full to the top. If it had been warmer, we would have immediately stripped off and splashed around, but even the thought that day made us shiver.

We tossed a coin and took the more direct route downhill to the Winay Wayna ruins that were scattered over a long series of Inca terraces. The path became very steep and narrowed into a thin earth track with a deep trench in the middle. It made walking very difficult. If you put a foot either side of the trench, the slope down either side towards the dip made the ankles ache painfully. If you waded through the trench, your feet sank in the dust, making each step a real effort. If you tried to squeeze both feet on one side, you were in constant fear of sliding in the earth down the cliff-face. Many times, the three of us gave up completely and tried to slide through the trench sitting on our bums. Our ankles and knees were aching terribly with the effort when we finally came into sight of a village, where we collapsed on the ground in front of a café and drank Coca-Cola, for four times the normal price.

We were on the homeward stretch now and agreed to press on to get the whole torture over and done with. We set off at a brisk pace along the muddy path, signposted either side with warnings of snakes, bears, deer and dangerous bridges. An Australian backpacker walking towards us told us there was no camping allowed at Inti Punku, the last knot of ruins before Machu Picchu itself. He'd been turned back by the caretaker and was now walking back to Winay Wayna to sleep the night. He advised us to turn back and do the same. We refused, point blank, to retrace a single step. As he walked off, he threw over his shoulder: 'Maybe as girls you'll have more luck. You could always cry when the keeper tells you to go back.' We stuck two fingers up behind his back. Mind you, we agreed, that might be an idea...

It's strange how so many men think travelling around Latin America is a cinch as a woman, we grumbled. If only they knew. Both Sue and Robin were similarly sick of men trying their luck with them at every opportunity.

'I wear a wedding ring,' I told them. 'But it doesn't seem to do much good.'

Sue laughed. 'No, I think I've found the best way to put men off.'

'What's that?' I asked, eagerly.

She smiled. 'I say I'm a widow. It's incredible how effective that is. They're immediately respectful, and leave you alone.' It sounded like a bloody good idea. I resolved to try it at the first sign of trouble.

We fell silent as we climbed the old Inca steps up the hillside. Then, as we passed through a gateway and caught our first sight of Machu Picchu far below, we each caught our breath. It looked beautiful, spread on the saddle of a high mountain, and completely hidden by the hillside from any other point. We were exhausted, but overcome with emotion. We had made it.

As the sun set over Machu Picchu, we found our first dry firewood and toasted the Incas in asparagus soup cooked with whole cloves of garlic and our only alcohol, a small bottle of anisette. We made a bed in the absent keeper's hut and hung up our tents along the walls to keep out the wind blowing through the wooden slats. We chatted and laughed. It had been a wonderful experience—especially in retrospect. I slept beautifully, warm in our three sleeping bags zipped together. We rose early to catch the sunrise filtering light down onto Machu Picchu and smiled warmly at the Australian backpacker striding by on his second walk from Winay Wayna to Inti Punku. He spat loudly at our feet. We didn't care. We were there.

chapter fourteen
PEANUTS IN A SEX MOTEL
destination: Iguazu Falls, Brazil

I got off the bus and looked around me. I could see nothing; everything was pitch black. I didn't know what to do. Making an early start in order to hitchhike the 1500 kilometres north-east to the Argentinian capital, Buenos Aires, had seemed eminently sensible when I'd planned it the night before. But I'd overlooked one small detail: sunrise wasn't until 8.30am.

Now it was still only 6.20am and here I was—presumably on the outskirts of the swish ski town of Bariloche in Argentina's south, near the Chilean border—standing in a little pool of light which the cheerily bright bus threw on my feet, wondering just where the road even started. This was utterly ridiculous. I made the snap decision to ride the bus back into town, have some breakfast and start again in a couple of hours.

I picked up my pack, and turned towards the bus, only to see the doors thwack shut. I yelled to the driver and waved my arms, but my voice was lost in the roar of his revving engine as he pulled away, traced a wide half-circle and roared back off to town, leaving me alone and lost and feeling utterly stupid.

I trudged off up the tarmac towards a pinpoint of light I could see in the far distance. With luck, it might be a café, a house, even a truck stop. I brightened. I could feel my optimism slowly dissipate, however, as I trudged on and on towards the light, stumbling off the road every ten metres onto the soft verges at either side. Each time I looked behind me, just to check nothing might be coming as I tried to keep in the middle of the road, I somehow veered off course.

Finally I arrived at a police checkpoint. The barrier was down, cutting off the road completely to traffic. Even worse, there was no-one there. A notice on the side of the little guard box said the road would be closed until further notice. This was as far as anyone, excluding road maintenance engineers, could go. There was nothing to do but turn straight around and walk back to where the bus had dropped me. Hopefully, there might be another one along in half-an-hour, or an hour. At least then I'd be able to get back to town and start again.

I waited an hour-and-a-half before the bus finally turned up again, just as a few pale streaks of light were threading their way across the sky. It was the same driver. He didn't look at all surprised to see me. 'There is nowhere to go from here,' I told him, sulkily, wondering why he hadn't warned me when I'd actually got on the bus. After all, surely it was obvious what I had been planning to do? You don't actually catch a bus with a heavy rucksack two hours before dawn to take a look at a police checkpoint.

He smiled genially. 'You people,' he said, 'you people.' He threw his hands into the air in a gesture of wonderment. 'You like to see the strangest things. I met one man who travelled for two days just to see a big tree. A big tree!' He laughed and shook his head. 'Don't you have big trees in your home? Maybe you don't have police roadblocks either. What do I know?'

I paid my money silently and was dropped back where I'd started two hours before. The sun was almost completely up. No time for breakfast now. I asked at the bus station, now bustling with people, for the best bus to catch out of town that could drop me on the main road. By the time I'd actually stuck my thumb out to try for the first ride, it was 10am.

Despite the difficulties, hitchhiking is always my preferred mode of travel. Sure, it's often slow and inconvenient, punctuated by long periods of inactivity waiting by the roadside. It can also, occasionally, be dangerous if you're unlucky enough to get picked up by a maniac. But at its best, it's a wonderful way to get places, and to meet and get to know people along the way.

I'd heard Argentina was a pretty good place to pick up lifts. Unlike countries such as Bolivia, there was plenty of petrol and many people could afford vehicles, so there was no shortage of cars around. The roads were also very good. And, with huge distances between places on the wide, green *pampas*, drivers were often making long journeys themselves, so were only too keen to find company along the way. With a bit of luck, I thought, I could hitch all the way to Buenos Aires, then north through Uruguay and Paraguay, and straight up to the mighty

Iguazu Falls, one of the world's greatest waterfalls, on the Argentine–Brazilian border.

It was said to be a magnificent sight, one which moved former First Lady Eleanor Roosevelt—a woman not known for her lack of patriotic pride—to remark that, 'the Iguazu Falls makes Niagra look like a kitchen faucet'.

After just a few minutes, a sports car pulled up beside me. Fantastic! My luck must finally be turning. I jumped in and had the breath knocked out of me as we took off with a squeal of tyres on the empty road. His name was Carlos and he drove like a demon. Happily, he was only going the 200-odd kilometres to Neuquen, which was quite far enough for me. I was exhausted after spending the entire hour-and-a-half hanging, in a white knuckle grip, onto the handle above the window, only letting go when cramp made me fear I might lose the use of my hand completely.

Carlos tried a couple of times to start a conversation, but I mumbled only one-word replies. If he was going to drive this fast, I wanted him to keep his mind on the road ahead. I didn't want to provide any distractions at all. Just as we neared Neuquen, however, he seemed to notice how set my face had become and how tensely I was sitting in the seat beside him. 'Hey relax!' he said. 'I am a good driver!' I said I was sure he was, but I really didn't like travelling this fast, even with the best driver in the world. At that, he smiled enigmatically. 'I am a Formula One driver,' he said. 'Maybe, one day, I will be the best.'

You're not practising at my expense though, matey, I thought, as I smiled weakly at him. Only later, did I discover my ride had been courtesy of Carlos Reuteman who, six years previously, had lost the world drivers' championship to Nelson Piquet by a single point.

It was with immense relief, and jelly knees, that I eventually climbed out of his car, and stood happily back on firm land, waiting for the next ride. Again, it didn't take long. A great truck hissed and puffed to a stop beside me. 'I'm going to Plata!' shouted the driver. I checked the map hurriedly. 'Great!' I said, noting the name of the little town just outside the capital, La Plata. 'Thanks very much!'

His must have been the slowest truck on earth. He didn't have much conversation, either. We went through the usual questions, before things started getting sticky. 'Where is your husband?' he asked me.

'He isn't with me,' I replied.

'Ah, that is a shame,' he said, putting a hand on my knee, 'I think you are very pretty.'

I tried to look sad. 'Thank you,' I replied. 'But my husband died three months ago. I am a widow.'

His hand shot back onto the wheel. 'I am very sorry,' he said gravely. 'That is very bad.'

Mentally, I thanked my old Machu Picchu walking buddy Sue for the 'widow' tip. For the next fourteen hours, he drove in silence. It felt so much better than fending off advances for half a day and night.

In the early hours of the next morning, we finally arrived. The driver dropped me off in the centre of town, where he said there were plenty of decent cheap hotels. He was off to his depot to get a good night's sleep there. He shook my hand gravely. 'Good luck to you,' he said. 'God bless you.' I thanked him and followed his directions, through a surprisingly large town, to a cluster of hotels. I checked into one and immediately fell asleep.

I woke late the next morning, but didn't mind. I'd had enough of early starts. I thought I'd even have a bite of breakfast and a bit of a wander around La Plata before I headed off into Buenos Aires. It must only be an hour away, if that. At the bottom of the road, however, I stopped dead. I couldn't believe my eyes. There was a huge expanse of blue sea just beyond it. Strange. According to my map, La Plata was miles from the ocean.

I went into the nearest café. 'How far to Buenos Aires?' I asked the waitress after ordering coffee and eggs.

She rolled her eyes. 'Far, far,' she said. 'Maybe 250 miles.'

I couldn't understand it. Suddenly, a thought occurred to me. 'This town, it's called La Plata, isn't it?' I asked. She looked mystified.

'No,' she replied, 'this is Mar del Plata.'

Horrified, I grabbed my map. Instead of the direct road north, we'd gone due east to the coast. It had added miles onto my journey.

Back on the road, I stood for a couple of hours without seeing a single vehicle. When one at last appeared in the distance, I smiled sweetly—and watched it zoom straight past. And another, and another. Just as I started thinking about walking back to town and catching the train, the fourth, a little mini groaning slowly along, stopped. I only hesitated a moment before getting in.

The driver was called Julio, a short, fat man who found it quite absurd that a foreign woman should be hitching alone such a long way. His eyebrows rose into his hairline when I said exactly how far I'd already come.

'But why come via Mar del Plata?' he asked. 'That's a long way round.'

When I explained, he laughed until tears rolled down his face. I soon joined in. From that moment on, we laughed a great deal. He talked about his life as a teacher with a principal who hated him so much, he always gave him the worst-behaved classes to teach. I thought that was very funny. I told him how I'd always wanted to travel but had never reckoned with not so much an appalling sense of direction, but a non-existent one. When I talked about the time I'd once travelled for two days back the way I'd already come, while hitching through Zaire (only realising my mistake when a bunch of kids in a village, where I stopped the second night, seemed strangely to already know my name) he pulled over so he could laugh properly. And then he snatched the map of the route to Buenos Aires off my lap.

Halfway there, we stopped at a *parrilla*, a typical Argentinian grill house where great slabs of meat are slapped onto an upright grill over a roaring fire, for lunch. After looking at the menu, with its awkwardly translated delights—chicken small matters and pig's testicles highlighted as particular delicacies—I happened to mention the word 'pork' to the waiter, or at least the word I'd fondly believed to have meant pork. The waiter looked at me as if I were mad, and Julio let out a little scream and sank his head into his arms.

'What did I say?' I asked when he'd finally recovered his breath.

'You asked if he'd give you sex!' replied Julio. Turned out the Chilean word for pork meant something quite different across the border.

We continued laughing all the way to Buenos Aires, and arranged to meet up the next day for him to show me some of the city. It's only occasionally in a lifetime you meet people with whom you strike up an instant rapport and neither of us wanted to give it away so quickly. The next morning, Julio turned up at my hotel and, true to his word, walked me around the churches, museums, statues, city streets, coffee bars and tango clubs. We talked about his little son, his wife who'd died the year before, the joys of living alone and the way most Argentinians live at home with their parents until they marry, often well into their thirties.

'Isn't that a bit difficult?' I asked. 'What if you want to bring a girlfriend home for the night? But then again, you're mostly Catholics. You probably don't have sex until you marry.'

He looked puzzled, then understood. 'Oh no,' he said. 'We have the perfect arrangement for that.'

Julio laughed again, and led me to the next street, to an innocuous-looking front door. He pressed a silent bell and the door was immediately opened by a man in a dark suit and glasses. He bade us both good afternoon, then led us into another room and closed the door. Inside, everything was pink—the walls, the carpet, the lighting and a counter. 'Hello, there. Welcome!' came a voice, making me start. I hadn't noticed the woman standing behind the counter, since she was also dressed, head to toe, in the same colour. Julio said something to her and handed over his credit card. She copied down the numbers, and gave him a key. He winked at me.

'One moment,' said the woman. She walked to the door, opened it a fraction and peered out. The coast seemed to be clear. She opened it fully, and motioned at us to follow her. We padded down the darkened corridor until she indicated a room, and disappeared.

Julio put the key in and swung open the door. Inside, was a large, softly-lit room, with a large bed in the centre, swathed in a furry leopard-skin print fabric. Slowly, I realised the room wasn't really large, it was just that every wall was covered with mirrors. Julio pointed to the ceiling—that too was a mirror. He laughed at the expression on my face. 'Welcome,' he said. 'Welcome to an authentic Argentinian sex motel. If you could see what your face looks like...'

I soon joined in his laughter. I wandered around, peering into the little bathroom through another door, and marvelling at the array of perfumes, shampoos and condoms ranged on the shelves. When I came back, Julio was sitting on the bed and patting the other side. 'Sit down,' he said, 'there's one more thing to show you.' I must have looked wary, because he exploded into loud guffaws. 'No,' he said. 'Really, don't worry.

I just wanted to show you this place.' He flicked a switch on a panel to the side of the bed. Immediately on the screen just above our heads, a porn video started. I was astonished.

We sat and drank beers and ate peanuts from the mini-bar for two hours, until we judged a respectable enough time had passed to preserve Julio's pride. He pressed a bell beside the bed. A few moments later, there was a soft knock on the door. We were escorted out a different way, with just as much care being taken to make sure no-one could possibly see us. 'Everyone uses these places,' said Julio. 'Young people living at home, housewives, lawyers, politicians...it's so discreet, they even cover your numberplates if you drive into the car park at the bottom. Don't you think it's a fantastic idea?'

A few days later, I said a sad goodbye to Julio, ready to take the train, ferry and bus over the border to Uruguay. 'Why don't you stay?' he said, suddenly, grabbing my arm. 'You can live with me and Jose in our flat. You could find work easily. No strings,' he suddenly added. It was tempting, but hey, what could I honestly do in Argentina? I smiled and promised to write. By the time we left each other, we were both in tears.

•••

Montevideo, Uruguay's capital, seemed sombre, gloomy and terribly old-fashioned by comparison with Buenos Aires. After a few days lonely exploration, I made my way on to the main road north out of the city, ready to move on to Paraguay. My first lift was with an elderly couple in a beautifully preserved, wood-panelled Morris Traveller. 'How do you find Uruguay?' the man asked. I mumbled that I found it very pleasant. 'Ah,' he said, sadly, 'but you should have been here before. We were once a very wealthy country, full of proud people. But that was before the military.' It was a common story across the whole of Latin America. The struggles between the right and left all too often left the economy decimated, the population forcibly subdued and the country devastated.

Nowhere, indeed, was that more evident than in neighbouring Paraguay. It had a tragic history: not only was there the constant trauma of political coup and counter-coup, but slave traders ravaged the native Indian populations; the war against Uruguay, Argentina and Brazil in the 1860s killed half the population; and, finally, the iron rule of military dictator Alfredo Stroessner, the world's longest-reigning dictator, lasted from 1954 to 1989.

Yet I'd been looking forward to Paraguay for reasons other than merely being able to have a closer look at a country which only seems to be known outside South America as a friendly refuge for fascist criminals from all over the globe. Strangely enough, I had two friends from university who'd both settled in the capital Asunción. I'd written to them both and had replies demanding I drop in. Andy, a close friend until he'd found God, had gone to Paraguay to become a missionary. His family had rarely heard from him, and they begged me to look him up and report back. He seemed to want to sever all contact with them, they said. The other person, Michael, I didn't know so well as he'd been a year ahead of me at uni, but he sounded equally eager to see me.

Getting to Asunción, however, proved far more difficult than it looked on the map. I caught a bus to Encarnación, a large town in the middle of the country, from where I planned to catch the old steam train to Asunción. I'd been warned it was a slow journey ('Are you sure?' the ticket seller asked me at the station. 'The bus is much better.'), but I had no idea it could possibly be as slow as it proved. Leaving three hours after the scheduled departure time, we came to a halt just 100 metres along the track. 'Breakdown! Breakdown!' the cry went through the carriages. 'Five hours to fix!' I got off the train and went for a wander along the side. Dozens of corn-on-the-cob, banana and soft drink sellers from the station platform were hastily setting up shop alongside the track. The rest were still struggling along the lines, carrying braziers, boxes and vats of drink. 'This happens very often,' one old man told me sadly, as he slowly ate a banana. 'The bus is much better.'

A short, thickset Englishman carrying an assortment of plastic bags and wearing a startling yellow shirt, festooned with pictures of bananas, joined us. 'This is a right game, ain't it?' he said in a broad Cockney accent, indicating the crowd of Paraguayans now standing around the ancient steam engine, looking puzzled. 'D'ya reckon we'll get there?'

His name was Leo and this was his first time out of England. He'd ended up in Paraguay after a drunken night in the pub when he'd got out a world map and pledged to go wherever he stuck his pin after turning round with his eyes closed three times. The next day, his mates held him to his promise. He'd had to look up Paraguay in his encyclopedia as he'd never even heard of it before. He'd now been in the country two weeks, and already he was regretting his haste. 'Brazil might 'ave been better', he said. 'All that sand and sun and...' he hesitated '...samba'. Even Argentina he'd heard wasn't bad. Or Spain would have been nice, and a hell of a lot nearer to home. He didn't think much of Paraguay. 'No-one speaks bleedin' English,' he said. 'And they don't even 'ave a proper train.'

Day turned to night, with no sign of the engine being fixed, and we all settled back into our seats to sleep. At about 3am, there was a piercing shriek of a whistle, and the train jolted forward. And again. And again. We couldn't have travelled more than three yards before the humming stopped and we were stationary once more. The next day, there seemed to have been little progress.

By nightfall, I was growing as restless as Leo. 'Let's catch the bus,' I suggested.

He nodded. 'I've 'eard it's much better,' he said.

Asunción was a pleasant town, full of pretty green squares, white buildings and the purple blooms of dozens of jacaranda trees. Leo tagged along as I wandered through in search of a cheap hotel, stopping along the way for a cup of coffee in a little café on a corner. As I went to pay, he begged me for a loan. It was just a temporary cash crisis, he said. He'd be sure to pay me back. I handed over some money, telling him to be careful not to run out—the next day was Sunday and there might not be many money-changers around.

The advice, I knew, would be lost on Leo. He was quite possibly the least equipped traveller I had ever met. For a start, his Cockney accent was so broad and his vocabulary so eccentric, that even other European backpackers had trouble understanding him, let alone the Paraguayans. He didn't possess a single word of Spanish either, preferring simply to repeat his original sentence more loudly when anyone failed to understand him the first time round. Also, he seemed not to have even considered buying a backpack before he left home, merely tossing a few things into an assortment of plastic bags. Finally, he didn't have a clue about how to organise himself to catch a bus on time, or find out about a rail timetable. It was only people persistently taking pity on him and helping him that allowed him to survive in this strange environment. And he was plainly so inept at finding his way around anywhere, he made me feel like David Livingstone, which was quite an achievement in itself.

I found a hotel, and suggested Leo check in too. That way, I knew he'd be safe for that night at least. We then both decided to have a further look around. We walked the dark, empty streets, until we saw a sign for a bar. It was the kind of tatty little place down two flights of stairs that looks so much better because it's so dark and smoky. In daylight, it would probably have been ghastly. But with loud blues coming from the jukebox and ice cold beer, it felt like a haven. Looking around, however, I couldn't understand why it had so many tall, stunningly dressed women milling around. There were only a couple of guys among them. While I figured it out, one gorgeous woman in a silver dress slit to the thigh asked Leo to dance. His eyes fairly bulged. Despite only coming up to her

peanuts in a sex motel / 247

breasts, they were soon smooching in time to the music. After an hour, I tapped him on the shoulder and said I was off. I hardly knew Leo and it hadn't occurred to me that he didn't know they were all transsexuals.

The next morning, he appeared at around lunchtime with a black eye. Apparently, he'd gone back to her place and only at a crucial moment in their relationship had he discovered 'she' had been a 'he'. It must have been just like *The Crying Game*. I giggled, but Leo silenced me with a filthy look. Horrified at this turn-up, he'd tried to deck his date but, full of beer, he'd missed. 'She', on the other hand, hadn't.

I thought my missionary friend Andy might provide a good antidote to this sleaze. I rang and left a message, and he called back. We arranged to meet in a café in the city. I hurried over—I was looking forward to seeing him again. He'd always been a gorgeous man, in both looks—tall and craggy-jawed with a mop of black curls and laughing brown eyes—and temperament. At uni, he was the life and soul of every party, a permanent fixture on the rugby side and one of the most popular men around, until he'd suddenly undergone a complete change of heart and found religion. Then he became quiet and withdrawn, and his eyes grew sad. Somehow, whatever he'd found, he seemed lost. I hoped he might get over this 'God' phase, but obviously he hadn't. Still, I hoped he was happy.

I spotted him immediately in the crowd and rushed over to give him a hug. I was taken aback when he stepped away to avoid me. He motioned to a woman standing, frowning, by his side. 'Sorry,' he said, quietly. 'I can't be with you on my own.

I have to have a married escort with me. And we can't physically touch.' He seemed sombre and subdued, nothing like the exuberant, up-beat Andy of old. As I took a seat, he explained his order was very traditional. In fact, would I mind putting my bag on my lap, rather than on the floor? He looked pained. A woman setting her bag on the floor was akin to announcing herself a prostitute. 'And if you wouldn't mind, could you do up the top button of your shirt?'

This wasn't going anything at all like I'd imagined. I fixed a smile on my face. 'So, how are things?' I asked. 'Are you happy here?'

He stirred his tea with a spoon, even though he'd put neither milk nor sugar in. 'Yes, my work here is terribly rewarding,' he said. 'I've made lots of friends and I am very happy.' He didn't look it at all.

He asked if I'd come to a church service he was conducting the following evening. I wasn't sure, I wasn't at all religious. 'No, I remember that,' he said softly. 'But it would mean a lot to me if you came. Please.' I agreed, and after half-an-hour of desultory conversation, he stood up and announced he had to go. He said goodbye gravely as his escort watched us like a hawk.

The next morning, I called Michael. He'd only met with Andy once, he said, and that once was enough. They hadn't spoken since, they'd just had nothing left in common. He said he was coming into town in an hour, and he'd pick me up. He arrived in a bright red open-top Mercedes, wearing a white suit and a straw hat over his floppy blond hair, looking as if he'd just stepped out of the pages of *The Great Gatsby*.

We drove back to his place. He'd been in Paraguay two years now, working for an oil company, and he loved it. The reason soon became apparent. 'This country is just ripe for the picking,' he said. 'There's so much money to be made here. Labour's dirt cheap and you can get anyone to do anything for a fraction of the price of anywhere else in South America. Last week, we had to get rid of a few trouble-makers...' He went on and on, talking non-stop about quick profits, low wages, and the cash that was readily available for anyone—of European extraction, presumably—with a little bit of nous and initiative. By the time we pulled up at a grand, white-washed mansion, and had the doors of the car opened for us by Paraguayan servants (bizarrely wearing black morning suits) I was heartily sick of him. I could see why Andy and Michael would have very little to talk about at all.

Late in the afternoon, Michael ordered one of his servants to drive me back to the hotel as I struggled gamely to stop looking so disapproving. But it must have been obvious that I was more than happy to leave. 'You must come back and stay a few days next time,' said Michael, as I went. I think he knew I wouldn't.

That evening, I caught a bus to Andy's church. It was a little wood-and-thatch affair in a poor part of town, but already packed as I arrived. I took a pew in the middle and returned everyone's smiles. Andy came in and walked up the aisle, shaking men's hands and nodding to me as he passed. It was strange to see him in a full black gown and white collar. There were a couple of hymns, and then we got down to the real business of the evening.

'Do we have any sinners with us tonight?' called Andy to the congregation. 'I can feel the presence of evil here!'

There were downcast looks. I held my breath. What? Evil among these nice people dressed in their best clothes, looking so eager to please? But Andy was adamant. 'Evil is here, it is among us,' he said, walking back down the aisle, fixing various members of his audience with a hard glare. 'It is perverting our souls. It is turning us away from God. It must be banished.' Whoa! I thought to myself. This is a bit heavy.

Andy suddenly spun around on his heel and pointed to a woman in a gay orange and green floral dress. 'You!' he thundered. 'It's you who are harbouring evil!' The woman visibly paled. He took her shoulder and propelled her towards the front, made her kneel in front of him, then shouted at her. Her shoulders sagged and he called for two helpers. Two men came forward and held her still. Andy started chanting something at her, and very soon she started shaking.

'It is the devil inside her!' he yelled.

'The devil!' cried the congregation in unison. 'The devil!' The two men were now holding her down on the floor as she screamed and wept, quite probably in fear.

'The devil!' shouted Andy.

'The devil!' cried his audience.

I felt myself shaking, but with anger. Great! That's all these people need. It's not enough that they're among the poorest on the continent, they're now being told they're infected by the devil and being used as fodder for foreign do-gooders to practise primitive exorcism techniques. My face was wet with tears. I could stand it no longer. I ran from the hall. It was the last time I ever saw Andy.

'He seems fine,' I wrote later to his family. 'He looks as if he's very much at home.'

•••

The next day, with Leo again tagging along, I caught a bus to the point where Paraguay, Argentina and Brazil meet. He'd decided to see the falls and then catch the next plane he could find back to London. 'This place ain't for me,' he explained. He had an abscess developing under a tooth and was in a lot of pain but refused point-blank to visit a dentist. 'I wouldn't bloody trust them 'ere.' It hadn't helped his mood that the bus stopped for lunch and, after ordering what he'd believed to have been soup, he was served a huge dish on which stood half an animal's torso. I had to admit it did look nightmarish, even for someone who could open their mouth properly. 'Next time, I'm sticking to the Costa Brava,' he announced. 'It's civilised there.'

The next morning, I could hear the thunder of the 4 kilometre-long jagged stretch of river pounding over the precipice to the water below before I could even see it. I'd finally arrived at Iguazu Falls. I felt the excitement catch in my throat. Leo said he was excited too, but would have to dash after 'a quick gander'. 'But I have something for you,' he announced. 'I've got that money I owe you.' He handed me a 10 000 Paraguayan *guarani* note and I thanked him warmly, never having expected to see the cash again. We hugged goodbye.

With that, I set my face towards the falls and started walking. It was only when I stopped to buy a lemonade that I discovered that the note was forged.

chapter fifteen
JUST WHEN YOU THINK THINGS CAN'T GET ANY WORSE...

destination: Angel Falls, Venezuela

It was a bad sign. The bus to Belem—in the north of Brazil, by the mouth of the mighty Amazon River—had broken down between the garage and the bus station. I was told it would be an hour late. I felt glum—this wasn't a great start.

I'd been in Brazil for more than two months now, and I'd had enough. It was an astonishingly stunning country, with fabulous beaches, picture book jungle and a huge variety of people. But the waves did tend to dump the unwary—i.e. me—crashing back into the sand; the jungle was full of creepy-crawlies that always seemed, somehow, to want to raise their young in my pack; and the contrast between the hedonistic wealthy and the ragged kids limping around the restaurants begging for the leftovers from your plate was shocking. In addition, the country was so very big. Every journey between interesting places would take a gruelling twelve, twenty-four or thirty-six hours by bus. It was exhausting. I was eager to get out of Brazil and on to Venezuela, a mellower, gentler place, and home to the next great sight I was looking forward to: the Angel Falls, the highest waterfall in the world, twice the height of the Empire State Building, with water crashing nearly a kilometre from the top of the Auyantepui into the thick jungle below.

On the map, it looked straightforward. A bus from Fortaleza to Belém—a snip at a mere twenty-eight hours—a boat to Manaus, deep within the Amazon rainforest, hitch a ride north to Boa Vista and up across the Venezuela border, then bus to Ciudad Bolivar and a plane ride to view the falls. Neat. That's if the first bus ever arrived.

Two hours later, it limped into the bus station. We all piled on and set off. Three hours on, the bus shuddered to a halt. There was something wrong with the steering. The driver and his mechanic went underneath the bus and fiddled around. After an hour-and-a-half, they emerged to declare the emergency over. Everyone cheered. We set off again, but soon slowed down to a snail-like crawl. A couple of passengers got out and walked alongside the bus. They had to keep stopping to let the bus keep up. We pulled over again, finally, and the men welded something to the bus's underside. Two hours of jerky driving later, and the bus stopped for the last time. The damage, it appeared, was irreparable, and we'd have to wait for a new bus.

So we waited by the roadside. And waited. And waited. When at last a rickety old bus appeared around the bend in the road, everyone scrambled to their feet. Immediately, a shout went up. This new bus was much smaller than the original, with only thirty-seven seats between the forty-six passengers. I steeled myself, ready for the mad charge on board, but what happened next surprised me. A few people went into a huddle and emerged, punching their fists into the air.

'No-one will leave until we can all go,' announced a burly middle-aged man to the rest of us. There was a cheer and a disgruntled muttering from a couple of the passengers who had rushed to the bus door, planning to be first on. 'The passengers, united,' shouted our new leader, 'will never be defeated!'

Everyone else quickly took up the cry. 'The passengers, united, will never be defeated! The passengers, united, will never be defeated!'

I was thrilled to see a spontaneous show of Brazilian democracy in action. Not everyone was so pleased. The two drivers had faces like thunder as they each took out their radios to relay the news back to base that they had a troublesome bunch of passengers here, and what the hell should they do now?

Another bus arrived at about 2am, just after the skies had opened to a massive tropical downpour. Soaked, we marched onto the new bus. This had the right number of seats, true enough, but they were tiny, very old and mostly broken. My seat wouldn't lean back, while the one in front of me would *only* lean back. In addition, the luggage hold was far too small, so most of us held our bags and cases on our laps. It was hot, cramped and extremely uncomfortable. My seat was just by the engine, which blasted me with constant gusts of hot air. The seats had plastic covers, so every time I managed to fall asleep, I'd wake up drenched in sweat. In addition, I had only oranges to eat, so very soon I was hot, sweaty *and* sticky.

I was also feeling intensely irritated by the man beside me.

After a few desultory attempts at conversation—'Do you have cheese in your country? Do you have oranges? How many days by bus to your country?'—he'd obviously decided on a more physical approach, and kept letting his hand rest casually on my knee. My ploy of confiding in lecherous men that I was a widow didn't appear to be working very well on him. Every time I took his hand off my knee, it took him only twenty minutes to put it back again.

Eventually, I tried to read by the light of my torch in a desperate bid to mentally escape the misery. I had Henry James' *The Portrait of a Lady* with me, but somehow reading it only made me feel worse. He did so insist on creating extra-ordinarily mellow little English scenarios all the time, with afternoon tea in the old country mansion, Gardencourt, when, 'part of the afternoon had waned, but much of it was left, and what was left was of the finest and rarest quality.' I snapped the book shut. The gentle conversation of the tea parties, the chink of fine china, the refinement of the guests, and the pretty dresses of the ladies, all contrasted far too sharply with the hot, foul-smelling, sweaty bus.

Still, there was one plus. In the breaks where we had to stop for the overheated engine to cool down, my neighbour finally, happily, began wooing the woman behind us who had been showing him dirty photos of herself, hidden inside her Bible. At least that was one less annoyance.

After what felt like a lifetime, I started seeing ponds, palms and green forest, all signs we were getting closer and closer to Belém. Just outside, we pulled over and were ordered off at a checkpoint. There we stood in a queue to have, I assumed, our papers checked. But as a screaming and wailing broke out from the front of the queue, I peered around to see two doctors walking down the line jabbing the passengers with needles—the same needle, I noted. Yellow Fever vaccinations, I was told. I hastily pulled out my doctor's note to say I'd had one and, after a long and extremely passionate (from me) argument over whether a note was as valid as a certificate (my doctor had assured me there'd be no problem, but I don't think he'd exactly foreseen this situation), I was excused.

Belém was an agreeable melee of old, run-down, dirty docks, and rat-infested warehouses where muscle-bound men dressed in shorts and, dripping with sweat, carried impossible loads on their heads. The other side of town looked like a museum of faded elegance with tiled plazas, graceful statues of mermaids and heroes, and pretty churches, all a little the worse for wear. I didn't have too long to look around, however. The boat to Manaus was leaving the next day and I wanted to stock up on food at the market and also, most importantly, to buy a hammock ready for the seven-night trip.

The next day, I arrived at 7am at the boat terminal. It wasn't leaving until 10pm, but I'd been told to get there well in advance to make sure of snaring a space for me and my hammock. Fifteen hours early should do it nicely, I thought, even if I do run the risk of looking rather silly. Nine o'clock came around and, strangely enough, I was still the only one waiting there. I started to fret. Surely I couldn't be the only one anxious to find a good space?

Eventually, I went over to a woman who was struggling with a suitcase the same size as her, two small children and, rather bizarrely, a caged parrot. 'The boat to Manaus?' she echoed. 'It's over the other side. I don't know if you'll find a place though, it's been there for hours. Everyone else has already boarded.'

I rushed around to the other side of the terminal, cursing myself. Sure enough, there was the ship, looking full to bursting with passengers. I pushed my way on and then wondered what to do next. I had my hammock tucked neatly into the top of my pack, but how were you meant to get a space to sleep, and, most importantly, *where*? Two young girls must have noticed my bewilderment because they came over and grabbed me by the arm, steering me upstairs, where row after row of hammocks had already been strung up between railings, often criss-crossing each other to fit in.

'You are single?' one asked.

'No,' I answered, my reaction automatic after months of being quizzed the same by over-amorous men. I felt embarrassed. 'Er...yes. I'm alone. I forgot,' I quickly corrected myself.

They looked at me oddly, then guided me to the section for single women. As they unwrapped my hammock and deftly tied it up between the rails in a space that looked far too narrow for me even to lie down in, they explained the pecking order. The area next to us, they explained, was for women with children, the next one married couples with children, then couples, then finally single men towards the furthest wall. The whole deck was divided into two by a long trough of a sink with six taps, women's and men's toilets and showers. The trough was already blocked with chicken bones and discarded rice, over which soupy water slopped over the sides. I could see the showers were already ankle-deep in water, and I could smell the toilets from where I stood. Babies screamed a few hammocks away. I smiled gamely.

My two new friends, who were going home to Manaus after visiting relatives in Belém, took me on a quick tour of the boat, visiting the restaurant downstairs and the café upstairs selling toasted sandwiches, burgers, coffee and soft drinks. Even these decks were looking pretty tatty. As I'd found they did all the way through Brazil, everyone was simply throwing their rubbish on the floor where they stood, ignoring completely the rubbish bins posted at strategic intervals. If this was the state of the place before we'd cast off, I shuddered to think of the mountains of rubbish we'd be wading through by the fourth day.

I bought my helpers a Coke in the café, then I went back downstairs to watch the cheerful lights of Belém slide off into the distance. Soon, they were replaced by the dark outlines of trees as we stole deeper and deeper into the Amazon basin. I went to find my hammock, only to discover it was now squeezed between the rails three deep—one tied both above and below— with barely enough room for me to scramble in. Once in, I didn't even have the space to turn over, so I spent the night lying rigid, being kicked by women either side, and listening to a great cacophony of snores mingling with babies' wails and the excited whispering of single men who'd crept over to our section to eye up the available talent.

The days quickly melded into each other. Showers were taken quickly, with clothes either carefully balanced on the rail above, or fished out of the water lapping around our ankles in the shower rooms. Breakfast started at 6am, when a long queue would wind around the boat for a cup of sweet coffee, another of maize porridge and a sweet soft bread roll. Most of the rest of the morning would then be spent queuing for lunch when huge sweating men, wiping their brows with dirty cloths, would slop beans, rice and stew onto metal trays. Any spare moments were taken up with scrambling for the dozen or so highly prized chairs on the deck which would vanish from beneath you if you so much as stood up to adjust your dress, let alone look at the deep green jungle slipping by or the occasional little village where everyone would stop whatever they were doing to stare at the boat and its passengers.

The political complexities of the boat slowly revealed themselves. At first, I couldn't understand how some people got their meals first each day, without apparently having to wait in the interminable queues. They, I later discovered, had either tipped the sailors or, if they were women, had slept with them. The captain of the boat, in his stiff white uniform and nice peaked cap with the word 'Capitaine' proudly emblazoned, was always surrounded by the most beautiful of the female passengers. Everyone, it seemed, was nervous of the enormous power he wielded. On the third day, when food rations were halved, an Italian backpacker organised a delegation to the captain to complain. When they arrived in his office, the others shrank away, leaving him alone to argue. He did, however, extract a promise that the business of tipping be looked into. He became an instant hero among those passengers who couldn't afford to hand out extra money.

His name was Mario, and he was travelling with Gloria, a woman he'd met in Argentina. They were a nice pair, but both terrifyingly hot tempered. In the couples section of the sleeping deck, other passengers had complained about the rows they had, conducted at the top of their voices. Everywhere they went, they seemed to become embroiled in an incredible number of fights: with a man Mario spotted weeing in the showers; another who pushed in front of them in the breakfast line; a woman who Gloria had seen throwing rubbish into the sink; and a man who'd spat at their feet. One young tearaway who tipped his tray of leftover food onto the table when he'd finished his lunch, Mario actually reported to the captain. He was locked in the ship's cell for the day. I marvelled at our different approaches: I'd merely assume it was intrinsically Brazilian to do certain things, and accepted them; they took a strong line that anti-social behaviour, from whomever, should not be tolerated. As a couple, they could be enormously entertaining, but they could also be quite tiring.

The other passengers were generally a friendly lot. My two friends in the singles' hammock section regaled me with questions whenever I saw them. 'How often do you have periods? Do you find Brazilian men handsome? How many times a day do you have sex? Do you like white skin best, or black skin?'

One plump, smiling woman told me she had twenty-one children, by four different men. When I asked why, she smiled, indulgently. 'If God had given me a plantation, I would sow seeds,' she explained, patiently. 'But he gave me a womb. It is only right I give Him something in return.'

The little thirteen-year-old girl I'd seen around the boat nursing a child I'd assumed was her little brother or sister, turned out to be the mother herself. No-one else was in the least surprised. It didn't seem an uncommon phenomenon at all.

There was one passenger who was just a little too friendly, though. Nathan, from Brasilia, a good-looking young man whose line of work seemed to be transporting merchandise from one part of the country to another (he'd had twenty cases of whisky contraband confiscated at Belém) followed me around the boat like a puppy. Asking him to go away seemed to have little effect. When I played cards with any of the others, he always tried to barge in and shuffle for me. When I joined the food queue, he was always just in front, urging me to stand with him. When I tried to take part in a game of dominoes with the men, he gently explained that women weren't allowed to play. When I read, he sat at my feet, staring up at me. I tried hard to shake him off but, in the end, it seemed easier just to ignore him.

The declarations of eternal devotion were, however, becoming quite wearying. Mario and Gloria found it very funny. 'I only have eyes for you,' Nathan would tell me each day. 'You are the most beautiful woman on this boat. Just one kiss will make me happy.' I doubted it, somehow. At meal times, he chastised me for eating onion. 'Many Brazilian women don't eat onion. They believe it makes their vaginas stretch.'

As the trip went on, his ardour became fiercer. 'Look at you, living like the poor people,' he said one day. 'If you were with me, I would always have you travelling by plane. I will buy a big house and you will wear nice clothes.' I laughed, and tried to explain that I enjoyed travelling in this way, and I quite liked the clothes I had, thanks. But he would not be put off. Even when I accused him of lying, after I was invited to join a dominoes game and it became obvious that women *were* allowed to play, he remained totally unruffled. 'I didn't want you to play,' he said. 'I would be jealous of the other men looking at you.' But he'd saved his trump card for last. 'I have great trouble with women,' he told me towards the end of the journey, with a pained expression on his face. 'Once I have made love to a woman, she keeps coming back for more and never wants to let go.' I couldn't help a sneaking admiration for his ability to keep a straight face.

On our last day aboard, everyone was up and cleaning their teeth by 4am, even though we weren't due to arrive until late afternoon. But the excitement was infectious. By 9am, the whole boat was standing on the top deck to watch the legendary meeting of the waters—the blue-black Rio Negro and the brown-yellow of the Solimoes—forming the Amazon River. The two distinctive rivers flow strangely side-by-side for four miles (some say it's water density that stops them mixing, others, water velocity). When we finally docked in the remote free port of Manaus, there was a mad rush to get ashore. I was right there in the middle. I only had the relatively short trip north to go before I'd be out of Brazil and into Venezuela and on to Angel Falls. And I could hardly wait.

In that frame of mind, I wasn't likely to fall in love with Manaus. But, I soon had to admit, it was an interesting place. It felt like a distant outpost of the country, a pocket of civilisation in the middle of nowhere which, I suppose, it was. At its heart was a surprisingly smart commercial centre, with shops full of TVs, stereos and expensive motor-bikes (to go where, I wondered); some grand colonial build-ings from the boom days of the rubber industry; and a handful of up-market tourists, looking horribly self-conscious in faun safari suits. There were startling contrasts all the way: from the beggar sitting patiently by a shop window that was showing a state-of-the-art US$150 000 huge-screen TV set; to the man outside a shop displaying a powerboat, trying to sell passers-by one of the little goldfish he kept in a tin bowl balanced on his head. And, everywhere, there was rubbish piled high in the gutters, smelling over-poweringly rancid in the heat and humidity.

I revelled, however, in the chance to floss my teeth without a dozen other people curiously looking at me, to shower comfortably alone and to sleep in a real bed once more. I went to see all the sights; took long walks; tried some of the strangest foods; hitched to a village deep in the rainforest; and paddled around nervously in a canoe, wondering how big the piranhas under me might be. One day, I even went along to the cinema to watch a Star Trek movie, just for the chance to escape the blistering heat outside and sit for a couple of hours in air-conditioned luxury. It wasn't the greatest success. At first, I couldn't understand why, in a near-empty picture theatre, a man would choose the seat next to mine. Twenty minutes into the film, I felt my seat tremble and, to my horror, realised he was masturbating next to me. Incensed, I decided not to move, to pretend I hadn't noticed. Why should I let him force me out of my place? I continued steadfastly ignoring him, although my discomfort grew by the minute. I couldn't even concentrate on the film, worrying he might jump on me at any moment. Still, I was determined not to budge. The film seemed to go on forever, and he got up and left just ten minutes from the end. Only later did I realise how seriously stupid I had been. He'd wanted me to stay in that seat. By sitting and sweating it out, I'd hurt no-one but myself.

•••

Eventually, the heat made me feel drained and lethargic. I had to get out of Manuas, but that was harder than I'd imagined. I went to the port captain's office to see if there were any boats due to leave for Boa Vista. No, no boats because the river was too low. I went over to the bus station to inquire about the roads out. No, no buses because the roads were too wet. I was stuck. I caught a bus to the second port on the other side of the city. Here, the chief was more optimistic. There might be a boat two days away, he said. I came back in two days, only to hear it was now three days away. I returned again two days later. He looked glum. 'No, no boats this week,' he said. It was as much as I could do to stop myself bursting into tears. I checked out the airfares. They were astronomical from Manaus. Would I ever be able to get out of this Godforsaken place? I decided to try hitching a ride if there were any vehicles going north.

The next day, I caught a bus early to the first truck stop on the road to Boa Vista, and was delighted to see half-a-dozen trucks standing on the road. I wandered around them, asking each of the drivers for a lift. Two weren't planning to go anywhere, two were on their way into Manaus and another had broken down. The sixth was fully laden with tins of food stacked high into the sky, covered with a tarpaulin secured by a rope, and a VW Beetle balanced on top. Apparently five others had already booked a seat each in the Beetle, which I didn't fancy anyway. The more I looked at the stacks of tins, the more I didn't like the thought of balancing on top, even with the driver's kind offer to secure me there with a rope.

As I stood on the tarmac, wondering what my next move should be, another open truck pulled up. I raced over to the driver. The truck was leaving at midday with no load, just passengers for a minimal fee. I paid up, and sat and waited. We left at about 2.30pm, as I and the nine other passengers scrabbled for a good place to sit near the cab among the packing cases of flour, sweets, fish and clothes that everyone else had carried on. I sat on my sleeping bag and looked back out on Manuas, disappearing into the distance as the lorry jolted, rocked and bumped over the dirt road. Clouds of pink dust enveloped us, and butterflies scattered around as other trucks came the opposite way. Slowly, the scenery changed from thick, dark, dense foliage of palms, trees and bushes, with rivers, inlets and swamps, to desolate, wide, clear green spaces with only the stumps of trees left from clearing operations, or eerie lakes where tall, dead palm trees stood defiant at their lack of fronds. The road gradually turned deep rust red, with the damp dust clinging to our skins.

At around 6pm we stopped on the edge of an Indian reservation we weren't allowed to pass through at night, at a little gas station and the shell of a building with low walls and no roof that seemed to serve as a restaurant. There was only one thing on the menu—rice, beans and meat—so I ordered a plate. When the place emptied, I strung up my hammock between two walls in the corner, and slept like a baby.

The next morning, I dreamt I was falling and woke when I hit the floor with a thud. It wasn't a dream. Two of the truck's passengers, apparently nervous about waking me up or actually speaking to me, had simply untied my hammock with me inside. I gathered we were in a rush to be off. I went outside to see around twenty people now crushed in the back of the truck, taking up all the space near the driver's cab. I took a spot at the back end and waited. After three hours, we were finally allowed to pass into the reservation. My back ached from my fall, and I felt angry that I could have carried on sleeping in my hammock, instead of sitting on the hot metal of the truck, under the burning sun.

Finally, we set off and I was immediately thrown around violently in the back. The road here was broken and muddy, and showers of mucky water splattered up over the back from the wheels, streaking me with orange. As the truck roared through deep trenches and over ruts, I realised why everyone else was sitting squeezed up at the front near the cab. The back end lifted up and came crashing back down again with each rut we drove over. I was then hurled from side to side as we dipped in the trenches. I tried to anticipate what the driver was going to do by whether he slowed, blistering my hands by holding on tight to the back panel, and would each time hunch myself forward in a ball to hold in my insides. It was hellish. I felt like my organs were slapping around, and I had a sharp pain in my side that was steadily growing worse. Some of the other passengers, comfortably up by the front of the truck, smiled sympathetically at me as I was bounced around; others merely laughed as I groaned.

I started bitterly regretting not splashing out for a flight. But how could I have known it would get this bad? I wondered how long I could stand it. Every bone hurt. When the truck driver stopped to take a drink, I could hardly stand. The blisters on the palms of both my hands had already broken, so it was even painful to hold on. I tried to immerse myself in the passing green countryside and the occasional wooden huts and groups of children playing in the dirt outside. It didn't work. Getting off and spending a few days scratching around in the dirt, hoping another truck might chance along, would be better than this pain. At that point, the truck slowed again, and one of the passengers jumped down over the side. As if in a daze, I watched the others throw his luggage down to him below. Then one of them came over, seized me by the arm and led me to the space on a rice bag that had just been vacated. 'Here sister, this would be better,' he said. I felt like offering to have his children.

As we set off again, I could hardly believe this was the same ride. I was still bounced, sure enough, but so much more gently. I had a few sips of water and bites of a dried-up old biscuit I'd found lodged in a forgotten side pocket of my pack. I felt I was riding in absolute luxury. But my pleasure was short-lived. Very soon, we drove into two deep, sticky, muddy ruts in the road and, after trying to get out backwards, then forwards, then backwards again, we trembled to a final, miserable stop. Everyone jumped out to help push, and lay tree branches along the metre-high grooves for the tyres to find a grip. We slithered around in the ankle-deep mud. Nothing would budge that truck. A few hours later, a truck coming the other way stopped and pulled over. Since he couldn't get past us, he had to help haul us free. We set off again, this time at 15 kilometres-per-hour, negotiating the sodden road.

I'd been hoping we'd reach Boa Vista that night, but it was 9.30pm by the time we reached the nearby Mucajai River, long after the ferry had finished for the day. On the banks, there was a tatty little restaurant. I ate there, then asked if I could put my hammock up over the tables. Even better, the owner told me, for an exorbitant fee I could even take a shower. A shower! I'd caught sight of myself in a mirror on the wall and the image of an orange-streaked face, with hair standing thickly on end from the dust and my forehead and neck caked in mud, had shocked me. I excitedly handed over the cash.

270 / getting there

The shower room only had two walls, but I didn't care. It was also dark, but I managed to fumble in the dim glow of the restaurant and find the hose pipe against the side. I peeled off my filthy clothes and turned the tap on. The cool water felt blissful on my body. I took a handful of shampoo and lathered up my hair. Heaven. Then, disaster. The water stopped and the lights from the restaurant went out. It was suddenly pitch black. I waited for a few minutes, hoping the water and light might come back on. They didn't. Gloomily, I dressed, pulled back on my muddy clothes, ran my fingers through my sticky, soapy hair, slithered my way back to the restaurant and crawled into my hammock, feeling as if things couldn't possibly get any worse.

But, of course, they could and they did. In the middle of the night, I felt an odd pressure on my body. Turning over and opening one eye, I found myself looking straight into the face of a man who'd strung his hammock right next to mine. I kicked him as if in my sleep and the pressure eased off. I turned over again, but then I felt a hand come over and pluck at my hammock. At first, I thought he might be trying to get his balance. But when he did it a second and third time, tired, hot, sticky and absolutely fed up, I sat up and screamed abuse at him. I could see his dark form recoil. He didn't dare try to touch me again.

The next morning, we crossed the river on the little wooden ferry and drove into town. I checked into a hotel and had the best shower I'd ever had. Venezuela was so close now, I could almost smell it. After getting dressed again, I headed straight for the Venezuelan consulate nearby for my visa to the country. I'd been told to leave it until here to apply, but I always felt anxious whenever I left anything to the last minute—if there was ever room for a problem to occur in Latin America, you could bet your bottom dollar it would. And, of course, it did. The Consul was off-hand. No, he said, I couldn't have a visa as I didn't have an onward ticket from the capital, Caracas.

'But I'm travelling overland,' I protested.

He wouldn't budge. 'No, you need an onward air ticket,' he insisted. It was a catastrophic blow.

There was a travel agent nearby and I went in to ask if I could buy a ticket from Caracas to...well...anywhere. Not possible. I could either buy one from Caracas—pretty impossible I pointed out if I wasn't going to be allowed in—or I'd have to go back to Brasilia or Rio and buy one there. I crumpled. The thought of doing that journey again, in reverse, was too much to bear. I went back to the consulate. It had closed for the day.

At 10am the next day, I was standing on the doorstep, again arguing with all my might. But the Consul was totally uninterested in my dilemma. Back at the travel agent's, I tried to bribe the salesperson to make me up a false ticket, but no go. She wouldn't even phone the Consul for me to confirm that I couldn't buy a ticket. My only hope was to personally wear the Consul down.

For the next three days, I knocked politely on his office door and explained my problem over and over. At the end of the third day, he was looking grey and bored. Finally, he threw his hands in the air. 'You win!' he shouted, wearily. 'I'll give it to you. But you might still be stopped at the border.'

It was a chance I was happy to take. I needed a doctor's certificate to say I was healthy, so dashed to the doctor's where my finger was cut with a razor blade for a blood sample to check I wasn't carrying malaria, and answered questions like, 'So, do you have any infections down under?' presumably checking for STDs. I shook my head vigorously and was given a note for the Consul saying I was perfectly fit.

I ran back all the way to the consulate and presented the letter. 'Yes, yes,' he said, begrudgingly. 'I'll do it for you now.' He almost threw my passport back at me, with the precious visa stamped inside.

I left early in the morning by bus, and reached the border at lunchtime. As the Brazilian customs officer stamped me out of Brazil, I peered over to the other side of the no-man's land between the two countries. In the distance, Venezuela shimmered with promise. Even the grass looked greener at the next customs block. I felt a new bounce in my step. Venezuela was going to be wonderful, I knew it in my bones.

•••

The border town on the other side, Santa Elena, was a pretty little place with low white-washed buildings, painted soft yellow, pink and powder blue. Everywhere, there were trees, heavy with red, pink and orange blossoms. Even the people were friendly. At the local police station, there was no hesitation about stamping my passport, and they even gave me directions to the bus for Ciudad Bolivar. I was tempted to stay for a couple of days in order to properly absorb the atmosphere, but I was eager to see Angel Falls.

The next morning, I took the bus to Ciudad Bolivar and hitched a ride to the airport to check out sight-seeing planes going over the falls. I was in luck. Standing at the same counter was a group of three tourists who had just hired a five-seater Cessna to do the jaunt, and were happy to have me share the cost. We sat and waited for the pilot to come back from his last trip. He came back sooner than we thought. 'There was a problem with the engine,' he called over to us, after taxiing right over to the airport door, jumping out and striding past, leaving his passengers to shakily scuttle out after him. 'We'll get it fixed in a minute.' We all looked at each other. It didn't exactly inspire us with confidence. Still, I hadn't come all this way just to bottle out at the last minute.

Two hours later, he returned, saying everything should be all right now. I didn't much like that word 'should'. His former passengers obviously felt the same. They looked wary. He went over to reassure them, then came back over to us. 'They say you can go up first,' he said. 'They want to have lunch now.' Yeah, sure they did. We looked at each other. Oh well, he seemed pretty confident. We agreed to go up first.

The plane felt tiny inside as we shuddered up through the bloated clouds and bumped through them, dipping down intermittently to see the dark green forests and the inky dark waters of the Orinoco River, trickling into the swamplands. After about an hour, we approached the high, flat-topped, marbled brown mountaintops of the Zona Auyantepuy. I took a breath when I glimpsed the narrow aisle between the mountains we were heading for, the Callejon del Diablo. I started feeling sick. We swooped in, darting from side to side of the alleyway, looking at the waterfalls gushing from the tops and trickling down the sides all the way along. The sunlight caught the drops so they looked like twinkling gossamer caught on the sharp surfaces.

'Is that it?' I asked hopefully, reaching for a paper bag on the back of the seat in front of me. 'It's lovely,' I added, apologetically.

'No, not quite yet,' barked the pilot. 'But soon now, soon. This is Churumeru just in front.'

I looked ahead. We couldn't see the top, but I could see a thin stream of water running all the way down, as if the peak had pierced the cloud. He was obviously planning to go right up to it. He swerved and tilted the plane to give us a better view and I pulled open the bag on my lap just in time.

chapter sixteen
A FELLOW BACKPACKER
DISAPPEARS

destination: The Corn Islands, Nicaragua

The bus stopped in what looked like the middle of a field and passengers started getting out. I sat tight until I realised I was the only one left. It could only be me the driver was wildly gesticulating at. 'Last stop!' he was shouting. 'Last stop! Goodbye. Goodbye.'

I looked around. Nothing but green fields, a few stony paths trickling off into the distance and the hurriedly departing backs of my fellow travellers, laden down with hessian sacks of sugar and maize. There must be some mistake. I thought this bus had supposed to be stopping in Managua, the capital of Nicaragua, another dusty, dirty, polluted Central American city, no doubt, with a ragged skyline of tower blocks and grimy streets bustling with shoe shops and undertakers. I must have caught the wrong one.

I walked up to the driver. 'Managua,' I said. 'Managua.'

He carried on gesturing at me to get off his bus. 'Yes, yes,' he replied. 'Managua. Welcome. Now, GOODBYE!'

I obviously wasn't going to get anywhere there. But, still

unconvinced I wasn't in the middle of nowhere, I grabbed my pack, jumped off the bus and trundled off after the stragglers. I caught up with an old man at the back and tapped him on the shoulder. 'Managua?' I asked. 'Managua?'

He stopped and turned to look at me. 'Yes, sister, this is Managua,' he said, solemnly. 'God save us.'

I looked about me. Beyond the fields, I could see a few white brick houses, a long low brown shed, a couple of trees and more dirt. Surely this couldn't be it? An old car rattled up, swaying, with six people crammed onto the back seat and three in the front. The driver peered out of the front window. 'Taxi?' he yelled. Well, I couldn't see how on earth he was going to fit me in, but it sure as hell looked a better bet than wandering around these fields looking for a hotel I wouldn't have the slightest clue how to find. I nodded, eagerly. He said something to his front seat passengers and one of them opened the door and climbed out, giving me a filthy look. I squashed in with my pack on my lap, trying hard not to catch his eye again as he stood disconsolately on the roadside. I felt terrible, but still probably not half as bad as he did. I told the driver the name of the hotel I wanted and he pulled away. Three minutes later, he stopped beside the long brown shed with a line of doors on the front. I looked at him quizzically, but he nodded his head reassuringly. This was one of the best hotels in the city.

I checked into a windowless dark room, and went to find the hotel restaurant. I walked twice past a neighbouring garage, with two tables and some chairs inside, before I realised that was it. I decided to go to bed. Maybe things would look better in the morning. Besides, I hadn't planned to spend too long in Managua, I reassured myself. My main aim was the Corn Islands in the Caribbean Sea just off the east coast of Nicaragua. I'd been told that the two little islands, fringed with white coral, dusted with golden sand and adorned with gently swaying coconut palms, were Paradise on earth. Untouched, unspoilt and absolutely beautiful. I slept well that night, dreaming of swimming in clear turquoise water and lying on creamy sands, sipping milk through a straw in a chilled coconut.

The next day, Managua still looked much the same. It was simply astonishing that this was a capital city. Of course, much of it had been destroyed by the massive earthquakes in 1931 and 1972, but I was expecting great sprawling ruins, construction sites, new buildings rising up from the ashes to take the place of the old. Really, it didn't look as if there was terribly much here in the first place. Obviously it hadn't helped either that the country had been in the grip of civil war since 1979, when the US-supported right-wing Somoza Government was over-thrown. It had been a brutal reign by a family well-recognised for its tyranny. One-time US President Franklin Roosevelt, indeed, was once said to have remarked, 'Somoza is a son of a bitch...but at least he is *our* son of a bitch.' The Somozas were then replaced by the increasingly left-wing Sandinistas. From that time on, President Ronald Reagan funded the guerilla group, the Contras, who were working to destabilise the country and bring down the government. Yet little Nicaragua survived the Goliath's assault—kind of. On the one hand, President Daniel Ortega became the toast of libertarians worldwide with land reforms, an education system, health care and a literacy rate that was one of the highest in the world. On the other, his nation was desperately poor with chronic shortages of anything that had to be bought in hard currency, like fuel, machinery, and spare parts.

Walking down the dirt roads, hearing crows shrieking to each other, and cicadas humming in the long grass, it was hard to believe Managua was a real city. Even in the centre, there were houses, garages and businesses often with roofs, or a wall or two, missing. The walls that were left, however, were often nicely adorned with artwork showing women cradling babies and machine guns, or slogans like 'Yankees Go Home!' In the one proper square there was left, with a couple of proper shops and a supermarket, it was still impossible to comprehend the place as a twentieth century city with more than one million people. The shelves of the supermarket, true enough, were all full of goods, but only of four types: Cuban rum; peanuts; an array of revolutionary literature; and, inexplicably, jar after jar of mayonnaise. Outside the Intercontinental Hotel—a massive white building perched incongruously like a space ship on a moonscape—groups of women sold Pepsi emptied into plastic bags, which you drank by biting off the corner and sucking, because of a national shortage of bottles. Others sold sugary fruit drinks, *frescos*, also in plastic bags with a straw that invariably split on the first suck. One man stood selling his wares—three plastic wallets and a box of matches. The locally made matches were of variable quality; the only guarantee was that their heads would always explode and end up burning in your lap.

The cafés were usually the broken down shells of people's homes, with one table, a few stools and broken-armed chairs, and a crowd of women cooking little sweet maize cakes over a wood fire. Always, they'd sell *frescos*, sometimes coffee and, occasionally, they'd even have an egg. Invariably, they'd only have stained white plastic knives, forks and spoons to eat with. 'We may not have much, sister,' one elderly woman said to me, handing me a plastic beaker of cold coffee as she'd just run out of wood. 'But at least what we have is ours. We don't have to rely on those Yankees' (and she spat noisily on the ground at that point) 'for our lives. We will overcome.'

A middle-aged man, who insisted I share his family's evening beans-and-rice meal after I'd greeted him as I walked past his home, was similarly enthusiastic. 'Welcome to our country,' he said. 'We have to look after our visitors. They will tell the rest of the world how we are suffering, but how we are proud of what we are doing.'

One afternoon, I went to a rally in support of Ortega, at the Plaza del Revolucion. Rows of children with black and white kerchiefs around their necks marched behind banners proclaiming, 'We Want Peace' and 'No Amnesty For Terrorists!' In the square, 4000 supporters congregated under banners congratulating the FSLN party for surviving twenty-six years to 1989, while great portraits of the patriot Augusto Sandino—who waged a guerilla resistance war against the US occupation of Nicaragua, but who was murdered by Anastasio Somoza when the two agreed to meet for peace talks—fluttered in the wind. Ortega eventually took the stage to speak, in a roar of cheers and applause, announcing his plans for an amnesty for Contras who'd joined up since 1981, thereby still signalling his intention to pursue the old Somoza guard. He was a genuinely charismatic man. I could see why he was rapidly becoming one of Central America's best-loved folk heroes.

Outside Managua, however, the critics of the regime seemed to grow either more numerous, or more vocal. On a boat crossing Lake Nicaragua to get to the western side of the country, in between trying to wave away clouds of tiny black flies and picking them out of my ears, nose and eyes, I noticed a man glowering at me from the other side of the boat. I tried to ignore him, but he didn't stop. Finally, I went over to him and said a pleasant good day. It was like a red rag to a bull.

'Good?' he snarled. 'Good? What's bloody good about it? You bloody people...you're all communists. You come to our country and then go back to your nice houses and warm fires far away saying we're poor but happy. Poor but happy. What's so bloody happy about being poor?' Well, he had a point.

I put out my hand. 'My name's Sue,' I said. 'What's yours?'

He looked at my outstretched hand and, for a moment, I thought he might refuse to shake it. But then he visibly softened, seized it and gave it a hearty shake. 'Hernandez,' he said. 'Victor.' He was a farmer, growing coffee and bananas near the Pacific coast. He'd been much better off under Somoza, he explained, when labour was dirt cheap, and there were eight *cordoba* to the US dollar, rather than the current 18 000. I took a deep breath. Pot-bellied and red-faced in a New York City baseball cap and a smart pair of linen shorts, he didn't look all that poor today to me, I ventured.

'That's only because I work hard for my living,' he said sharply. 'But listen to me. Name me one socialist country that isn't poor.'

'But there are poor people in the US,' I replied.

'Aha!' he said, slapping his knee in triumph. 'You can't tell me that! I have been to America. There are no poor people there. You should not believe everything you hear on the radio.' He leaned closer and whispered. 'The radio is controlled by the Sandinistas.' He put his arm around my shoulders, and whispered again in my ear. 'Do you like sex?'

It was interesting, too, to talk to the *brigadistas*, the idealistic young men and women from Australia, Europe and the US usually taking a year off their university studies to help the cause. They'd be teaching English, working on engineering projects or drafted out to villages to help with well-digging or anything else that needed to be done. Some of them would treat us tourists with ill-disguised contempt; others would be glad of the English-speaking company. I met one Australian called Mike in Rivas. He had been in the country for only three weeks, but in that time he'd had his every possession stolen by the family he'd been living with. His second day there, his Walkman had disappeared. The third day, his jacket. Now he was left with only the clothes he stood up in, and a few text books that obviously had little value on the burgeoning black market. He was managing to remain astonishingly cheerful, considering.

'But, really, it's not a problem,' he insisted, good-humouredly. 'These people have so little, and I have so much.'

I grimaced. 'They *had* so little and you *had* so much,' I corrected him.

He shrugged, laughing. 'But I'm here to help. If they think that's the best help I can be, then maybe that's all right.'

Certainly, the extreme poverty of life for so many corrupted everything. The shortages of fuel meant there were few vehicles plying the long distances between towns and villages, and people stood by the side of the road hitching with the world-weary patience of those who knew that they might still be waiting tomorrow, or the next day, for a lift. The roads, and some of the boats, had been destroyed in Contra attacks. The buses, when they ran, were packed to overflowing with more than one hundred passengers routinely riding in a vehicle designed to take a maximum number of fifty-four. With great holes in the floors and ceilings, it was often safer to cling to the sides, perch on the roof racks and hold on, for dear life, to the hands of friends inside hanging out of the windows. And even if people managed to get to work, it was for little reward. The average daily wage of 2000 *cordobas* (about fourteen Australian cents) for farm labourers didn't stretch to much, considering galloping inflation. One man who owned a shoe shop where I went to have my sandals repaired—his assets comprising two pairs of shoes, a sheet of rubber and some glue—was pessimistic, or optimistic, depending on how you saw it. 'The Yankees will invade in about seven months,' he said, confidently. 'Then the Sandinistas will be finished.'

I thought it might be as well to get over to the Corn Islands before anything too dramatic happened. My application for a permit to visit had been approved for the bigger of the two islands. The smaller one, I was told, was these days strictly off limits to everyone. In Somoza's day, it had been used as his own private fiefdom. Now it had particular political significance. No matter. The big one was still pretty small and sounded a fascinating place. The islands had been originally settled by Africans from wrecked slave ships, missionaries, pirates and the odd settler. It made the population a pretty mixed bag. The missionaries, often from Scotland, had been extremely strict, with members of their congregation threatened with expulsion for an impressive list of sins that stretched from good old-fashioned fornication to the more mean-spirited dancing at weddings. The pirates were a law unto themselves and the rest of the settlers a potentially explosive mix of refugees from the Somoza and Sandinista governments alike.

I hitched along the terribly dilapidated road to Rama, and took a boat over to Bluefields on the eastern coast of Nicaragua, on the Caribbean Sea, the departure point for the islands. It was stunningly different to the rest of the country. The town was just as run down and higgledy-piggledy, its muddy streets lined with rickety wooden houses on stilts from which blared an endless medley of reggae songs, but it did look as if it had once been a thriving metropolis. And it had. Somoza had traditionally left this side of the country alone, and had thus enjoyed some degree of popularity there. The Sandinistas, on the other hand, were viewed with extreme suspicion when they came to power. No-one knew them on this coastline, and none of the locals were in their army. Yet the Sandinistas were paranoid about the region, as the US had always declared its intention to build a beachhead on the Atlantic coast. They pursued land expropriation more rigorously here than anywhere, and put up pictures of their martyrs, not realising that the local Misquitos Indians found displaying photos of the dead extremely disrespectful. Resistance built up, until the Sandinistas finally decided to loosen up.

Yet hostility lingered. On the way to find a hotel on my first night, a man sprung into my path. 'You white people,' he said, pushing his face close to mine. 'What whores! You came here and robbed us and now you don't want to know us. We are left poor, while you grow rich on our misery.' I could smell the rum on his breath. 'We end up here, eating shit, while you stand well-dressed in front of me.' It seemed pointless trying to reason with him.

I checked into an old hotel with a wooden verandah and a rocking chair, to share a room with Keith, an American, and John, an Englishman, I'd met on the boat over. They were good company. Keith was a blond, strapping ex-sailor, who'd left the US Navy a few months before and had decided to travel the world for a year. John was simply taking a month-long holiday. We wandered over to a nearby square, where posters were advertising a dance display that evening by a visiting group of black artistes from Atlanta, Georgia. We waited, and waited, until it had grown quite dark. Finally, a voice cut through the gloom. The evening had been cancelled, it said, because there was a power cut and no lights. On the way back to the hotel, I noticed my Mr Angry now lying full-length in a gutter. I thought it wise not to wake him up to offer help.

The next morning, we took turns to suss out a means of getting to the Corn Islands. John discovered there might be a boat from El Bluff, another harbour you had to reach by boat. I volunteered to go over there to check it out. There was a little speedboat plying the twenty-minute journey across the bay, which might have been quite fun, had there been fewer than ten passengers crushed in, with all their luggage. As it was, the boat was lying low in the water, and looked perilously close to being swamped several times on the trip. Once in El Bluff, though, there was good news and bad. The good news was that there was a boat to the islands, leaving at 6am. The bad news was that the first boat from Bluefields to El Bluff left at 6am. I went back to Bluefields and reported my news. We all decided to go over that evening to El Bluff, and catch the 6am boat the next morning.

Back at El Bluff, we knocked on the door of a nice house just off the harbour and asked if we could pay to sleep on the floor. The woman inside, Shirley, was happy with the deal. Since her Honduran husband had left her to return to his homeland with three of their four children—he left the girl and took the boys—every extra *cordoba* of income helped.

We were up at the crack of dawn ready for the boat. But down at the harbour, there was a problem: no sign of any boat. We sat around all morning until a speck in the distance came closer and closer to reveal a barge piled high with concrete slabs and pieces of wood. 'No passengers,' barked the captain, as he came up to the side. 'No room.' The harbourmaster said he'd heard there might be a boat leaving from Bluefields.

Back at the house, Shirley was sympathetic. 'Yes, travel here is very difficult,' she said. 'But then think how it is for us. When I fly to Managua, I can't take any clothes. You are allowed one bag and you have to fill it to the top with money. Our largest note is 5000 *cordobas*. You are only allowed to carry 25lb, and the money you need for the trip weighs that.' We took the boat back to Bluefields to try for the next boat. When we arrived, we were told it had just left. We checked back into the hotel.

There was supposed to be another boat in four days, so we decided to wait. The second night back in Bluefields, however, Keith didn't come back to the room. By the next night, John and I wondered if something had happened to him, and whether we should do something. I went through his pack and found his money-belt and passport. I knew there was no way he would have left without those.

The next morning, we went to the police station and reported his disappearance. We showed them the photo in his passport.

'Ah yes,' said the officer at the desk. 'We know where he is. He's in our jail. He's a Contra.' Keith had been stopped walking near a Sandinista camp and, unable to produce any ID, was arrested as a guerilla. He'd been locked up there now for two days.

'No, he's not a Contra,' I protested. 'He's a tourist, like us. He's an American, but a *good* American.'

The man went off to consult with his superiors. A little while later, he came back and asked us to produce more of Keith's documents. We scurried back to the hotel and picked up his rucksack. The police went through it minutely. After four hours, Keith was finally marched to the front door. He was predictably pleased to see us. 'Thank you so much,' he said, hugging us both. 'I don't think I would have ever got out of there otherwise.'

Back at the hotel, he told us the whole story. He'd been grabbed while out walking, arrested and taken into an interrogation room for questioning. He hadn't fared so well there, not fitting neatly into any of their categories. Job? No. Address? No. Family? No. He'd noticed blood on the walls. There was no bulb in the light fitting, so his interrogators had been forced to keep moving him around the room to catch the dying light of the day through the doorway. One man cataloguing the few possessions he'd had on him had played with his penknife and cut his finger so badly, he'd had to retype all the questions and answers all over again because the form had become so badly stained with blood. Then the guards had taken away Keith's shoelaces and, since there were no empty cells left, had left him handcuffed in the corridor to sleep at night. He was looking forward enormously to catching the boat the next day to the islands, far away from Bluefields.

It didn't arrive. It would be leaving in two days' time instead, because of rough seas, the harbourmaster told us. The hotel didn't seem at all surprised to see us return.

'You wanna go by *boat*?' one of the other guests cried when she heard that we planned to leave the next day. 'Man, you must be mad. It's just too rough. The waves are way too high. Hey! One time it took twelve hours and a woman had a baby on board. No-one could help her because they were all too busy being sick. But it was a healthy boy.' We smiled weakly back. A boat—any boat—however high the waves, sounded pretty good to us.

At 6.30am the next morning, all hell broke loose around Bluefields. The radio had just broadcast that the Bluefields Express was about to leave. All around town, people madly packed their bags and raced down to the harbour. We did too, only to find when we'd got there that the radio station was publicising an old timetable. The boat would still leave the next day. The hotel owner didn't even look up as we picked up our key.

The next morning, an old metal boat was actually there, waiting. It had seats for thirty people, but had sold tickets for eighty, all of whom had come loaded down with sacks of vegetables and fruit, and great drums of coconut oil. I squeezed in between bags of sugar and salt, to find a place to sit on the floor by the side of the boat, and idly gazed at a rash of little holes in the metal. A tall young man with a beret pulled at a jaunty angle noticed me looking. 'Contra attack,' he said, flatly. 'They know if they sink this boat there might not be another.'

I looked off at the view of the water. We'd be passing along the narrow river way with trees either side first, because the harbour was too shallow for a more direct route to the open ocean. We pulled away dead on 7am. Under the flap to the engine room below, I could see men toiling away. They pushed a pipe through the flap, and I leapt up and out of the way when it started pouring water onto the deck. Everyone laughed. Then, gradually, the water turned to thick black oil. People squealed and tried to snatch their bags out of the way. Everything was soaked. Just as we entered the mouth of the sea, however, thick black, foul-smelling smoke started to belch out from the room below. I found another place to crouch on the floor, away from the fumes. We ploughed on for about an hour-and-a-half. One woman fell asleep, sprawled on my pack. Then the engine shuddered and the boat started to turn around. The captain walked out onto the deck. There was a problem, he said. We'd have to go back to the harbour. I wondered if I'd ever actually make it to the Corn Islands.

The sleeping woman woke up just as we were docking in Bluefields. 'Are we there?' she asked hopefully.

We sat around the harbour, watching mechanics tinker with the boat. After three hours, the news filtered round. The boat would now leave at 5am the next day. I checked into a different hotel; I just couldn't face going back to our regular place. That evening, I persuaded Keith to come to the cinema with me. It turned out to be a huge, high, bare hall with rows of wooden slatted benches, looking more like a church than anything else. I wasn't quite sure which way to face when I sat down as there was no sign of a screen. One wall, though, was painted white and, underneath, there was a single old speaker, covered in dust and spiders' webs. The place filled up. *Young Doctors in Love* had been, it seemed, a film eagerly awaited in Bluefields. It started well enough, but the picture started getting fainter and fainter until it disappeared completely after about ten minutes. There was an angry chorus of cat-calls, whistles and boos, a space of three minutes, and then the picture appeared again, having missed out several scenes of the story. Every ten minutes, the same thing would happen again. At the same time, the sound seemed to be coming from six feet underwater, with the dialogue quite inaudible. The Spanish subtitles were printed white on a white background so were similarly impossible to make out. The audience, unperturbed, cheerfully shouted out suggestions of what might be happening before us. Halfway through, someone switched on their radio, playing a pop tune very loudly.

Then, suddenly, something huge and black appeared, blotting out half of the picture. At first, I thought it was part of the film, then I realised it must be a moth on the projector. Most of the audience stood on the bench to yell to the projectionist to remove the moth. It took him fifteen minutes to respond. He then stopped the film, took away the moth and came out to apologise. He'd apparently played some of the reels in the wrong order.

I had an early night and was up by 3.30am ready to get down to the harbour. If the boat didn't go this time, I would give the islands a miss. They probably weren't all that wonderful anyway. It was still dark when we got down to the harbour.

Our boat was two boats away, so everyone was crawling on all fours—with babies and more luggage balanced on their backs—in the pitch-black, over the other boats to get to ours. It felt grim. There was a stench of rotting vegetables coming from some of the sacks, while the deck was awash with black, from the coal in sacks which had become soaked with water, and then oil, the day before. I took a deep breath and found a place to squat. At 7am, we pulled away, with black fumes still billowing from the engine room. No-one complained. We all hoped, I'm sure, that the captain wouldn't notice.

The ride to El Bluff was smooth but, as soon as we hit the open sea, I started to feel ghastly. Not only were the waves throwing us up and down, but the swell was rolling us from side to side. Each time, I was thrown in the air to fall rapidly down to the deck, leaving my stomach somewhere two feet above. I threw up three times into my precious spare plastic bags I'd been saving so carefully for special occasions. The boat felt tiny as it was tossed around by those towering waves.

'Hey!' said one man cheerfully. 'This is not bad. You should feel what it's like when it's *rough*!' He laughed uproariously at his own joke, as I fixed my eyes firmly on the horizon. My stomach, however, still wouldn't be calmed. I threw up again and again. The journey was feeling like a nightmare from which I would never awake. It went on and on. Another woman started throwing up over the side, but the wind whipped it back onto the boat. Immediately, five or six others joined her. The man who'd made the joke about rough seas, I noted not without some small measure of satisfaction, was among them.

After what felt like days, someone shouted that the island was up ahead. I could just make out a fuzzy green dot. Our progress towards it was painfully slow. I tried to make a joke to someone hanging over the side of the boat near me that I'd catch the plane back.

He shook his head, sadly. 'Not possible,' he said. 'Even if there is one, it is booked up two months ahead.' What was left of my stomach shrank still further. The Corn Islands had better live up to their promise. If I had to do this journey twice, they *had* to be paradise on earth.

'But the islands are lovely, eh?' I asked the man, more as a rhetorical question than anything else.

'No, not really,' he said, gloomily. 'No food, not much to drink. And the waves...too, too rough.' He moved his hand up and down to indicate towering peaks. 'And our nicest beach, they are taking it away for concrete.'

I didn't want to hear any more. I stared back at the dot moving ever closer. I could make out trees, sand and a horde of people standing there, either waiting for us passengers—or eager to jump on the boat to beat their own retreat. I'd soon find out.

chapter seventeen
A ONE-SIDED LOVE AFFAIR
destination: The Pyramid of the Sun,
Teotihuacán, Mexico

It was wonderful to hear a friendly voice on the phone.
'Suzannah!' he exclaimed. 'Oh Suzannah! You have made it!
It is so good to speak to you. Where are you now? Where are
you calling from?'

I was actually in a laundrette close to my hotel, thoroughly
enjoying the novelty of watching my washing going round in
a machine after ten months of scrubbing clothes in cold water.
It was just off a main road in one of the shabbier parts of
Mexico City.

There was a sharp intake of breath at the other end of the
line as he heard the name of the suburb. 'Oh Suzannah!' he
cried. 'You cannot stay there! It is not right. It is not good
there. Suzannah, in fact, you must stay here with my family.
I will come and pick you up right away.'

I laughed at the anxiety in his voice. 'That's very kind of you,
Emilio,' I said. 'But I'm fine. I like it here. Maybe I'll visit you
tomorrow. We could have lunch or something. How about that?'

He, however, clucked his tongue in a way that suggested he
would stand for no nonsense from someone who was obviously

too dumb to know any better. 'No, Suzannah, no,' he said, firmly. 'In fact, I am going to get in my car now. Don't move. I will be there in half-an-hour, Suzannah.' He put the phone down with a determined click.

I felt my first stab of regret that I'd phoned Emilio so soon after arriving in Mexico City. I didn't want to stay with him and his family. I wanted to be free to explore the place on my own, and then head north to Teotihuacán, the site of the great pyramids of the sun and the moon, the most marvellous monuments on the continent. Besides, I didn't know him *that* well. And all this Suzannah business was beginning to get on my nerves already. But apart from grabbing my wet washing from the machine mid-cycle and making a dash for it, I really had little choice but to stay there and await his arrival. I wondered if I'd even recognise him after all this time.

I'd met Emilio a few years before, on a train going from Xian in central China to Beijing in the north. He'd been sick and, after spending the whole journey getting sicker and sicker, ended up being whisked to hospital with an acute case of pneumonia. Since I was the only friendly non-Chinese face around, I'd visited him in hospital every day until he'd finally been flown home to Mexico.

Since that week, we'd written to each other every so often, and sent cards at Christmas. Emilio was an architect with budding political aspirations. He'd forever be grateful to me, he wrote often, 'for saving me'. I thought that was a little bit over-dramatic, but very Latin. When I'd finally written to him the previous year, saying I was planning a trip around Latin

America, he said I must make sure to contact him as soon as I got to Mexico City. Now I had, and I shouldn't be so mean as to start resenting him before we'd even set eyes on each other again.

I put my faded wet clothes into the dryer and sat back. It wasn't long before I heard him.

'SUZANNAH!!!' yelled a tall, thin man in a dark three-piece suit, with a droopy dark moustache. He rushed over and gripped me in a bony bear hug. 'It is so wonderful to see you again! Wonderful, wonderful.' Then he pulled away and held me at arm's length ostensibly to smile at me, but I could see him surreptitiously looking me up and down. When I met his eyes again, I was astonished to see them wet with tears. 'It is so good to see you,' he said, sniffing. 'Forgive me. I am just overwhelmed.' Clutching my plastic bag of damp knickers, we went back to my hotel where I hurriedly re-packed. He then drove me back to his place.

His family was hardly large. It consisted, apparently, of just his brother, uni student Carlos, and their elderly aunt, whom they fondly, and rather unimaginatively, called 'Tia', the Spanish word for aunt. His mother apparently lived in another state and his father had died ten years before. Both Carlos and Tia seemed inordinately pleased to meet me. I supposed Emilio had embroidered his version of how I had saved his life as he lay dying in a foreign land. Tia hugged me warmly and welcomed me to the family; Carlos shook my hand solemnly and said how much he had heard about me. Then I was given a pleasant bedroom at the back of the house and told to unpack and hand over any dirty laundry to one of the two maids (one was sixty and stone deaf, and the other was seventeen and in disgrace for having had a baby while still unmarried). It was a bit late for the laundry, and I tried to protest about staying there, saying I didn't want to put them out, and would be just as happy at a hotel. To no avail. None of them would hear of it.

Emilio took me on a tour of the stately old place, stuffed with silk armchairs and walnut tables, nervously stroking his moustache all the way. He showed me the three bathrooms, Tia's quarters, Carlos's rooms, and then his own bedroom and study next door. He threw open one of the doors to a massive wardrobe in the corner, to reveal a row of women's dresses.

'They're my sister's,' he explained, hurriedly. 'I told her to bring them over in case you needed extra clothes to wear.'

I was dumbfounded. He'd obviously been planning my stay carefully. I smiled and sorted through the rack, touching the silk low-waisted dresses I knew would make me look 104-years-old and shuddering at the sight of the kaftans. 'Very nice of you,' I mumbled.

Gazing at his noticeboard, full of political posters and invitations to meetings, I was then startled to see the postcards and letters I'd written him also pinned up, next to a blurry photo of me he'd taken in the hospital.

•••

Every morning, I was left on my own to go off and explore the city, until Emilio came home from work at about 4pm to drive me further afield. It was quite a pleasant arrangement, I had to admit. By myself, I dived each day into the teeming city—-

at 18 million people, Latin America's biggest and certainly its most polluted. While there were still remnants everywhere of the devastating 1985 earthquake, I constantly marvelled at the vibrancy and variety of the place. I listened to blind men singing in strong, sweet voices on the metro. I ate tacos sizzling on street stalls. I marvelled at the sight of dark, swarthy figures in the hugest hats ever seen outside of cartoons. I visited the palace, the churches, the squares, the museums, the parks, the markets, the house where Trotsky was axed through the head and the shops in the fashionable Zona Rosa. I read more about the pyramids of Teotihuacán, in preparation for the last leg of my journey north.

When Emilio came home, we went along to many of the outlying districts. Sometimes, we ate in little restaurants he knew. Always, just as we were about to leave, he'd ask me solicitously if I'd like to visit the bathroom. On the Sunday, we went as a family to Xochimilco, a separate town in the city's south, criss-crossed with canals and flower markets. There, Emilio embarrassed me hugely by paying a *mariachi* band to serenade me noisily, much to the amusement of Carlos and Tia.

On the Monday morning, I decided to stay in and get to know Tia. That, I'd already discovered, was a better idea in the morning. By lunchtime every day, she'd be much the worse for wear after tippling copious quantities of gin from a beautifully engraved silver flask she kept in the folds of her dress. She did it in a slow, methodical way, then went straight to bed, so she'd be right again for when Emilio returned home.

She was an amazing woman. A fading Mexican celebrity, she was about seventy yet still wore full make-up in bed. She reminded me enormously of Joan Crawford. The sister of the boys' mother, Tia had brought them up when their mother ran off with another man, and their father died, she said, of a broken heart. Recently, their mother had contacted her, asking if Carlos and Emilio would be prepared to see her again. Carlos had met up with her; Emilio had resolutely refused. 'But you know what he is like,' she said, sadly.

Indeed, I did. I'd only known him a week, really, but I'd already learned how stubborn he could be. Despite the fact that I was only a couple of years younger than him, he insisted on treating me like a child, checking if I needed the bathroom after every meal, and saying I should be chaperoned everywhere in the evenings. He had even come along, disapproving and stiff-lipped, to a dance I said I was going to in a local hall one night merely because he said it would be 'dangerous' for me alone. 'You do not know what these Latin men are like,' he said pompously, shaking his head with world-weary sadness.

Of course I did. Hadn't I been travelling, alone, among them, for nearly a year? But still Emilio would have nothing of it. He knew best, he said gently, as if to a four year old. He didn't even like me going out alone before he got home from work but he must have reasoned there was little he could do about it. Instead, he seemed determined to make up for it late every afternoon by showing me as much of his city as he could, accompanied by a dour, monotone commentary, often with his arm looped through mine, fiddling with his moustache with his other hand, or guiding me along laneways with a hand in the small of my back. It made me feel uncomfortable to have him touch me like that, but he was never anything but the perfect gentleman. This was obviously how he always treated women and maybe I was being oversensitive after enduring so many months of unwelcome male attention.

Yet my wandering around alone during the days wasn't the only thing he disapproved of. Tia, I soon realised, sorely tried his patience. He knew all about her drinking and frequently took her to task over it. She endured his lectures stoically—after all, she pointed out, she was dependent on his charity for a place to live these days—and then always promptly ignored them. By the next morning, she'd be back sipping delicately at her flask whenever there was a spare moment. Live and let live, I felt. After all, she'd raised Emilio and Carlos and these days still cooked, cleaned and ironed for the pair. You could hardly say that letting her stay at Emilio's house was charity.

At that, Tia just smiled demurely. 'Ah, but with you here, I am afraid,' she said.

'Afraid?' I asked, startled.

'Well, you know...' she said, but refused, point-blank to say any more.

The next morning, I talked to her again. We giggled over old photos of the boys when they were young, and took the mickey out of Emilio's political ambitions that he'd talked about gravely over dinner the previous night. He was a member of a newly formed right-wing political party that was planning to launch in a couple of months. He was one of their best candidates for office. 'There will be many changes in Mexico in the years to come,' he'd said, self-importantly, wagging his finger at the rest of us around the table. 'We will show people how they *should* live.'

I hadn't liked the sound of that one bit. Tia hadn't either, she confessed. 'Just think,' she said, 'of a world filled with people who have been taught by Emilio how to live.' We both exploded into laughter.

'Ah, but we shouldn't be speaking like this of Emilio,' said Tia, wiping her eyes. 'We shouldn't be so disrespectful. It must only be a matter of time now.'

'Until what?' I asked.

'Until, well, you know,' she replied, starting to look nervous.

'No, I don't know,' I said. 'Tell me.'

She grimaced. 'I know you two are very close and soon...'

'Soon, what?' I demanded. Suddenly, I realised what she was avoiding saying. I laughed. 'No, no, you've got it all wrong,' I said. 'Emilio and I are just friends. Nothing more than that.' Her eyes grew round. 'Honestly!' I said. 'There's nothing going on.' Something struck me. 'But has he told you any different?' There was real alarm in her eyes now, but I pressed on. 'Tell me, what has he said?'

She swore me to secrecy first, then confessed everything. Emilio had been talking about nothing else since he'd received the letter from me saying I was set to travel around Latin America. He'd been marking off the weeks. He'd called Carlos and Tia together and told them the woman he was going to marry would be arriving in Mexico soon. He said I'd be coming to stay for a while, and later we would announce our engagement. Instantly, everything fell into place: the chatty letters from Emilio asking how come I was in my mid-to-late twenties yet still not married and my jokey replies that I was still looking for a husband; the overly warm welcome I'd received and the constant attentiveness; the odd looks from Carlos whenever I laughed at how pompous Emilio was; and the nervousness of Tia at the thought that she might be put out of the house, presumably by the new mistress of the place.

The bastard! How dare he! I was pacing the kitchen now, but Tia begged me to sit down and say nothing. He'd be so angry if he knew she'd told me. But Emilio barely knew me, how could he even *think* of marrying me? Unless he had an ulterior motive. I mulled that one over and a light, somewhere in my mind, snapped on. Yes, I could see it clearly now—a new political career and a marriage to an Anglo. How neat and tidy. On the right, connections were everything. It would give him added status to have a white wife.

I told Tia my side of the story: a brief friendship based on a chance meeting on a train, and running errands to his hospital bed. A few letters over the years, a call from the phone box at the laundrette and my belief that he was simply being hospitable by offering me a place to stay while I visited Mexico City.

She could hardly believe it. 'And that is all there is?' she asked, aghast. 'It is amazing.'

'It's more than amazing,' I said, 'it's bloody ridiculous.'

But I was pledged to silence, and I reassured her I would say nothing. I as sure as hell wasn't going to be so polite to Emilio again, though, and put up with that arm through mine all the time. I stewed all afternoon and evening, and went to bed early, saying I had a headache. Emilio offered to come to my room and sit beside me with a wet cloth to stroke my forehead. I refused, and locked the door behind me.

The next morning, Tia was in high spirits. 'I have a friend who wants to meet you,' she said to me. 'She is coming to tea this morning.'

Her friend arrived, accompanied by her son, a dashingly handsome man, probably a little older than Emilio, in a well-cut cream linen suit. I tried to catch Tia's eye but she seemed to be avoiding me. He started chatting. Juan was a political candidate for the PRI, the political party of the left. By day, he worked in finance. He was funny and smart and seemed genuinely to care for the Mexican people, rather than just for their vote. I just couldn't help warming to him. Before the pair left, he asked me to accompany him to dinner that evening. I said yes. When Tia eventually closed the door behind them, she turned to me with a huge smile. I instantly knew she'd planned the whole thing. Emilio would be ropable to hear I'd be going out with another man, let alone a member of the opposition party. Tia had been unable to resist after he'd tried to trick me, and treated her so badly for years.

When Emilio came back that afternoon, he said he had been worrying all day about my headache. How was I feeling now?

What had I been doing all morning? His brow darkened, however, when I casually mentioned I had a date that evening. It darkened to thunder when I threw in Juan's name. He stormed off to his study 'to do some work'. Carlos winked at me. It seemed Tia had let him into the joke, too.

That evening, Juan was great company. He talked about the struggling Mexican economy, the unbridled optimism of the people that, it seemed, could be dulled neither by the prospect of imminent ruin nor by natural disasters like floods and earthquakes, and the image of Mexico overseas—he was astonished by pictures of sombreros and corn chips in foreign magazines. For my part, it felt wonderful to have an intelligent conversation with a man who neither treated me as a child, nor as something to be hustled into bed at the first possible opportunity.

Later, he asked about my travels, and my stay with my hosts. 'How do you find Emilio?' he asked at one point.

'Oh, fine,' I said, noncommittally.

'I just wondered,' he replied. 'His political career isn't going too well. In fact, he looks a little like he may be dumped by his party. He's going to have to pull something quite dramatic out of the bag to stay in the running. He must be under enormous strain at the moment.'

When I finally got back to the house, the strain was all too apparent. Emilio was sitting up waiting for me, stony-faced. It looked as if it cost him every ounce of self-control to resist slamming the front door on Juan's face. But I merely smiled at Juan, thanked him for a lovely evening and gave him a peck on the cheek goodnight. Beside me, I could see Emilio's face turn purple. Even as I waved Juan goodbye, I could hear Emilio licking his lips, and knew he'd be puffing out his chest and twiddling his moustache. With a sinking feeling, I knew our moment had come. Hoping to head it off, I turned round, bade him a quick good night and made a dash for my bedroom.

He was too quick. 'Suzannah, oh Suzannah,' he breathed, as he followed me through the door before I had the chance to close it behind me. 'I must confess something.' He sat down on the bed and patted the bedclothes close to him. 'Suzannah, sit down.'

I sat, obediently, but as far from him as the single bed allowed. Confess? Was he finally going to admit to having designs on me, even apologise? I didn't have to wait for long to find out.

'Suzannah,' he twisted his lips into a ghastly smile, 'I think I love you. No, in fact, I *know* I love you. My darling, I love you more each day.'

I sat and looked, dumbfounded, at him. This was an intelligent man. Surely he couldn't expect me to fall for such a line? He most certainly did.

'In fact, I have something to ask you,' he continued, not missing a beat. It seemed like we'd switched into slow motion as he stroked his moustache nervously, got up off the bed, then folded his body to crouch down on one knee. I could only just see his head over the side of the bed. 'I want, Suzannah,' he said, gravely, 'for you to marry me.'

I didn't say a word. He stayed there, frozen to the spot. It felt like ten minutes had passed before I had the confidence to say something without dissolving into giggles. That would have been just too, too cruel.

'Emilio, I'm very honoured,' I said, finally. 'But give me a day to think about it.' Much as I'd have loved to refuse him point-blank, experience had taught me that it might not be so wise openly to scorn a man on his own territory in a country where you might not be the best predictor of human behaviour.

He looked annoyed, but tried to smile softly in a kind of understanding way. He succeeded only in grimacing. 'OK, my sweet,' he said, standing back up and stroking his moustache. 'We will speak again tomorrow. Until then,' he reached across, grabbed my hand and yanked it to his lips, 'I will dream of you alone.' I cast my eyes chastely to the ground until I heard the door close.

The following morning, I was up early. I joined Tia for breakfast. She shook her head, smiling, when she heard about Emilio's performance. 'He was so, so angry about Juan,' she said. 'He paced all evening, waiting for you to come home. What are you going to do now?' I told her I'd already packed. Tears sprung into her eyes, but she nodded.

'Perhaps it is for the best,' she said. 'He will be very angry if you say no. But I will miss you.' We hugged warmly. At that moment, Carlos came down the stairs. He seemed to have been expecting something to happen. He offered to drive me to the bus station, but I'd have to hurry in case Emilio came back unexpectedly and discovered his family's collusion.

I said goodbye to Tia again, and climbed into the car. 'What shall I tell him when he gets back?' she called from the front step.

'Tell him...tell him...you think I've gone to stay at Juan's,' I yelled back. She clapped in delight. Carlos smiled.

At the station, I shook Carlos' hand, then gave him a hug. He beamed. 'I am so sorry about my brother,' he said. I shrugged. I'd lost one friend but had made three more. I watched him drive away, feeling strangely elated. I was back on my own again, and it felt good.

I turned and started searching for the right bus stand. It wouldn't do at all to still be standing in the same spot when Emilio came home, in case he managed to extract a confession from Tia and Carlos, and decided to look for me. I wandered up and down the aisles, getting increasingly frustrated.

'Teotihuacán?' I asked the man sweeping the ground, bending every so often to pick up any cigarette ends he spotted larger than his fingernail. He looked puzzled and shook his head.

'Teotihuacán?' I repeated to a woman with plastic bags of corn sitting at her feet. She shrugged.

'Teotihuacán?' I asked a little kid who might, I thought, prove more helpful. He took one look at me and ran off towards the big brother I suddenly noticed scowling at me from a few metres away.

Writer Graeme Sparkes described Teotihuacán as three-and-a-half million tonnes of stone lying over the chamber 'in which the universe was created'. Surely it couldn't be *that* hard to find after travelling so many thousands of kilometres around South and Central America to get there? I'd been spoilt by having Emilio looking after me. I'd forgotten how tricky it could be getting around on your own, when obviously your pronunciation of difficult words sounded to locals like the mutterings of an alien from another planet. And out of the corner of my eye, I could see big brother approaching me. I wondered if this meant trouble. 'Teotihuacán?' I said, by way of explanation, just in case he'd thought I was hounding his kid brother for no reason. 'Teotihuacán!'

He stood and frowned, then his face cleared. 'Ah!' he said. '*Piramides!*' I nodded vigorously as he laughed and looked around him. '*Piramides!*' he called over to the sweeper and the corn woman. 'Teotihuacán!' He said it quite differently to the way I'd been struggling with the word. Obviously that had been my problem. He took hold of my elbow and steered me towards an old bus, filled with passengers, revving up as if ready to leave at any moment. He hammered on the doors and they creaked open. '*Piramides!*' he shouted to the driver, obviously just in case I couldn't manage that word either.

I climbed on board and squashed myself into a tiny space between two women juggling enormous bundles in the air. My rucksack pressed against one of them and she spluttered her annoyance. I apologised hastily but, as the bus lurched off, I stumbled and whacked her right in the face with it. She narrowed her eyes at me.

Luckily, this last journey of my trip around Latin America was only going to be an hour-and-a-half long. Once there, I'd explore the marvels of Teotihuacán for a few days and then head off north to catch a bus over the border to the US, from where I'd buy a cheap air ticket to New Zealand. It was hard to think much beyond the pyramids, however. For so long they'd been my destination, and now I was so close.

The woman to my side stepped back onto my foot. I could hardly blame her. She'd staked out her territory long before I'd arrived. I moved my foot as far away as I could, and bent my knees, so I wouldn't be caught off balance again when the bus bumped over holes in the road or swayed from side to side. That ninety minutes passed slowly. We seemed to stop at every suburb along the way, and waited, even if no-one wanted to get on or off. Close to Teotihuacán, we stopped once more and my neighbour pushed past me to disembark, making sure to give me one last prod with her bundle. I smiled sweetly. I was almost there. No point in losing my rag now.

I looked out of the window at the rows of houses. I gazed at the faces of everyone else on the bus. I looked down at my battered shoes. And at last, the driver yelled something that, again, sounded nothing like the Teotihuacán I'd come to know and love, and there was a stampede to get off. I was carried along in the rush, missed my footing off the bus and fell, face first, into the dirt. Several willing hands pulled me back to my feet. I thanked them and smiled back. Nothing was going to dampen my spirits now. The pyramids could only be metres away, and I knew the sight was going to be absolutely incredible.

chapter eighteen
AND HERE IS YOUR GUIDE

destination: The Taj Mahal, India

It was still the dead of night when the banging on the door started. Wrenched from a deep sleep, I hoped it might just go away. It didn't. The banging simply grew louder.

Who could it be? We'd only just arrived at our hotel in the Indian capital Delhi, planning a few hours sleep before travelling on to Agra and the Taj Mahal. The sole people we'd met were the hotel receptionist and porter. They'd hardly have followed us to the room, sat tight for two hours until we'd be sure to be asleep and then think it might be a good idea to wake us to check we didn't need anything.

The thudding became more insistent and, wearily, I dragged myself from bed to answer the door. I threw it open: no-one. I looked up and down the corridor: nothing. Sleepily, I wandered back to bed. But the knocking on the door continued. I opened it again to find no-one there. *Strange.* I walked over to the window. My partner, Jimmy, was leaning against the frame. Together, we looked out onto the dark city, a couple of lone four-storey buildings standing out against the dusky sky. Then I jumped back in alarm. It felt as though the window frame was shaking and, yes, I could have sworn one of the buildings moved.

Finally, the truth dawned. We were in the middle of an earthquake. If there's one rule about visiting India, it is to expect the oddest things always to happen just when you're convinced everything's running smoothly.

•••

On paper, it had looked a simple trip. First, persuade a partner whose idea of roughing it would be a stay in a four-star hotel without CNN, to come along and sample the joy of it. And, second, just fly to Delhi and then catch the daily train to Agra to visit the Taj Mahal, a glorious marble mausoleum to love built by the great Mughal Shah Jahan in memory of his beloved wife. It was one of the great man-made wonders of the world I'd always longed to see. The reality was quite different, on both counts.

Persuading my partner Jimmy to come along was much tougher than I'd thought. 'How about New York?' he'd suggested hopefully when the subject had first come up. 'There are parts of that you could go to that'd be pretty rough. I'll stay in that day.'

He paled visibly when he heard inoculations were involved, too. It didn't help that the doctor snorted loudly at the news we were visiting India. 'You wouldn't catch me anywhere near a place like that,' he said. 'I've seen some of those diseases first-hand. If you want adventure, what's wrong with New York?'

As for that simple, straightforward journey... The divergence of what should happen, and what actually does, began early—at Delhi airport. With 300 passengers all clustered around the carousel we'd been told would deliver our cases, we all stood patiently for it to start. Suddenly, great parts of the crowd split off and ran to a carousel at the far end of the arrivals hall. It started a stampede. Soon, panting and sweating, we were all waiting around another carousel. After another half-an-hour, a group of soldiers approached a few members of the crowd, who then rushed off back to the first carousel. We followed, breathlessly, to find our luggage at last emerging.

Even the taxi ride to the hotel was not as it seemed. Buying a pre-paid ticket to our hotel, we thought we'd be safe from the taxi touts who ply the airport. We followed the man who'd snatched the pre-paid ticket from my hands as we trudged wearily out of the airport, insisting he'd been sent by the taxi police to collect us, but my heart slumped as we made our way past the crowds jammed against a mesh fence to meet the new arrivals, cows sleeping along the verges and cycle rickshaws full of sleeping bodies, to his 'taxi': an ancient Ambassador with his friend sitting at the wheel.

After a few minutes, the friend eventually managed to start the car, apparently without the need of a key, and we set off, in a black burst of billowing smoke and petrol fumes, along a wide freeway which soon became a narrow, dusty road, choked with traffic. The driver didn't seem to notice. He careened past the traffic queues on the outside and then darted back in, milliseconds before the roaring oncoming traffic could smash us out of existence. He cut off other cars and forced great thundering trucks to veer away. He went through red lights in a cacophony of horns and invective. He peeled left out of a queue, rocked up a muddy bank and down a ditch on the other side, then tried to squeeze back in ahead of a haulage lorry, but the lorry driver refused to slow down to let us in. We approached a narrow bridge, both hurtling along side by side, and the driver leant out of his cab and swore fruitily at us. It was a test of nerves. Jimmy and I swapped worried glances. Our nerves were shot, at least. But, thankfully, our driver backed down, seconds before we were set to be wiped out, under fifteen tonnes of steel and determination.

Gradually, the road narrowed into a muddy path through rows of grimy buildings. Dogs scattered as we roared through. Cars driving towards us with no lights emerged ghost-like out of the gloom. After forty-five minutes, and with still no sign of a big, bustling city in sight, I asked the driver if he was sure he knew where he was going. His mate replied there was no such hotel as the one we'd booked into, but he'd try and find us an alternative. We groaned. 'No, no,' I said as firmly as I could, 'I want the Oberoi Maidens.'

He turned round and smiled. 'No, no, it is not possible,' he said, brightly.

I started getting nervous. I had no idea where we were. Where could he be taking us? And this was obviously not a proper taxi, just two guys earning a bit of extra money on the side by camping outside the airport and preying on gullible new arrivals. Our guidebook had warned us, chapter and verse, about such scams but we'd still been hoodwinked, just the same, by a text-book example. I shut up and tried to peer through the night for some landmarks that might come in useful later. The problem was, I could see nothing.

Unperturbed, the driver and his mate chatted cheerfully as we continued bumping through the dark streets. Eventually, we pulled up outside a small, brightly lit office. 'They tell us,' he said, jabbing a finger towards it. 'Tourist information. Then we go.'

The man inside was adamant. There was no hotel with the name we'd mentioned. When we pulled out the fax on which my booking had been confirmed, he insisted it was a fake. When I found the address, he said it no longer existed. When I suggested calling them, he changed his mind. Yes, there was a hotel of that name, he miraculously remembered, without even a hint of embarrassment, but they were full.

'But I've booked,' I pointed out.

'Oh yes,' he replied, without missing a beat, 'but they've now had an unexpected arrival of a lot of guests. You will have to go to another hotel. We will take you to a much more lovely—and cheaper—place.'

It was the oldest trick in the book, I knew. They'd take us to some grotty, overpriced hotel where we'd pay anything in order to get to sleep. They'd pocket the commission. There was even a chance that we'd end up staying there for days at some vastly inflated cost. Their commission would double, but we had no intention of giving in. We stood, quietly holding our ground, as they moved through every possible reason they could think of to stop us proceeding.

Eventually, tired, hungry and utterly worn down, Jimmy

pulled out the guidebook, opened it to the page about getting to your hotel from the airport and jabbed a section with his finger. 'Look at this!' he said, thrusting it under their noses. 'This is the trick you are trying to play! And this trick! And this one!'

They read the words, nodding their heads with interest and obvious pleasure, presumably gratified at this official recognition of such initiative. We, meanwhile, marched outside, opened the taxi boot and started unloading our luggage. If they would not take us to our hotel, we would find someone else who would. They turned up at the final slam of the boot and held a hurried little conference. They then handed back the book and, without another word, piled our cases back into the car. 'We will go now,' said the driver's mate. We arrived at the hotel a quarter-of-an-hour later. Both men were, however, still completely unfazed by the incident. The driver was nothing but sweetness and light as we grumpily unloaded the boot. 'You need a driver tomorrow?' he enquired cheerfully. 'We pick you up.' We ignored him.

•••

But now, standing in the hotel room feeling the walls shiver in that March 1999 earthquake (which, we later discovered, measured 6.8 on the Richter Scale and killed at least 100 in the remote villages of Chamoli in the hills), I knew getting to the Taj Mahal would be much more difficult than it looked. I vowed to try to get there the very next day.

'Do we have to?' asked Jimmy plaintively. 'I thought it might be nice just to stay in the hotel all day. Do I *have* to go outside again?'

Early the next morning, we caught an auto-rickshaw, a kind of motorbike with a little passenger cage built onto the back, to the train station. The driver offered to help us, for a fee, to buy a ticket. I demurred. We were quite capable, thank you, of buying one ourselves. But I'd reckoned without India.

Stepping out of the rickshaw and making our way towards the station, I felt the waves of 44°C heat roll in to wash over me. The air was thick with fumes. Spiralling dust from the dry mud under my feet blew into my eyes. Stopping to rub them, we were immediately ambushed by a group of men. 'A ticket to Agra?' they echoed. 'No, to buy tickets, you go to the ticket office over there.' I looked, confused, towards the vague direction they'd indicated. It was *away* from the station. They assured us that was correct, however. 'Look, I will show you,' volunteered one, helpfully.

We followed him back across the road from the busy station, towards a row of shops on the other side, behind those stores and, at last, into a grimy little office with the words, 'Government Tourist Bureau' written on a banner stuck onto the wall. The man inside looked pleased to see us. Agra? The Taj Mahal? Wonderful! He looked up his train timetable and a price list he kept hidden, inexplicably, under his desk. The final figure he announced was some eight times higher than the one my guidebook had advised.

We declined, politely, and, as he stood shouting at us to

come back so we might be able to work out a better price, we made our way determinedly through the tangle of narrow alleyways once again towards the station. Just a few metres from the entrance, we were stopped by another man. 'The ticket office has moved,' he said. 'Come, I show you.' As he grasped my arm and tried to push us back away from the station, I resisted. I was wise to the game now. I knew that if I bought the ticket through an agent, whoever took me there would earn himself a handsome commission. It was in their interests to have me charged way too much.

This time, we made it through the entrance and all the way up the stairs to a platform before we were stopped by a man in a smart linen shirt, dark trousers and a jaunty tie.

'Where are you going?' he asked.

'To buy a ticket to Agra,' I replied.

'Oh no,' he said, 'The ticket office is no longer here.' I snorted with derision. He was gently persuasive. 'No, it moved a few months ago,' he insisted. 'It is now about a mile away. Wait a moment. I will find someone to show you.'

He looked as if he was in a position of some authority with the railway. While he called over to a young boy to fetch someone else, he advised passengers of which platform was theirs, where to buy tickets, and who was, and wasn't, allowed to pass him. I relaxed. At last we'd find the right place.

After a few minutes, a smart young man ran to his side. He told him to take us to the ticket office. We walked back down the stairs and out of the station. He beckoned over an auto-rickshaw and we both climbed in. The driver then darted for ten minutes around the city, before coming to rest outside another travel agent's. 'No, no,' I protested. 'This isn't a ticket office. This is a travel agent.' We argued; we refused to get out. Finally, he agreed to take us to the right place.

We arrived ten minutes later and he tilted his head, now decidedly surly, towards another office. We wandered in. 'Government-Approved Travel Agency' it said on the wall. I felt anger and frustration well up inside me, and the feeling of helplessness brought hot tears pricking at the inside of my eyelids.

I walked up to the desk. 'Do you sell train tickets to Agra?' I asked, miserably.

'Oh yes,' came the reply from a cheerful fat man squashed into a tiny space between the desk and the wall. 'Would you like a Coca-Cola?'

I declined, and frowned at Jimmy who'd been nodding. Once you'd accepted a drink, you were theirs, I felt. Sorry, but we were in a rush, I said, could he just tell us the price of a ticket?

'Ah, yes, there are many things we have to consider...' he started. He looked through books; he scoured timetables; he made a few phone calls. Finally, he smiled, showing greying teeth. 'I'm afraid there are no tickets left,' he said. 'But if you would like to pay a little extra, I'm sure we could find you two.' He looked from me to Jimmy and back again. He was anxious to find a crack in the veneer of our determination not to be taken for a ride.

'A little extra?' I asked. 'Who to?'

'Ah,' he looked carefully around and dropped his voice, 'we would approach the railway clerk.'

'Ahhhh,' I said, realisation slowly dawning, 'you mean a bribe?'

He nodded vigorously. 'Maybe fifty US dollars or 100 could get you a ticket.'

I stood up. If only we could find a railway clerk ourselves who was able to issue tickets, I thought to myself, surely we'd be able to buy a ticket fairly and squarely from him. We bade him farewell and went back to the door where the same auto-rickshaw was waiting. The sun was now high in the sky, and the heat was making my vision shimmer. The dust was suffocating.

'No tickets,' we barked to the man who had shown us there. 'NOW, we go to the ticket office.' He mumbled something and nodded his head. We set off once more. This time, the building we pulled up outside looked a great deal more promising. 'Government Tickets' said a sign over the door. 'Train, Bus and Plane'.

We marched over and were ushered into a poky little room identical to the last three. Slowly, we began to realise it was yet another travel agent's. But this time I knew when we were beaten. We could continue racing around Delhi all day, from agency to agency, or we could just give up gracefully and agree to buy a ticket, whatever it took, from an agent. I hung my head.

'What do you think?' I asked Jimmy. He looked equally exhausted. We waited our turn. After two more customers were dealt with, we were beckoned over to the desk.

'A ticket to Agra?' I whispered. 'Please?'

He brought out the railway timetable and frowned. 'No tickets tomorrow,' he said. 'It's Monday. That's the day they clean the Taj Mahal. It's shut.'

I sighed, reluctant to believe him. But the fight was all drained out of me.

'How about the next day then?' Jimmy asked.

The agent picked up the phone, dialled a number and held a conversation. Then he cupped his hand over the mouthpiece. 'You're number ninety-one on the waiting list for a ticket there,' he hissed. 'But there are no seats back. Because it is closed on Monday, Tuesday is very, very busy.'

I shook my head. 'So how do we get there?' I asked.

'Ah ha,' he said, puffing out his chest. 'I have a much better idea.' He shouted over my head to the man standing by the door, who shouted to another man outside. A tall, dark Sikh walked into the office. 'This is Ajit,' said the travel agent, 'he will be your driver.'

We agreed to everything he suggested. We would be picked up the next day from our hotel. Ajit would drive us to the Taj Mahal and then back to Delhi. We would have a marvellous time in fast, air-conditioned comfort. Ajit would be a wonderful driver and a very good guide. And, of course, he would appreciate a tip if we were delighted with the service he offered us.

The next day, Ajit arrived bright and early. As we drove through Delhi's streets, full of families beating the dust out of mats they'd slept on along the freeway's central reservation, Ajit started his travelogue. He spoke as if he were addressing an entire coach party. His voice was deafening. His English was very good, but the accent was strong and the sing-song delivery made it hard to follow. If I tuned in and listened hard to every word, I found I could follow him. If I let up the concentration, all was lost. Jimmy sounded as if he was having less trouble as the pair chatted. I worked out how to block him out as he went on and on. He, it seemed, was determined to give us value for money. His tip, after all, depended on it.

Delhi's suburbs felt as if they stretched forever. We passed shanty towns of flapping sheets of plastic; barbers squatting on the roadside, carefully cutting hair and beards and shaving people's armpits; water buffalo wallowing in muddy ponds or pulling wooden wagons heaped high with truck tyres; donkeys trundling carts of bricks, and even camels hauling great loads of hay. As we finally emerged into the countryside, everything looked fresh from the Stone Age. Children bathed in the rivers alongside the road, men soaped up their bodies on the rivers' *ghats* (steps into the water) while their womenfolk beat the dirt out of great piles of washing. Every time we stopped, the car was surrounded by little children tapping on the windows to sell dusters, newspapers or fizzy drinks. Sometimes they begged for money for their little brothers and sisters, desperately sick mother or to feed themselves. Stalls lined the road, peddling snake beans, water melons fattened by a good soaking in the filthy river, cold drinks, dishes of *dhal* and, bizarrely, chandeliers tinkling and winking as they danced on lines of rope.

In the fields, women waved scythes at ripened wheat or carried bundles away on their heads, still dressed gorgeously in brightly-coloured, intricately embroidered saris tinged with gold and silver. They glowed purple, cerise, blue and violent green against the dust as the women stepped gracefully around hillocks of rubbish piled by the road and swayed past massive sewer pipes, waiting to be placed in freshly dug trenches now full of water. Over it all hung a dense brown pall of pollution and smoke. The rich, ripe smells of rubbish, manure, urine and petrol fumes mixed and mingled, then were sucked heartily into the car by the much-vaunted air conditioning.

Finally, we arrived in Agra, the big, dusty, dirty and completely charmless city of the Taj Mahal. It used to be a major industrial centre for the country, but all the industry had been closed down a few years before because of the pollution damage to the Taj. As we drove closer, I could feel my excitement growing. Just a few minutes more, and we'd be at one of the great modern wonders of the world. Finished in 1653 by Shah Jahan to show the world how much he loved his wife, Mumtaz Mahal, who died giving birth to their fourteenth child, it was supposed to be a place of astonishing beauty, an incredible monument to the power of love. 'He loved her too much,' Ajit informed us helpfully. 'Too, too much.'

I felt my irritation at being trapped in such a small place with a man determined to deliver the longest monologue in history begin to ebb away. I felt my annoyance at not having been able to spend this journey sitting quietly in a train, watching the world slide by, start to mellow. I felt serene, peaceful and even a little stirring of affection towards this man talking incessantly up in front.

Suddenly, I realised he had stopped. We were pulling into a car park. Ajit switched off the engine and turned to us, just as the passenger door was wrenched open and a hand reached in to shake his. 'This is your guide,' said Ajit, cheerfully. 'You will stay with him. He will show you everything and tell you everything about this place.'

The bile bubbled up once more in my chest. 'Oh no,' I said. 'I don't want a guide. We want to enjoy this place on our own.'

Ajit fixed me with a fierce stare. I hadn't understood. He had just arranged it. The guide would be with us every step of the way. That way we would be guaranteed to *really* enjoy the experience. There would be no arguments.

Beaten once more, we slid out of our seats and into the dazzling sunlight. Our new guide, Raj, beamed and welcomed us in a high-pitched whine. He took hold of our arms firmly and propelled us towards the little pollution-free electric bus that was to take us to the gate of our wondrous destination. I bit my lip. We were almost there. Once we got inside, surely we'd be able to shake him off.

We pulled up a few minutes later and stepped out of the bus. 'This way,' motioned Raj. 'This way.' We trotted along, like obedient schoolchildren. We almost bumped into him when he stopped suddenly, just by the gates. 'And this is my friend,' he said, putting his arm around another man. 'He will take your photograph. Very beautiful photograph.'

'No thanks,' I said immediately, 'we have our own cameras.' I pointed out the one slung around my neck and the other over Jimmy's shoulder. 'We don't need a photographer.'

Raj seemed unmoved. 'No, you *must* have a photographer,' he said. 'Very cheap. Very beautiful.'

I felt my shoulders slump again. Okay. It seemed easier not to argue. 'How much?' I said in a sad little tired voice.

'Fifty *rupees*,' said the photographer. 'Very cheap.'

Well, it certainly wasn't very cheap, but it suddenly seemed a small price to get rid of him. We went through the gate and posed, arm-in-arm, against the backdrop of the Taj Mahal in the distance. He took one photo. And then another, and then another. 'Hey!' I said. 'We only want one. That's enough. We pay you, you go now.'

The photographer frowned. 'No,' he said, firmly. 'You buy ten photos. Fifty *rupees* each.'

'No,' I said, realising how close I was to breaking point when I heard how shaky my voice was. 'No. One. Fifty *rupees*.'

He shook his head sadly. 'No, madam,' he replied. 'I have started new film now. You *have* to buy ten.'

'No!' I shouted. 'No! No!'

Raj came running over and no doubt realised immediately the problem. After all, he'd probably rehearsed this scenario a thousand times before with his mate. He suggested we buy three, as a compromise. The photographer didn't seem too happy with this, but probably understood that, if it had been left to me, I wouldn't have budged from one. He sneered. 'Give me the money,' he said, his hand outstretched. 'I give them to you when you come back from looking.' We handed it over and made a dash for freedom.

As we walked towards the timeless monument to love and peace and devotion, I could still feel my blood boiling, my rage a hard little lump in my throat. Travelling hopefully, I thought ruefully, is often truly a far, far better thing than finally actually arriving.

On reflection, I'd had some hellish experiences over the years and at times I thought I just wasn't going to survive, but, because I was prepared to put myself in those situations, I'd seen things that defied explanation and met people of all races who had enriched my life in ways I'd never have imagined. Every life we pass through, I thought philosophically, we leave something of ourselves but take so much more with us.

•••

I breathed in deeply. There was a man who had started trotting beside us, repeating over and over in a sing-song voice, 'Guide? Please? Guide? Please? Guide? Please?'

I ignored him, and successfully managed to block out his voice from my head. I squeezed Jimmy's hand, and felt the squeeze in return. I felt the bile slowly subside. The Taj Mahal looked magnificent up ahead. Its white marble curves were glowing gently, softly, invitingly in the late afternoon sun. This really was, after all, going to be an amazing experience.

epilogue
THE RULES OF TRAVEL

1. Never travel in a group.
2. Never travel with just one other person.
3. Never travel alone.
4. Always take as much money as you can afford—then double it.
5. Travel with as little as you need, but as much as you can carry.
6. Always hope for the best, but expect the worst.
7. Don't be too cautious.
8. Never take risks.
9. View with suspicion any man who sits next to you in a cinema; offers to show you the sights...at night; won't let you play dominoes; needs to marry you to bolster his political career; or plays 'spin the bottle' with a loaded revolver.
10. Always lock your hotel room door, preferably with your own padlock.
11. Plan ahead but make sure you can still be spontaneous.
12. Remember you can never carry too many cans of sardines, medical certificates or packets of dried mashed potatoes.
13. Don't hit the locals.
14. Do give them water.

ABOUT THE AUTHOR

Sue Williams was born in England and studied economics and politics at Durham University. Following her student days, she worked in a variety of dead end jobs for many years to support her travels around the world, starting in Europe and moving further and further afield each time. In between, she trained as a journalist and has worked in newspapers, magazines, radio and television.

Her wanderlust has taken her on many trips, from North Africa to Kenya, from Cape Town to Cairo, around South and Central America, through the United States, China, Borneo, Indonesia, Malaysia, Fiji, India, Pakistan and New Zealand. In 1989, she arrived in Australia and loved it so much she couldn't bear to leave again. Three years later, Sue became an Australian citizen and is now a high-profile journalist, based in Sydney. She writes for *The Sun-Herald* newspaper, in which she also has a weekly column, and for a number of magazines. Her previous book, *Powering Up*, was about women's health.